KOREA

THE IMPOSSIBLE COUNTRY

DANIEL TUDOR

TUTTLE Publishing

Tokyo | Rutland, Vermont | Singapore

ABOUT TUTTLE
"Books to Span the East and West"

Our core mission at Tuttle Publishing is to create books which bring people together one page at a time. Tuttle was founded in 1832 in the small New England town of Rutland, Vermont (USA). Our fundamental values remain as strong today as they were then—to publish best-in-class books informing the English-speaking world about the countries and peoples of Asia. The world has become a smaller place today and Asia's economic, cultural and political influence has expanded, yet the need for meaningful dialogue and information about this diverse region has never been greater. Since 1948, Tuttle has been a leader in publishing books on the cultures, arts, cuisines, languages and literatures of Asia. Our authors and photographers have won numerous awards and Tuttle has published thousands of books on subjects ranging from martial arts to paper crafts. We welcome you to explore the wealth of information available on Asia at **www.tuttlepublishing.com**.

Published by Tuttle Publishing, an imprint of Periplus Editions (HK) Ltd.

www.tuttlepublishing.com

Copyright © 2012 by Daniel Tudor.
Photographs not credited in the photo insert between pages 96 and 97 are by the author.

Library of Congress Cataloging-in-Publication Data
Tudor, Daniel, 1982-
  Korea : the impossible country / Daniel Tudor.
-- 1st ed.
    320 p., [16] p. of plates : ill. (some col.) ; 21 cm.
  ISBN 978-0-8048-4252-5 (hardcover)
  1. Korea (South)--Civilization--20th century. 2. Korea (South)--Civilization--21st century. I. Title.
  DS916.27.T84 2012
  951.9--dc23
                    2012017071

ISBN 978-0-8048-4252-5

Distributed by

North America, Latin America & Europe
Tuttle Publishing
364 Innovation Drive
North Clarendon, VT 05759-9436 U.S.A.
Tel: 1 (802) 773-8930
Fax: 1 (802) 773-6993
info@tuttlepublishing.com
www.tuttlepublishing.com

Asia Pacific
Berkeley Books Pte. Ltd.
61 Tai Seng Avenue #02-12
Singapore 534167
Tel: (65) 6280-1330
Fax: (65) 6280-6290
inquiries@periplus.com.sg
www.periplus.com

First edition
20 18 17 16   8 7 6 5   1602CM

Printed in China

TUTTLE PUBLISHING® is a registered trademark of Tuttle Publishing, a division of Periplus Editions (HK) Ltd.

Contents

Acknowledgments, Caveats, and a Note on Names   7

Introduction   9

A Brief History of Korea   12

Part I: FOUNDATIONS

Chapter 1   Shamanism and the Spirit World   24

Chapter 2   Buddhism   34

Chapter 3   Confucianism   42

Chapter 4   Christianity   54

Chapter 5   Capitalism with a Korean Face   66

Chapter 6   Democracy: Beyond Asian Values   78

Part II: CULTURAL CODES

Chapter 7   *Jeong*—The "Invisible Hug"   92

Chapter 8   Competition   101

Chapter 9   *Chemyon*, or Face   112

Chapter 10   *Han* and *Heung*   120

Chapter 11   From Clan to Nuclear Family   128

Chapter 12   Neophilia   139

Part III: *HYUN-SHIL*: COLD REALITY

Chapter 13 North Korea: Friend, Foe, or Foreigner?   148

Chapter 14 Politics and the Media   158

Chapter 15 Onward, Industrial Soldiers   170

Chapter 16 "More Important than the Business Itself"   182

Chapter 17 Introducing Mr. and Mrs. Perfect   192

Chapter 18 English Mania   202

Part IV: IN THE HOURS NOT SPENT WORKING

Chapter 19 Living Space: From *Hanok* to Apartment
Houses and Back Again   212

Chapter 20 Four Seasons at the Dinner Table   220

Chapter 21 Cinema: Boom, Bust, and Brilliance   229

Chapter 22 More Than K-Pop   240

Chapter 23 Work All Day, Stay Out All Night   250

Part V: MORE OF "US," LESS OF "THEM"

Chapter 24 Defensive Nationalism   260

Chapter 25 Multicultural Korea?   271

Chapter 26 "It's Our Turn"   279

Chapter 27 "We Are Not Aliens, From Another Cosmos"   291

Chapter 28 A Woman's Place Is in the Office   298

Epilogue: Where Is the Champagne?   309

Index   313

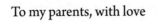
To my parents, with love

Acknowledgments, Caveats, and a Note on Names

The following people provided interviews, helped me in some way over the past year, or are simply friends I wish to express my appreciation to. There are a few others I would have liked to mention here, but their help has to remain secret:

In alphabetical order: Ahn Seong-hee, Alex Travelli, Andrew Barbour, Angela Yoon, Andrew Salmon, Antti Hellgren, 'Ask the Korean', Bae Yeong-jin, Cal Barksdale, Choi Min-sik, Chris Kelly, Chun Su-jin, Cynthia Yoo, Darcy Paquet, Darren Long, David Maltby, Dominic Ziegler, Don O'Brien, Eric Oey, Gady Epstein, Han Sun-Kyung, Han Young-yong and Lee Jun-ho, Henry Tricks, Hong Joo-hee, Hong Myung-bo, Hong Seok-chon, Hwang Doo-jin, 'Hyun-ju', Jason Lee, Ji Bae and family, Jooch Nam, Jung Eun-sung, Jung Yoon-sun, Jung Young-sun, Kang Hye-ran, Kang Jeong-im, Kang Se-ree, Kang Ye-won, Kate English, Kim Bo-yeon, Kim Ou-joon, Kim Hye-jeong, Kim Kkobbi, Ko Un and Lee Sang-hwa, Krys Lee, Kwon Yong-ho, Kwon Young-se, Lee Hye-ryeong, Lee Ji-eun, Lee Seong-hee, Lee Seul, Lee Yoo-jin and family, Lee Yun-hee, Lin Lin, Marcus Haggers, Marisa Muscari, Mary Jane Liddicoat, Michael Breen, Michael Freeman, Moon Jung-hee and Lee Young-joon, Nam Sang-ah and Third Line Butterfly, Naomi Rovnick, Nick Watney, Oh Kwan-soo, Park So-young and family, Park Won-soon, Patrick Lee, Peter Underwood, Prof. Chang Ha-joon, Prof. Chung Duk-ae, Prof. Jang Hoon, Prof. Jin Y. Park, Prof. Kim Ui-cheol, Prof. Michael Shin, Prof. Park Jung-sook, Pyo Chul-min, Rob Dickinson, Rob York, Seo Ji-hye, Shin Joong-hyun, Simon Long, Song Ji-hye, Song Yae-ri, TBS eFM (Ahn Jung-hyun, Ahn Jung-mi, Mike Weisbart, and friends), The LFG Family, Will Ennett, Yang Ik-jun, Yi Soyeon, Yoo Jae-hoon, Yoon Sun-oo, Zachi Schor, and Zander Lanfried.

Caveats: Many people were generous enough to share their knowledge and insight with me during the making of this book. However, all opinions—and mistakes—are my own. The presence of an interviewee in a particular chapter does not mean that he or she will necessarily agree with my conclusions, or indeed anything else I write. If anyone feels I have been unfair about of any aspect of their country or culture, then I can only say that it was absolutely not my intention to offend anyone. I wrote this book with sincerity and love for the subject, and I hope that shows.

A note on names: Korean names are ordered family name first, and given name (which is usually composed of two syllables and hyphenated when written in English) second. In this way, Manchester United's Korean player would be referred to as Park Ji-sung. I follow this convention, unless specifically asked to do otherwise by the person in question. Also, I try to follow generally accepted Romanization of Korean characters, but in cases where a famous person is known by a different spelling (Kim Jong-il, for instance), I defer to the general consensus.

Introduction

Though Hyundais and Kias are commonplace on Western streets and Korean technology is found in products from smart phones to the Dreamliner, South Korea remains something of an unknown quantity. Even those with an interest in Asian cultures tend to overlook this nation of fifty million in favor of its more powerful and populous neighbors. To its west, China, a nation that exacted tribute from Korea for centuries, is a reemerging regional hegemon. To its east lies Japan, the former colonizer and cultural powerhouse that has been exciting Western imaginations for decades. And directly to the north looms the so-called Democratic People's Republic of Korea, which, thanks to its nuclear weapons program and bizarre, monarchical leadership, utterly overshadows South Korea in the world's media.

What ideas do exist about South Korea tend to be heavily stereotypical. When this author visits any non-Asian country, one of the first questions people ask is, "Do all Koreans really eat dog?" The idea that no pet Alsatian would be safe wandering the streets of Seoul is surprisingly common. And though South Korean per-capita GDP (by purchasing power parity) has reached US$30,000, many in the West assume that South Koreans are still the poor third-world citizens depicted in the TV sitcom *M*A*S*H*.

Other misplaced assumptions include: Koreans are socially conservative; Koreans are shy and reserved, and do not know how to have fun; Koreans are excessively proud, and believe their country to be the best in the world; all Koreans want North-South reunification; all Koreans hate (or all Koreans love) the United States; Koreans lack creativity; and Koreans are untrustworthy and difficult to deal with in business. There is also one very important misunderstanding about the state of South Korea itself: many believe that this country has always been a bastion of free markets and democracy, which is not the case.

Existing English-language literature about Korea has done little to dispel these ideas. Western writers tend to focus on the old and the traditional, on the Korean War, or on North Korea. There are very few books that show modern South Korea as it is. This is unfortunate, because South Korea is already an important country in the community of nations and in this modern world—not just economically but also culturally and politically. It is time for us all to learn something more about this unique, vibrant, rising country. This book is intended as a way in—a starting point for those who wish to get to know South Korea.

The book is divided into five parts. The first concerns fundamental influences on human behavior in Korea, such as the Buddhist religion, Confucianism, millennia-old shamanism, capitalism, and Christianity. The second part discusses well-studied cultural codes such as *jeong* and *han* but also the less frequently discussed *heung* (a kind of pure joy) and South Koreans' obsession with anything new. The third section, *Hyun-shil: Cold Reality*, covers how Koreans do business and politics, work, date, and obsess over education, particularly the study of English. The fourth concerns Korean films, popular music, cuisine, and nightlife; and finally, the fifth part shows how South Korea is no longer an insular, conservative country but rather one that is opening up to the rest of the world and starting to shake off its Confucian-influenced, sexist past. The book begins with a brief synopsis of Korean history in order to give historical context to the chapters that follow.

Why "The Impossible Country"?

Fifty years ago, South Korea was an impoverished, war-torn country that lurched from brutal dictatorship to chaotic democracy and then dictatorship again. Few expected it to survive as a state, let alone graduate to becoming a prosperous and stable model for developing countries the world over—and one with an impressive list of achievements in popular culture, to boot. Quite simply, South Koreans have written the most unlikely and impressive story of nation building of the last century. For that reason alone, theirs deserves to be called "the impossible country."

South Korea is home to not one, but two miracles. The first is the often-referenced "miracle on the Han River," the extraordinary economic growth that led the country out of poverty and on the road to wealth, in the 1960s, '70s, and '80s. That South Korea had a GDP of less than US$100 per capita in 1960, precious few natural resources, and only the most basic (and war-ravaged) infrastructure seems scarcely believable looking around Seoul these days. The second miracle is just as precious, though. As recently as 1987, South Korea was a military dictatorship, but today, it has stable, democratic leadership. As other Asian nations like Singapore, and now China, promote a mix of authoritarianism and capitalism, South Korea stands out in the region as an example of a country that values not just wealth but also the rule of law and rights for its citizens.

There is another, more negative, source of inspiration for the subtitle, though. As we shall see, genuine contentment largely eludes the people of South Korea, despite all their material success and stability. This is a country that puts too much pressure on its citizens to conform to impossible standards of education, reputation, physical appearance, and career progress. Worldwide, South Korea is second only to Lithuania in terms of suicides per capita. The problem is getting worse, rather than better: between 1989 and 2009, the rate of suicide quintupled. South Korea therefore is "impossible" in its astonishing economic and political achievements but also in the way that it imposes unattainable targets on its people.

Korean independence fighter Kim Gu stated that, "I do not want our nation to become the richest and most powerful nation in the world. . . . It is sufficient that our wealth is such that it makes our lives abundant." Instead, he wanted Korea to become "the most beautiful nation in the world," one that provides happiness for its own people and others. Were he alive today, he would probably be disappointed with some of what he saw. But even he would have to admit that this impossible country has come a long way.

A Brief History of Korea

Prehistory and Gojoseon

Homo erectus made his appearance on the Korean peninsula as early as 400,000 years ago. Modern humans have existed in the region of northeast Asia for almost 40,000 years. The people identified by archaeologists as the ancestors of today's Koreans are believed to have arrived in successive waves from southern Siberia and Manchuria from around 6,000 BCE onwards. They were semi-nomadic, followed shamanistic religious practice, and spoke an Altaic language.

The foundation of the first state entity on the peninsula is shrouded in myth. According to the *Samguk Yusa*, a compendium of historical events, legends, and folktales from ancient Korea from the thirteenth century, the state of Gojoseon was founded by the demigod king, Dangun, in the fiftieth year of the reign of Chinese emperor Yao. This corresponds with the year 2333 BCE. The story goes that Hwanin, the Lord of Heaven, had a son named Hwanung, who wanted to live on earth. Hwanung descended from Heaven at Taebaek, now known as Baekdu, the highest mountain on the Korean peninsula. There he founded a city named Sinsi, the City of God. A tiger and a bear prayed to Hwanung that he make them human, and Hwanung instructed them to remain in a cave for one hundred days, eating only garlic and mugwort. The tiger soon gave up, but the bear kept to the bargain and was transformed into a woman. Hwanung took her as his wife, and together they produced a son, Dangun. After becoming king, Dangun built a city named Asadal (near present-day Pyongyang) and established the state of Gojoseon.

Archeological evidence suggests the existence of city-states on the peninsula from the eleventh century BCE onwards. Gojoseon, ruled by kings who claimed to descend from Dangun, became the most powerful and advanced of these. It absorbed other city-states in a kind of confederation structure and controlled territory from the

Daedong River to the Liao River in present-day China by the fourth century BCE.

Gojoseon had hostile relations with the Chinese state of Yan and lost much of its northern territory following a war around 300 BCE. Two centuries later, in 108 BCE, Emperor Wu of the Western Han dynasty destroyed Gojoseon completely and set up four command- eries to rule Gojoseon's former territory. Due to local resistance, though, three were recalled, leaving only one, the Lelang Command- ery ("Nakranggun" in Korean). The Lelang Commandery's exact location is the subject of controversy, but it survived until 313 AD, serving as a conduit by which Chinese culture—particularly Confu- cian thought and the Chinese writing system—entered the Korean peninsula.

The state responsible for ending the Lelang Commandery was Goguryeo, a pre-Korean state that began in southern Manchuria around the Yalu River. By the fifth century, the territorially and cul- turally ambitious Goguryeo had expanded its control to the north- ern part of Korea as well as almost all of Manchuria and parts of Inner Mongolia. Goguryeo established the Korean peninsula's first Confucian college in 372 and was also the first of Korea's kingdoms to adopt Buddhism, in the very same year.

The Three Kingdoms, and Unifying Shilla

While Goguryeo was building up its power in the north, two other states began to emerge in the southwest and southeast of the pen- insula. These were Baekje and Shilla, respectively. During this so- called proto-Three Kingdoms Period, Baekje began absorbing a set of less powerful states in the southwest known collectively as the Mahan Confederacy (between the first and third centuries), and Shilla achieved the same feat in the southeast with a collection of chiefdoms known as the Jinhan (between the first and fourth cen- turies). Shilla later conquered Gaya, another confederacy located around the Nakdong River Basin by the south coast, in 562.

Goguryeo, Baekje, and Shilla shared a common language (Old Korean, or Godae Gukeo), a shamanistic religious tradition that came from the Siberian heritage of ancient Korea, and an increasing acceptance of Chinese culture. However, these three states also existed in a state of political and military rivalry. Following the annexation of Gaya and the formation of an alliance with Tang China in 648, Shilla began to gain the upper hand. In 660, aided by the Tang, Shilla conquered Baekje. Together, the Tang and Shilla also attacked Goguryeo the following year but were repulsed. In 668, Goguryeo finally fell to Shilla, which thus became the state that unified the Korean peninsula.

Goguryeo's former territories in Manchuria were lost, however. Tang China's purpose in allying with Shilla had always been the eventual conquest of Korea, and so, following the Korean unification, the two former allies fell into conflict, fighting several battles throughout the 670s. Shilla eventually repelled the Tang but at the cost of all the land north of the Daedong River. Nationalistic Korean historians sometimes lament Shilla's alliance with the Tang because of this. Kim Yu-shin, the general who led Shilla's unification of Korea, has statues dedicated to him in South Korea, yet North Korean defectors report that General Kim is vilified there for his role in the forfeit of Goguryeo land.

Shilla led Korea through an era of prosperity and peace that lasted until around the mid-eighth century. It adopted Buddhism as state religion and encouraged the development of Confucianism, with the opening of a national Confucian college in 682. Despite the wars of the 670s, it also managed to rebuild relations with Tang China, which was at the time the most advanced state in the world, and certainly the most powerful in East Asia.

Fall of Shilla, and Koryo

Early pre-unification Shilla was marked by shifts in power between three competing clans, with the names of Park, Kim, and Seok. As the state developed, the Kim clan gained the upper hand and established a monarchy. They adopted a highly stratified social structure, based on so-called "bone rank." At the top was the "sacred bone" class, which comprised those directly related to the king. Beneath this was the "true bone" class of lesser royals and members of the Park and Seok clans. Below the true bone class were six further ranks.

Those at the top, at rank six, could become vice ministers of the government but rise no higher. Ranks five and four could become lower-level civil servants. Little is known about ranks one, two, and three, but they are assumed to represent the general populace. This system was entirely hereditary, and thus social mobility in the state of Shilla was nonexistent.

Those in level six, often highly educated and ambitious intellectuals, felt restricted by the system's rigidity, and by the eighth century, rebellions began to issue from this class. Peasant farmers also revolted in 889 over excessive taxation, and regional differences that had previously been held at bay began to resurface. Shilla started to crumble, and a former general, Gyeon Hwon, established the breakaway kingdom of Hubaekje (later Baekje) in 900. One year later, a Shilla noble named Gung Ye established Hugoguryeo (later Goguryeo). By 901, Korea was thus once again three separate kingdoms.

By 918, Hugoguryeo had become the strongest of the three. However, Gung Ye had grown into a paranoid despot, killing even his wife and two sons and proclaiming himself a Buddha. Four of his generals plotted to assassinate him and installed his chief minister, Wang Geon, as the new king. Wang Geon became King Taejo (Taejo means "The Great Progenitor"). He renamed his young state Koryo, from which the English-language name of Korea is derived.

In 935, a weakened Shilla submitted to Taejo; one year later, he defeated Hubaekje. Thus, Korea was reunified under a new dynasty. Taejo was careful to act as a benevolent ruler. He gave land and titles to those who submitted to him, including Gyeongsun, the last king of Shilla, though he extended no such privileges to anyone from Hubaekje, a state he despised. Skilled in diplomacy, Taejo maintained good relations with Song dynasty China. He reclaimed some of the land lost to China after the fall of Goguryeo, thus increasing Korea's territory. At the same time, Koryo underwent increased Sinicization. For instance, the Chinese civil service examination system, which selected would-be bureaucrats based on their knowledge of history, Confucian classics, and Confucian ethics, was adopted by the Koryo state. This examination system remained in place until 1894.

Theoretically, the examination system meant that anyone could rise to a position of authority. In practice though, Koryo did not of-fer real social mobility. Social classes were established based on pro-fession and were preserved by hereditary transfer. The children of a member of the artisan class would be artisans too. Children of the peasant classes were not allowed to hold government posts. An out-cast class, comprised of butchers, entertainers, and people performing other tasks considered base by the aristocracy, was forced to live in ghetto-like areas, away from the rest of society.

Confucianism as an ethical system and political ideology would increasingly dominate Koryo, but spiritual life remained Buddhist. Koryo sponsored the golden age of Korean Buddhism, with the erec-tion of many temples and the creation of masterpieces such as the Tripitaka Koreana, which remains the most complete corpus of Bud-dhist texts in existence, carved completely without error into more than eighty thousand wood blocks. Eventually, though, the admin-istrative elite, which was principally Confucian, grew tired of the power that the Buddhists had accumulated and sought to reduce the religion's role in the state. Buddhism and Confucianism had coexist-ed peacefully in Korea for centuries, but from the fourteenth century onwards, this was no longer to be the case.

Beginning in 1231 and continuing into 1258, the Mongols, who had conquered China and established the Yuan dynasty under Kub-lai Khan, invaded Korea repeatedly. Koryo was forced into a tribu-tary relationship with the powerful khans. Its kings were married off to Mongol princesses, which resulted in a string of half-Korean, half-Mongol monarchs. The khans' overlordship would last until the 1350s, by which time their influence had fundamentally weakened the stability of the Koryo state. Yet Mongol dominance also resulted in numerous cultural exchanges that would shape the history of the peninsula. Many elite Koreans either visited, or were held captive in, Beijing, the capital of the Mongol Yuan dynasty. The scholar An Hyang, for instance, was introduced to neo-Confucianism there and brought neo-Confucian texts back to Korea with him when he returned. This brand of Confucianism would become Korea's gov-erning philosophy and continues to influence Korean society to this day.

During the 1370s and 1380s, a talented general named Yi Seong-gye succeeded in driving the remaining Mongol garrisons out of the north of Korea, while also defeating the Japanese pirates who had been attacking the east coast. He became the leader of a faction within the Koryo court that favored allying with Ming dynasty China and opposing the Mongols, whose control of China was crumbling. In 1388, he was ordered by the government to attack Ming forces, but instead he launched a coup against the rulers of Koryo. In 1392, he declared himself king of the new Joseon dynasty. His descendents, the Yi family, would form the house that ruled Korea until 1910.

Joseon

Joseon Korea turned away from Buddhism and installed neo-Confucianism as the official state ideology. One critical change this ushered in was a reduction in the status of women. During the Koryo dynasty, women had equal rights to inheritance, and could be designated heads of households; under the Joseon state, this was no longer the case. Shamanism, the indigenous religion of the Koreans, was also marginalized: practitioners were relegated to the lowest social class, the *cheonmin*—a group that also included slaves.

The highest social class was known as the *yangban*. Members of this group owed their status to the civil service examination, since those who could pass it were awarded land and titles for three generations. In between the *yangban* and the *cheonmin* were the *jungin*, a middle class comprised of professionals, such as doctors, and the *sangmin*, the ordinary workers (usually farmers) who made up more than half of the total population.

The early Joseon period saw the reign of the king considered the most exemplary Korean ruler of all, King Sejong the Great (r. 1418–1450). Sejong expanded and secured Korea's northern territory to roughly where the North Korea-China border lies today. During his reign, great strides were made in agricultural output, literature, medicine, and science. Sejong was also responsible for the creation of *Hangul*, the native Korean alphabet. Prior to this, Koreans had only used Chinese characters, which were too complex and numerous for the masses to master, as they had no few real educational opportunities.

For these achievements, Sejong is the only king of a unified Korean state to have been posthumously acclaimed as "the Great."

Though the early Joseon period was a time of progress, by the late fifteenth century, infighting had broken out at court, weakening the power of the state. Later, in 1592, Japan launched the Imjin Waeran invasions against Korea, as the shogun Toyotomi Hideyoshi sought to use the peninsula as a stepping-stone on his way to conquer Ming China. The Koreans managed to finally repel the Japanese in 1598 with the assistance of China, as well as the metal-plated "turtle ships" of General Yi Sun-shin, whose defeat of the Japanese navy makes him one of Korea's greatest heroes. The cost of the war to Korea was vast, however: hundreds of thousands of Koreans are estimated to have died as a result of the invasion, and one-third of the nation's agricultural land was left unusable, causing poverty and famine.

Korea thus entered the seventeenth century extremely weakened, and fell into a tributary relationship with the Manchurian Qing dynasty that lasted until 1895. The rigid hierarchicalism of society also began to weaken during this portion of the Joseon period. The fortunes of many yangban had been ruined in the wake of the Japanese invasions, while the jungin professional class was beginning to rise. Some jungin managed to accumulate great fortunes through trading, an activity traditionally disdained by the yangban. Seeking to increase their social standing, many jungin began "buying in" to the yangban, swelling the ranks of the official elite and undermining the Joseon class system. Because of this practice, former yangban families such as the Kimhae Kim have millions of members today. It also explains the extraordinary prevalence of family names like Kim, Lee, Park, and Choi in Korea. Collectively, these four names account for half of the population.

Later Joseon was marked by rebellion, internal division, and increased outside influence. In the late eighteenth century, Christianity—brought in largely by Koreans who encountered the religion in China—began to attract its first converts, despite the opposition of a hostile government. A series of popular peasant revolts, such as one led by Hong Gyeong-nae in 1811, and the growth of a movement named Donghak, posed a serious challenge to the government toward the end of the century. Powerful families such as the Andong Kim reduced Joseon's ruling Yi family to mere figureheads and were draining the country's resources through corruption and outright thievery.

All of these factors weakened the government, while foreign powers were starting to exert influence and force trade on the peninsula. Though Korea attempted to pursue a policy of isolationism—which earned it the sobriquet of the Hermit Kingdom—France, Britain, the United States, and Russia all entered Korean waters without permission in the late 1800s, with sometimes violent results. Japan, then resurgent following the Meiji Restoration of 1868, also had designs on the country that had repelled them almost three hundred years before. In 1876, by means of the gunboat diplomacy first demonstrated by the West, Japan forced Korea into signing the unequal Treaty of Ganghwa, which opened the country to trade with the island nation.

In 1894–1895, China—Korea's long-standing "big brother" state—and Japan went to war, principally over control of Korea. Japan's victory ended Chinese influence over the peninsula and coincided with the official ending of the Joseon social structure based on yangban, jungin, sangmin, and cheonmin classes. A process of brutal colonization culminated in the Japan-Korea Treaty of 1910, granting Japan "all rights of sovereignty over the whole of Korea."

The Modern Era

The period of 1910–1945 represents a nadir in Korean history. It was the first time that this oft-invaded nation had fallen under the full control of a foreign power. Japan ruled the country through governors-general who imposed order via police and military force and punished dissenters severely. It is, however, an uncomfortable fact that Japanese political control was implemented not only by Japanese administrators but with the help of large numbers of Korean collaborators, who ranged from ex-Joseon officials and landowners in the governor-general's pay to people from the lower classes who took work in the police or as informers.

Particularly during the 1930s and early 1940s, Japan governed Korea with extreme cruelty. As many as 200,000 women were made into sex slaves. Men were used as forced laborers. All people were required to take Japanese names, speak Japanese, and worship at Shinto shrines. And while Japan did pursue industrialization, particularly in the north of Korea, the beneficiaries of the ensuing economic growth tended to be either Japanese, or their Korean collaborators.

Though the defeat of Imperial Japan in 1945 resulted in Korean liberation, joy was short-lived. The Allied victors, the United States and the Soviet Union, occupied and divided the country on a supposedly temporary basis (without consulting Koreans), with the former responsible for territory south of the 38th Parallel and the latter the north. The original intention was to reconstitute Korea as a free, independent country, and the newly formed UN drew up plans to hold elections to determine a Korean government. However, Moscow opposed this. Instead, in the North a new regime led by former independence fighter Kim Il-sung was formed, under the tutelage of Joseph Stalin. In the South, the U.S. military backed a staunchly anti-Communist, American-educated candidate named Syngman Rhee. Rhee would lead the South until 1960.

The two superpowers quickly turned from allies to enemies. By 1948, the U.S.-backed South was holding elections, which the Soviet-backed North boycotted. Rhee, the ultimate victor in this process, became president of South Korea and formally assumed power from the U.S. military, inaugurating the new Republic of Korea on the August 15, 1948, under a constitution promulgated one month previously. On September 9, the Democratic People's Republic of Korea was proclaimed, with Kim Il-sung as its prime minister. The formal establishment of two independent states completed the division of Korea.

Neither North nor South Korea viewed this division as acceptable in the long term. Both parties had launched border raids and skirmishes across the 38th parallel, but on June 25, 1950, the North began a full-scale invasion. Kim Il-sung's forces made rapid gains and by August controlled the entire Korean peninsula, save for a small area around the southeastern port city of Busan.

On September 15, acting for UN Command, U.S. general Douglas MacArthur staged a landing at the west coast city of Incheon, with

40,000 American and South Korean troops. By September 25, they had retaken Seoul and began pressing into North Korea, with the intention of reaching the Chinese border. China, which had been under Communist control since the previous year, sent 200,000 troops down into Korea across the Yalu River on October 25, in support of Kim Il-sung. For the rest of the war, the South Korea-UN and North Korea-China forces fought each other to a stalemate.

By the time the armistice agreement was signed on July 27, 1953, an estimated three million people had lost their lives as a result of the three-year conflict. Of this total, around 2.5 million were Korean civilians. The total combined population of North and South Korea at the time was just 30 million. Furthermore, the peninsula's infrastructure—roads, government buildings, bridges—was almost completely destroyed. The destruction of around half of all houses on the peninsula resulted in destitution for millions of those who had managed to survive the war itself.

South Korea was born into ruin and poverty. Even at the end of the 1950s, GDP per capita was well below $100. Life expectancy was around fifty-four years. The political situation was equally dismal: the nation was presided over by an authoritarian, corrupt regime under President Rhee. It could maintain power only through violence and did little to improve the people's standard of living.

In the intervening half-century though, South Korea has somehow overcome the weight of its tragic history to become arguably the greatest national success story of recent times. It is a story of rapid economic, political, cultural, and artistic achievements. These advances alone deserve our attention, but the overall story of the people and culture from which they sprang should also be more widely known.

PART ONE

Foundations

Chapter 1

Shamanism and the Spirit World

Primary colors blur as she spins repeatedly, entranced and led on by clanging cymbals and the insistent beat of drums. She sings and dances as a means of communicating with the spirit world. She enters into what appears to be a trance, speaking with the voice of the departed. This is her gift, and her curse—to be a *musok-in*, a Korean shaman. The ceremony she is performing, the *gut*, lasts all day long and may serve to calm malign spirits, purify the soul of the recently deceased, or ask the gods for a good harvest or success in a business venture. She is part of a tradition that stretches back forty thousand years and has its origins in Siberia. *Musok*, or shamanism, has been practiced on the Korean peninsula for far longer than the concept of Korea, the country, has existed.

Though *Musok* is ancient and seems remote from the South Korea of today—a wealthy, technologically advanced, and increasingly globalized country—it is woven into the fabric of Korean society and still exerts an influence over the most rational of city folk.

What is Korean Shamanism, and How Popular Is It?
Musok is a set of disparate religious or superstitious practices based in the belief of a natural world animated by spirits, and aimed at bridging between those spirits and living human beings. Usually, a believer will turn to *Musok* in order to produce some sort of benefit—good fortune or the removal of evil spirits—or to learn something about his or her destiny. Practitioners may follow a great many

different gods and spirits, and the way these are followed depends on a number of factors, including the practitioner's personality and the region she comes from. According to the *musok-in* Hyun-ju (her working name), who has practiced *Musok* for over twenty years for a large variety of clients, at the heart of *Musok* is simply a "belief in nature." As she explains, everything in nature—be it a person, an animal, a tree, or even a rock —has a spirit. *Musok* offers a way of communicating with those spirits, and possibly using them for some earthly benefit.

Since each *musok-in* follows different gods and spirits, there is a pantheon in only a very loose sense. Researchers have documented more than ten thousand gods worshipped by *Musok* practitioners, and, in reality, there are likely to be many more. Individual musok-in have their own principal gods—Hyun-ju's is an ancient Chinese monk. There have been those who have followed Jesus Christ; and, after his daring Incheon landing during the Korean War, some even worshipped General Douglas MacArthur.

Similarly, since there is no overarching set of rules and no bible or orthodoxy, ceremonies that have formalized rituals involving dances, songs, and incantations—such as the Seoul danggut, which calls for a good harvest—are recognized and transmitted on a regional or town level. *Musok-in* learn those that apply to their home regions. In addition, according to Hyun-ju, *musok-in* often find it hard to collaborate since they each believe "their gods are the best." While each *musok-in* is guided to some extent by millennia of shamanic tradition, specific traditions vary by region. Furthermore, much depends on who the novice learned from, the god she follows, and her own individual character.

Musok is very practical, as it is used as way of solving people's problems via communication with the spirit world. The *musok-in* is a go-between, mediating between ordinary Koreans and this other world, linking the person seeking advice or an understanding of their future or remediation of some sort with the spirits that can provide it. Hyun-ju, for instance, tells this author to avoid the color blue and, more specifically, not to buy a blue car at the age of thirty-four, based on the advice of spirits. But she does not impart the sort of moral counsel a pastor or priest might, for instance. There is no *Musok* Ten Commandments. (Hyun-ju does have her own personal rules, however, such as the need to refrain from lying and thoughtless speech. Her chosen name means "Be careful with your words.")

Followers do not describe themselves as adherents of *Musok*. In Korea, one simply visits a *musok-in* for advice with a big decision or dilemma, or when faced with illness or tragedy. Those who go for counsel are not typically aware of the specific character of the gods followed by the musok-in or the meaning of the rituals employed. They approach the musok-in in the way a Westerner may approach a psychiatrist: as a consultant, as and when required.

Musok is considered "feminine"—a legacy of Korean history and not simply due to the fact that most practitioners are women. During the Joseon dynasty (1392–1897), neo-Confucianism was the state ideology. This philosophical tradition was paternalistic and encouraged the marginalization of women in public life. Concerned with rationalism and the promotion of an orderly society, neo-Confucians considered *Musok* emotional and metaphysical and conflated it with the feminine, which may in fact have coincided with a tradition of shamans being mainly women. Consequently, they suppressed it, and relegated *musok-in* to the lowest social class, the *cheonmin*. Even so, practitioners continued to receive business from customers of all kinds, from humble farmers to royalty. In an era of male-dominated, non-spiritual formality, people demanded an outlet for the opposite side of their character—and *Musok* provided that. Queen Min of the late Joseon period herself employed two *musok-in* as advisors.

In the modern era, despite the advent of scientific rationalism and the rapid growth of Christianity in Korea, *Musok* has flourished. The New York Times reports there to be around 300,000 *musok-in* working in contemporary Korea. Many are drawn to the practice by the fact that it has become a very profitable business. A sought-after *musok-in* who pushes expensive ceremonies on her clients can become wealthy. Some are able to advertise in major newspapers, employ several apprentices and assistants, and buy multiple properties. The fact that millions of Koreans are prepared to pay for this sort of spiritual counsel does, of course, encourage fakes and frauds. This, according to Hyun-ju, has set the *Musok* world "at war with itself." A real *musok-in* is not rich, she says.

The Making of a *Musok-in*

The process of becoming a *musok-in* can start in one of two ways. The first is *seseupmu*, the inheritance of shaman status from one's family, with an older relative conferring the status on a younger one. Of such *musok-in*, there are two types, both traditionally found south of the Han River: *shimbang* and *tangol*. *Shimbang* are not considered to be in direct contact with spirits, but they have the ability to draw spirits into communion with others. A *tangol* may not believe in a particular god as her guide. Neither will maintain a personal shrine.

The second type of initiation, *gangshinmu*, occurs with no such hereditary connection. It begins with a kind of "spiritual sickness" known as a *shinbyeong*. The *shinbyeong* manifests itself in a variety of symptoms, such as loss of energy, hallucinations, the hearing of voices, and insomnia, which indicate that the woman who is stricken by them is possessed of the ability to communicate with spirits. This ability is considered a curse rather than a blessing—but it is also a matter of destiny: Hyun-ju states that she would not be a *musok-in* if she felt she had a choice. Her life is lonely, she says, and at least for her, incompatible with having a family. She remains unmarried and laments that she expects no one to turn up to her funeral, a consequence of people's superstition about the presence of hostile spirits at a *musok-in's* wake and her lack of a family.

Those judged to be proper candidates for *gangshinmu* induction into the ranks of *musok-in* are initiated by way of a special kind of *gut*, the *naerim gut*. *Naerim* refers to the physical entrance of a spirit into a new initiate; a particular god (for example, Hyun-ju's Chinese monk), will take possession of the new *musok-in*, and from then on be her spirit leader. This *naerim* ceremony cures the illness and signals the initiate's transformation from ordinary person to *musok-in*.

The conductor of the *naerim gut* will then likely serve as the new *musok-in's* master. Though the novice keeps her own god, she also forms a kind of spirit mother–spirit daughter apprentice relationship with the elder *musok-in*, learning her incantations and songs and working as a junior participant in her ceremonies. This period may last several years, and depending upon the strictness of the master, the trainee may also have to spend some of this time performing basic household chores.

The world of *Musok* is not uniform, however. Hyun-ju claims never to have suffered from any of the physical symptoms of *shinbyeong*, though she was visited by several spirits during her *naerim* stage. Her story is unusual: at the age of thirty-two, she was visited first by Jesus Christ, then the spirit of a Japanese samurai, then a Chinese monk. Each wanted her to accept *naerim* from him, and, following her instincts, she chose the monk. After this, the monk subjected her to a series of trials, such as having to repeatedly leap in the air, for six hours at a time. During this stage, which lasted several weeks, she also had to ward off the relentless entreaties of the samurai: in order to placate him, she spent another six hours per day bowing.

Because Hyun-ju never manifested *shinbyeong* symptoms, it was difficult for her to find an older *shaman* to perform her *naerim gut*. Those around her felt she had simply gone insane. She recounts becoming the subject of neighborhood gossip as a result of her unusual behavior. However, after she had approached several *musok-in* with her story, one established practitioner accepted her as an apprentice, thus beginning her initiation into Korea's oldest tradition.

Life as a *Musok-in*

Today, *musok-in* are not ostracized on class grounds, as they were during the Joseon era, for the social structures of old have disappeared. However, because of their perceived spiritual power, many people fear them and, as a result, refrain from socializing with them. For the ordinary person, the *musok-in* is someone to be visited in times of trouble and avoided at other times. A writer or anthropologist planning to visit one is likely be warned by friends to be careful.

The *musok-in* is called on to provide *gut*, dancing and singing to communicate with the spirits while dressed in the multicolored robes that denote her profession. She might "ride the blades" during such a ceremony. This is the most famously sensational *musok-in* act, performed in a state of deep entrancement or ecstasy, when the *musok-in* dances barefoot on the edge of a knife without cutting herself, to show her power and intimidate malign spirits. Other *musok-in* have different calling cards. Hyun-ju is said to have the ability to lift a cow off the ground and place it on a spike, in demonstration of the physical strength provided to her by her gods.

A *musok-in* will also perform smaller rituals at the home or place of business of a client. Those opening new enterprises, for example, may call upon the spirit world by inviting a *musok-in* to perform a ceremony for good luck. Practices include putting banknotes between the trotters of a dead pig (pigs symbolize money and fortune) and the ritual placement of a dried pollack on the premises. One sometimes sees such fish long after the ceremony is over, as it is supposed to bring good luck as long as it remains in place.

The most common service is *jeom*, which is a form of one-on-one spiritual counseling. If one has a particular query—for example, "When will I get married?" or "Should I start my own business?"— one may consult a *musok-in* for advice from the spirit world. For many *musok-in*, *jeom* is the starting point for subsequent services recommended to the client: for example, a follow-up *gut*. For Hyun-ju, however, *gut* is "only for rich people." Since it can be astonishingly expensive—a single ceremony may cost around 8 million won (about $7,500 U.S. dollars) or more—she never recommends it for people of ordinary means, opting instead to take them to the mountains for prayer. Much of Hyun-ju's practice simply consists in listening to people's problems and giving advice, much like a counselor.

Many of today's elite Koreans make use of *gut*, just as Queen Min did in the nineteenth century. Members of chaebol families (chaebol being the large family-run business groups that dominate the economy) have been reported to pay for services for purposes ranging from business success to personal matters, as have politicians seeking electoral success. Hyun-ju has had several business, politician, and celebrity clients; she claims to have foretold the bankruptcy of one of her wealthiest patrons, after having seen a vision of him in rags.

Animism and Mountain Spirits

Musok is so broad and practical it is very hard to pin down as a system of beliefs and behaviors. However, stemming from Korea's ancient past, it is fundamentally a form of animism. In animism, every natural entity in existence has a spirit or life force in the same way that people do—even things Westerners consider inanimate, like rocks and trees.

Some natural features hold more power than others. For instance, some multicentenarian pine trees are considered to have a character or personality of their own. A powerful tree can be a benefactor or village guardian, providing good fortune and serving as the focal point of the community. It was the practice of village elders to hold meetings around some of these trees in order to reach important decisions. Such venerable beings may have a temper when mistreated, though: one tree in the town of Gimje was said to bring bad luck on the house of anyone who took even one of its leaves. In the case of an angry tree, *musok-in* could offer *gut* ceremonies to it by way of placation.

Animals may also have a spiritual role. The tiger, which features prominently in the creation myth and is the national animal of Korea, was said to be a messenger of mountain spirits and a spiritual protector in its own right. However, the most important repositories of animist spirits in Korea are the mountains. Seventy percent of the peninsula is mountainous, so it seems natural that the tall peaks of Baekdu-san, Jiri-san, and Halla-san in particular have a great hold over the Korean psyche. Ascending the mountains has always been considered a way of getting closer to the spirit world, and thus there is a strong tradition of shamanistic practice at high altitude.

There is no ranking system for the spiritual power of mountains, and each *musok-in* will have her own auspicious peaks. However, certain mountains are widely understood to be more important than others. Halla-san, the tallest mountain in South Korea, is located on Jeju Island, a place known for its deep shamanistic culture and, according to some, for the historic use of gwangdae beoseot, magic mushrooms, in shamanic practice. Halla-san was so revered by locals that in 1901 a visiting journalist from Germany, Siegfried Genthe, was told by the governor, "You may at no price climb Halla." The people believed that such an act would anger the mountain god and bring ruinous weather and a bad harvest in revenge.

One mountain in Seoul—Inwang-san—is a hotbed of *gut* and other ritualistic activity, so much so that the local authorities have erected signs discouraging it. For, on its slopes is Guksadang, the former shamanic shrine of the royal family, which was relocated from Namsan, another mountain beloved of musok-in (including Hyun-ju, who lives there). Guksadang is believed to enshrine the spirit of King Taejo, the founder of the Joseon dynasty. As the royal shrine, it was once private and forbidden. In today's republic, however, it is open to all, and it is tended to by *musok-in* who visit it daily in order to practice their skills. There are many public shrines throughout Korea, and, like Guksadang, they are typically located on hills and mountains. They vary greatly in size and state of repair. Private shrines are also kept by gangshinmu *musok-in*. Hyun-ju, for instance, has one in her home, dedicated to her Chinese monk.

To the untrained eye, Guksadang resembles a small Korean Buddhist temple, but on virtually any day one can watch *musok-in* perform rituals such as the cutting of animal entrails (in place of a live sacrifice, which would be illegal), utter incantations, and dance. A small convenience store near Guksadang sells pollack, a fish commonly used in shamanic ceremonies, among its soft drinks and newspapers.

Inwang-san and the Guksadang shrine lie close by Cheong Wa Dae (the Blue House), South Korea's presidential mansion, which is located behind the main palace of the Joseon dynasty, Gyeongbok-gung. Just a short distance away from these focal points of power in the country's capital, this mountain is the busiest site in all of Korean shamanism. This fact is less widely acknowledged than one would expect, which is testament to the paradoxical status *Musok* retains as a mysterious, non-mainstream set of activities that are in fact integral to Korean culture.

The Enduring Influence

Unlike Japanese Shinto, another set of animistic beliefs that became a vehicle for the state's ideology in Meiji Japan and has been somewhat standardized in its rituals, *Musok* remains disparate. Its countless gods are worshipped in ways depending on the individual character of the *musok-in* and of the teachers who initiated her. Although a small number of deities are widely accepted, such as the Seven Star God (concerned with longevity), the Dragon King God (sailing and fishing), and the House-Beam God (household prosperity), even these are not worshipped in the same way by all.

This fluidity or malleability is amply shown by the nature of one of the most popular gods, Sanshin (the mountain god). While each mountain has its own god, which one may follow, it is also possible to worship this general mountain deity. He is usually represented as a bearded, old man, frequently accompanied by a tiger, but sometimes Sanshin is depicted as a woman. Since there are both male and female gods, and certain mountains are considered feminine—Gyeryong-san, for example—this is not inappropriate.

Pictures of Sanshin can be found at the majority of Buddhist temples in Korea, testament to the syncretic nature of spiritual practice in this country. Buddhism has blended with shamanism since it first arrived in the fourth century, and today a great many Buddhists consult with *musok-in* when they confront a dilemma or misfortune. The first interview this author sought with Hyun-ju had to be postponed because it coincided with the run-up to Buddha's Birthday, a period when many of her Buddhist clients seek to consult with her about the future. At Inwang-san, a rock formation called Seonbawi (Zen Rock) is important to Buddhists; it lies less than a stone's throw from Guksadang and is considered by local *musok-in* too to have spiritual power.

Even Korean Christians, who tend to disparage shamanism as "mumbo-jumbo" (in the words of one churchgoer) manifest certain *Musok*-derived influences in their activities. Christians have a tradition of holding prayer meetings in the mountains, for instance. Furthermore, materialism of the God-wants-you-to-be-rich variety appears to be much more prevalent in Christianity in Korea than elsewhere in Asia. Arguably, this relates the practical or materialistic aspect of shamanism that is still manifest today. Performing a *Musok* ritual at the opening of a shop is not so different from praying to God for long lines of customers.

Perhaps *Musok's* most important gifts to Korea are practicality and flexibility. Having no set of commandments, fixed set of practices, or hierarchy of authorized gods, it accommodates and encourages pragmatism. To the end of achieving one's goals, an adherent can consult different musok-in about the same problem and combine their counsel with the comfort taken from other religions. Hyun-ju even advises followers to "not believe (in *Musok*) too much", for it can become addictive, like a drug if taken too far and thus detrimental to the follower. After all, the true purpose of *Musok* should be simply to help people. She may question her own ability, granting that not all her prophecies are correct, and jokes that if she were right one hundred percent of the time, she would be extremely rich. The most common misunderstanding about *Musok*, according to Hyun-ju, is that the practitioner has unlimited power to know, and do, anything.

These aspects of *Musok*—flexibility, pragmatism, openness to doubt, and easy acceptance of other beliefs—have had a positive effect on religious tolerance in general in Korea, and probably on Korean culture as well. A willingness to adapt has proven to be one of this country's most fortunate possessions.

Chapter 2

Buddhism

One might expect a transplanted religion to find balance uneasily, antagonistically even, with existing beliefs in a new country, but that was not the case for Buddhism in Korea. The relative ease with which Buddhism blended into the religious landscape following its arrival in 372 CE is testament to both the fluid nature of shamanism and the philosophical openness of the newcomer.

Today it is possible for a woman to pray at a Buddhist temple that she fall pregnant, and to consult with a shaman when faced with a tough decision. The temple might well be located in the mountains and contain a painting of Sanshin. Koreans who turn to both religions are aware there are philosophical contradictions in doing so, but they tend to overlook them—it is simply a matter of employing whatever works in a moment of need.

The Growth of Buddhism

Buddhism originated in India and is a product of the teachings of Siddartha Gautama, who is believed to have come from the state of Kapilavastu (part of present-day Nepal) in around the fifth century BCE. The religion entered the Korean peninsula some eight centuries later, via China. At the time, there was no unified Korean nation. Three major kingdoms, Goguryeo, Baekje, and Shilla held sway on the peninsula. Goguryeo, the most northerly of the kingdoms and including territory that is now part of Manchuria in China, was the earliest to encounter Buddhist teachings. In 372 CE, Goguryeo received Sundo, a Chinese monk who came with Buddhist texts and statues.

By 384 CE, Buddhism had spread to the court of Baekje via Goguryeo, with Baekje later serving as the conduit through which the religion entered Japan. (Baekje and Japan had extensive trade and cultural links, and a contingent of monks carrying Buddhist literature and images undertook a mission to the island nation in the mid-sixth century.) In both Goguryeo and Baekje, it was the royal family who first adopted this new religion, while the majority of the people continued to follow shamanism exclusively. In Shilla, the state that would eventually do more than any other to spread Buddhism throughout Korea, the initial reaction from the authorities was antipathy.

It took a martyr to convince the Shilla court to adopt Buddhism. In 527, a court official named Ichadon announced to King Beopheung (r. 514–540) that he had become a Buddhist, and he implored the monarch to adopt his faith as the state religion. Though Beopheung himself had studied Buddhism, many of his ministers were vehemently opposed to Ichadon's request. Ichadon then requested to be executed and made into a martyr. When this was refused, he publicly insulted government officials in order to force them to punish him. He predicted that when his head was removed, the blood that flowed would be white, rather than red. According to tradition, this is what came to pass, and the shocked court made Buddhism Shilla's state religion.

The king who succeeded Beopheung, Jinheung (r. 540–576) established the Hwarang, an elite fighting force whose members were instructed in Buddhist as well as Confucian teaching. His rule was marked by victories against Goguryeo and Baekje, and the Hwarang later played a crucial role in the eventual unification of the three kingdoms, which Shilla achieved in 668. With the Shilla court now in command of the whole of Korea, their state religion became the central faith of the peninsula.

Today, the Shilla capital city of Gyeongju can seem a living museum, because of the number of Buddhist temples and artifacts preserved there. To enhance the state religion, the government poured labor and resources into sites like Bulguksa, which remains one of the largest and most impressive temples in the whole of Korea, and monuments like the Buddha statue at Seokguram Grotto, completed in 774 during the height of Shilla power. *Bulguksa* means "Buddha Country Temple", the word *Bulguk* (Buddha Country) being a by-word of sorts for Shilla.

Buddhism's zenith in Korea would not come until the fall of Shilla and the founding of the Koryo dynasty in 918. The founder, Wang Kon (later King Taejo), was a devout Buddhist and believed the creation of his kingdom was owing to the "protective powers of the many Buddhas." Koryo thus also proclaimed Buddhism to be state religion, and great expense was lavished on ceremonies, the construction of temples throughout the country, and the employment of increasing numbers of monks. Two editions of the Buddhist canon, the *Tripitaka*, were produced; one was destroyed in a Mongol invasion, but the other—carved on 81,258 wood blocks and still housed at Haeinsa Temple—has remained one of the most precious Buddhist artifacts in the world since its completion in 1259.

Yet, by the end of the Koryo period, Buddhism had fallen into disrepute. The religion had become mired in corruption. Becoming a monk brought certain privileges, such as exemption from taxes, and this encouraged a costly growth in the ranks of monks as well as bogus practitioners. Monasteries had become extremely powerful: tax exempt status and state support gave them the ability to amass money, land holdings, and influence. Some monasteries employed private armies composed of monks.

Shamanism too continued to flourish during the Shilla and Koryo eras. *Musok's* animistic nature-worship was not seen as contradictory to the state religion, and the two were able to blend. The practice of placing depictions of Sanshin and also *Chilseong* (the Seven Star God), in Buddhist temples is a vestige of this. It was always possible for villagers to practice Buddhism, and then visit *musok-in* when they wished to exhort the gods to produce a bountiful harvest. Thus, though shamanism held no official status, its practitioners could enjoy esteem of Korean society if they were judged to do their job well.

Years of Decline

Yi Seonggye, who overthrew Koryo and established the Joseon dynasty in 1392, was a Buddhist, but the kingdom he founded was to take a radical new turn. The philosophy of neo-Confucianism, not truly a religion but a kind of ethical code for social order and harmonious living, was to become the dominant state ideology. Its proponents—among them Jeong Do-jeon, one of the strongest supporters of the new king—saw Buddhism as both corrupt and wrong, and wanted it suppressed.

Thus, the long Joseon period saw the retreat of Buddhism, its practitioners pushed to the margins of society by the repression of the state apparatus. Though several of the period's monarchs were Buddhist, they were constrained by the elite Confucian administrative class around them. The role Buddhists like Master So-san (who led a band of five thousand warrior-monks) played in repelling the Japanese invasions of 1592–1598 won them some favor, but the path of the religion over the six-hundred-year-long Joseon period was one of decline. Like shamanism, Buddhism became associated with mountains. Several early Joseon kings had ordered the destruction of temples in towns and built-up areas, and the isolated mountains served as a natural refuge.

Also like shamanism, Buddhism became a religion mainly for the sangmin and cheonmin, the lowest classes, who made up at least 70 percent of the population but were the least powerful. It also became a religion for women of all classes. Joseon society was ruled by men, and any man of status or ambition did not want to be identified publicly as a Buddhist, as that would harm his estimation in the eyes of government officials. United in marginalization, Buddhism aligned with shamanism to a greater extent than before, and the people who practiced one also tended to practice the other. After the promulgation in 1485 of the *Gyeongguk Daejeon* (Grand Code of State Administration), the corpus of laws that would govern Joseon society for four hundred years, anyone holding rites at a shaman shrine could be flogged one hundred times.

The Modern Era: A Revival of Sorts

After many years of trying to colonize Korea, Japan succeeded in 1910. At that time, Buddhism was more prominent in Japan than in Korea, and some Japanese colonists started promoting the religion and establishing new temples. Centuries after the Joseon ban, Buddhists became active in cities again. However, while the colonizers brought Buddhism down from the mountains, their practices were not truly consistent with Korean Buddhism. In the dominant Korean Buddhist sect, the Jogye Order, the monks were celibate, but Japanese monks did not have to be. This set off a sometimes violent feud, with no doubt nationalistic overtones that continued into the 1950s, well after Japan had been defeated. During the colonial period, the Japanese looted Buddhist artifacts and removed them to Japan, depleting the cultural riches of Korean Buddhism and creating lasting resentment.

Following the division of Korea in the late 1940s, the Communist North officially renounced religion of any kind. South Korea entered into an era of American influence and began to embrace Protestantism, which saw rapid growth in the postwar period. However, Buddhism's relevance to Korean life persisted. President Park Chunghee, the military strongman who ruled from 1961 to 1979, ordered the restoration of temples such as Bulguksa, which was in a state of disrepair prior to his intervention in 1969.

Today, 23 percent of the population counts itself as Buddhist. Buddhism trails Christianity slightly in terms of its number of adherents, and it has less influence: according to the 2005 census, 29.2 percent are Christian, and the percentage of Christians in high-ranking government and corporate positions is higher. Notably, an estimated 40 percent of South Koreans are believed to have no religious faith at all. Yet, Korea still needs Buddhism, as can be witnessed every time one visits a beautifully restored temple and sees the devotees absorbed in prayer and meditation.

The Influence of Buddhism on Korea

Buddhism teaches that life is full of suffering, caused by the "three poisons" of desire, aversion, and delusion. These are the fundamental cause of the bad *karma* that traps us in a continuing cycle of rebirth and suffering. The way to escape this fate is to follow the Eightfold Path prescribed by the Buddha and consisting in "right intention," "right action," and so on—in other words, ways of thinking

and behaving that are selfless and bring one nearer to the path of enlightenment. The ultimate goal is to reach "awakening," breaking the
cycle of rebirth and achieving a kind of nothingness, thus escaping
from suffering.

Korean Buddhism follows the Mahayana tradition, one of the two
dominant divisions within Buddhism. In comparison to Theravada,
the other division, Mahayana is considered more theologically liberal and "universal," and even flexible or relativist, in that it allows
for "relative truth." Something is true or false depending on whether
it is spiritually positive or not; whether it is objectively true is of less
importance. From this perspective, other forms of belief could be accepted so long as they helped the believer on the path he or she needs
to be on. Buddha in this tradition is more than a mere human, and
there are different Buddhas for different purposes: a healing Buddha,
an education Buddha, and a compassionate Buddha, for instance. In
fact, there is a limitless potential number of Buddhas in Mahayana.
This relativism and the multiplication of Buddhas with semi-divine
qualities compares on some level to shamanism, in which people
worship different gods and spirits depending on what they want to
achieve.

Although philosophically different, the two belief systems of shamanism and Buddhism were spiritually compatible, because of their
practicality and openness. To the present day, Korea enjoys a high
level of tolerance for different faiths and an aptitude for syncretizing
them in combinations that may seem illogical to outsiders.

Mahayana also contains the concept of the bodhisattva—the en-
lightened person who is concerned not only with their own state
but with the enlightenment of others, too. In order to assist others
in reaching enlightenment, the bodhisattva must attain "six perfections," namely, the perfections of giving, discipline, forbearance, diligence, meditation, and transcendent wisdom. Mastery of these six
perfections encourages selflessness and devotion to others, yet with
a strong emphasis on personal development.

Another key aspect of Buddhism that has influenced Korean society and culture is the Sangha. Sangha, which means "assembly" or
"community," is understood in two ways. It either describes Buddhist

monks and nuns collectively, or it denotes the wider group of followers of Buddhism with higher levels of spiritual understanding. The members of the Sangha work together to help each other pursue improvement, rather than seek merely to benefit themselves as individuals.

Korean friendships can encompass an extraordinary level of self-sacrifice. There is also a strong degree of loyalty to group structures. For example, Koreans may feel obliged to extend a helping hand to a fellow graduate from their school or military unit, even when they may not have a close relationship with the person in question. This relates strongly to jeong, which is explored in detail in chapter 7. Among the reasons why the concept of jeong developed in Korea is the existence of the Sangha and the boddhisatva, which encouraged selflessness and group-mindedness.

According to Professor Kim Ui-cheol, president of the Asian Association of Social Psychology, the concept of Sangha carries over into and influences the way businesses are managed, as well. Indeed, the Sangha's efforts to collectively and continuously improve itself find their parallel in the corporate management philosophies of companies like Samsung of South Korea and Toyota of Japan. Western students of business will know the Japanese term kaizen (which translates as "gaeseon" in Korean), which is about making continuous, incremental improvements to one's business processes. This key business concept shows obvious Buddhist influence. The importance of collectivity is also reflected in Korean businesses, for the progress or success of a company is considered a reflection of group effort, not the triumph of a single leader. Unlike in the United States, there are no rock-star CEOs with nine-figure stock option payouts in Korea.

If one considers the products of Samsung, one may observe that they are never truly original, unlike those made by "individualistic" American firms like Apple. However, where Samsung excels is in taking the big ideas of others and refining them to near-perfection. This ability to perfect the products of others stems from a laser-like focus on continuous improvement, which owes as much to Buddhist thinking here as it does in Japan.

Overcoming

According to Professor Kim, Buddhism should be credited for Korea's higher than average capacity for overcoming obstacles. In Buddhism, one can escape one's karma through enlightenment, which comes about through continuous self-improvement and self-cultivation. Hinduism teaches an acceptance of fate, but at a deep level Buddhism is about transcending fate by improving oneself. As a consequence of their Buddhist (as well as Confucian) heritage, Koreans constantly seek to improve themselves and ameliorate their condition. Study doesn't stop with a college degree. Middle-aged people will engage in vocational study in order to get ahead at work, and even many older Koreans will take up the study of foreign languages. During the Korean War, up to one a third of the population was made homeless, yet the imperative to learn was so strong that universities set up tents in the mountains and students would receive lectures there by gaslight.

Generally tolerant and even receptive in the face of new religions and ideas, the Korean character does not resign itself in the face of tragedy and misfortune. People believe in their power to overcome almost any situation. Indeed, the greatest illustration of this Korean mindset is the way the nation has overcome the terrible consequences of war and poverty to forge a wealthy, stable democracy in just two generations. Buddhism may not be responsible for the Korean miracle, but it certainly contributed to the Koreans' ability to believe the miracle was achievable—and indeed to achieve it.

The desire for continuous improvement in Korean culture comes from Buddhism. However, the choice of method that Koreans usually take to effect their improvement—the relentless pursuit of education—is strongly influenced by another foreign belief system: Confucianism.

Chapter 3

Confucianism

Confucianism is the last of the three main ancient philosophical and religious influences on Korean society. However, while the last two established a syncretic relationship with each other, Confucianism at its peak allowed little room for competing traditions—despite having a certain complementariness with both of the other traditions. A form of Confucianism was the state ideology during the Joseon dynasty (1392–1910), and it left profound traces on Korean society in its hierarchicalism, age and gender bias, reverence for parents, and emphasis on education.

What is Confucianism?
Confucianism is not a religion but rather a system of moral philosophy that originated in China in the teachings of Kong Fuzi (558–471 BCE), a thinker known in the West as Confucius. It has exerted considerable influence over not just China but also Korea, Japan, Vietnam, and other East Asian states. At its heart is a belief that humans are improvable through cultivation and moral action, and that collectively, a harmonious society can be created when all members fulfill certain obligations.

There are several key obligations. The first is *ren*, the necessity to treat others within the community with humanity. In its essence, it is similar to the "golden rule" of doing as you would be done by. *Ren* has important implications for leaders. If a leader fails to show *ren*, for instance by treating his subjects brutally, he loses his mandate to govern them and may be disobeyed. If he behaves benevolently, then subjects are to accept his word as the law.

Then there is *li*, the observation of customs, proper etiquette, and the need to act in accordance with society's set of morals. Through the observance of social rituals—such as the correct way to mourn the dead, or even drink tea—people learn to show respect for each other and behave in socially harmonious ways. In this sense, the rationale for *li* is comparable to William of Wykeham's maxim, "Manners maketh man." However, *li* also involves a sort of hierarchy: in Confucianism, those who master *li* are considered to be especially wise. The ideal society is ruled by such a person, who also appoints fellow wise men as his advisors and administrators. This concept gave rise to the practice of national examinations, which were held to determine who would join the civil service in China, from 605 CE until 1911. The ruler who mastered *li* was, in theory, reminiscent of Socrates' rule by Philosopher Kings, who would likewise rule society in a wise and just fashion.

Loyalty is held as essential—to one's family, one's husband or wife, one's king, and one's friends. Family loyalty is most important of all: the concept of filial piety, or *xiao*, commands children to respect and honor their parents and ancestors above all others. There was no higher virtue in Confucian-influenced cultures than this. Ancestors were commemorated in rituals; parental wishes, including their choice of their child's occupation or marriage partner, were to be fulfilled without complaint; and those who committed crimes against their parents were held by society to be particularly reprehensible and subjected to greater punishment.

In Confucianism, relationships between people have certain rules. There are five relationships in all: those between ruler and subject, father and son, older and younger, husband and wife, and two friends of similar status. The last relationship is the only one in which equality prevails. In all of the others, the former party is superior, and the latter inferior. The superior partner should act with a duty of responsibility and benevolence to the lower, who should respond in turn with loyalty and obedience. Confucians believed that a society run on these lines would be harmonious and orderly.

Confucianism in Korea

Koreans were first exposed to Confucian thought during the Lelang Commandery era, and like Buddhism, its influence began to grow during the Three Kingdoms period. The elites of Goguryeo, Shilla, and Baekje all studied Chinese classics; Confucian texts were an important part of such an education. At the time, Buddhism and Confucianism were not mutually exclusive: the former dealt with the metaphysical, and the latter with one's conduct in the temporal realm, in relation to other members of society. A good scholar was expected to have a solid understanding of both. Shilla, a Buddhist state, established a Confucian college in 682.

During the Koryo Dynasty (918–1392), the role of Confucianism grew. King Gwangjeong (r. 949–975) introduced the national civil service examination, and King Songjeong (r. 981–997) established Gukgajam, a Confucian school, as the highest educational institution in the land. Again though, its increased role did not encroach on Buddhism. The established state religion continued to grow, as the creation of the Tripitaka Koreana, and the increasing power of the monasteries, would attest.

Buddhism and Confucianism in fact share a certain degree of commonality. Both belief systems assign importance to helping others and acting selflessly. Self-improvement is also a critical theme or ethic in both traditions. The two philosophies intermingled in popular practice long before the Joseon period. This blending can be seen in the creation of the *Hwarang*, an elite group of young fighters from the Shilla dynasty that existed from the sixth to the tenth centuries.

The *Hwarang* were teenage boys of good moral character drawn mainly from the aristocracy. They were trained in horsemanship, archery, martial arts, and intellectual disciplines and indoctrinated with an ethical code based on both Buddhism and Confucianism. Though they were considered a Buddhist fighting force, and were given their moral code by a Buddhist monk named Wongwang, the first two instructions the monk gave them as part of that code were to "be loyal to your Lord" and "love and respect your parents and teachers." Nothing could be more Confucian than instructions like these.

It was not until the growth of neo-Confucianism in the late Koryo period that Buddhism and Confucianism fell into conflict. Neo-Confucianism was a philosophical movement most closely associated with Chinese thinker Zhu Xi (1130–1200). It attached even greater importance to *li* and also to education, since neo-Confucian philosophers believed that all things could be understood via the application of reason, and that it was man's duty to work to attain such understanding.

Zhu was a heavy reader of Buddhist texts, and argued for an ultimate state of knowledge in which there are no bounds between the thinker, and other people and things. This "breakthrough to integral comprehension" is reminiscent of the kind of oneness of understanding pursued by Buddhists. However, Zhu was also a rationalistic and non-spiritual thinker, and was of the ultimate opinion that Buddhism was vacuous and deluding. He and his followers sought to reduce the influence of Buddhism on society. Whereas the old Confucianism could accommodate Buddhism, neo-Confucianism would not.

After An Hyang, a Korean scholar, read one of Zhu's works in 1286 and was inspired to transcribe it and bring it back from China to his own country, neo-Confucianism began to influence intellectuals in Korea. Due to the presence of Confucian academies, there was a ready-made scholarly class who would have been receptive to his ideas. Furthermore, the excessive power and corrupt behavior of the monasteries meant Zhu's anti-Buddhist approach arrived at the right time.

Though both the common people and most of the elite continued to follow Buddhism, the religion had some powerful opponents. Jeong Do-jeon (died 1398), the closest advisor to Yi Seong-gye (later King Taejo, the founder of the Joseon dynasty following his overthrow of Koryo), was the most notable of these. When Koryo fell and Yi established the new regime in 1392, Jeong—who some consider to have been the real leader in all but name—was given many administrative portfolios including education, taxation policy, diplomacy, and defense. He established a highly centralized bureaucracy, moved Korea's capital from the city of Kaesong to Seoul, and replaced Buddhism with neo-Confucianism as official state ideology.

He set about reordering Korean society on neo-Confucian lines. This meant that the upper class would be composed of bureaucrats—those who passed the civil service examination. Beneath them, there was to be a professional class, and then a class of ordinary laborers. Formerly powerful Buddhist monks did not even make it into the lower class: along with musicians, prostitutes, and other people he considered socially harmful, monks became part of the cheonmin, an outcast group who were forced to live away from mainstream society and were blocked from social advancement through measures such the inability to register for the civil service examination.

Several monarchs throughout the early Joseon period retained their Buddhism: Taejo himself, and King Sejong the Great (r. 1418–1450), for example, were both Buddhists and believed that there was no contradiction between being guided by Confucianism in one's thinking on social issues, and by Buddhism on the metaphysical. They were, however, constrained by powerful civil servants, who followed neo-Confucianism rather than the more accommodating form of Confucianism that had existed in Korea before Zhu Xi's influence began.

Shamanists also came under attack from the neo-Confucians; they too were relegated to cheonmin status. However, both the *musok-in* and the Buddhist monk remained in demand. Neo-Confucianism was non-spiritual, and naturally, the people required an outlet for their metaphysical questions and troubles. Furthermore, in the case of *Musok*, its use of colorful ceremonies full of music, dance, and emotional displays allowed people a sense of joy that neo-Confucianism, with its stifling hierarchicalism and emphasis on duty, could not. Throughout the Joseon era, many members of both the nobility and the common classes turned to both Buddhism and shamanism; Queen Min, in the late nineteenth century, was a devout Buddhist, and also employed two *musok-in* as advisors. According to Homer B. Hulbert, a nineteenth century American missionary to Korea, "The all-round Korean will be a Confucian in society, a Buddhist when he philosophizes, and a spirit worshipper when he is in trouble."

Aspects of Confucianism in Korea

As neo-Confucianism was the state ideology of the Joseon dynas-ty—a regime that lasted until 1910—it had many years in which to influence a variety of areas of human interaction in Korea. Perhaps its most powerful effect on Korean culture is to be found in the sense of hierarchy that pervades the five Confucian relationships that can exist between people.

Regarding the relationship between ruler and subject, the latter had to show absolute loyalty. The ruler, though, could expect to be removed if he did not respond with benevolence. This argument was used by pro-coup neo-Confucianists to justify Yi Seong-gye's over-throw of the Koryo Dynasty, which Joseon's founders believed was failing the people. The trading of benevolence in return for loyalty is still a factor in Korean offices: whistleblowing is rare, as it goes against the employee's obligation to his superior. A typical Korean boss is also more paternalistic than one from a non-Confucian soci-ety. He will take greater interest in the personal lives of his staff, and feel the need to treat them to lunch or dinner with regularity.

Within the home, the father held authority: his wife and children were expected to do as he commanded, and in return, he was to be a just ruler and provider. Males in this neo-Confucian order were priv-ileged over females, to the extent that a woman who had given birth was referred to simply as "X's mother." In a house where the father had died, the firstborn son rather than the mother became the new head or master. This was a consequence of the "three obediences" of the later Joseon period: daughters were obedient to their fathers, wives to their husbands, and widows to their sons. Women were de-nied all inheritance rights (prior to the Joseon era, women had equal right to inherit property, as well as noble titles), and restricted from access to education. Books distributed by the government ordered women to refrain from being *agnyeo* (immoral women), by staying out of public affairs. This latter commandment was part of *naewae-beop*, a set of rules delineating the "internal" sphere from the "exter-nal." The woman's realm was considered to be the former, and thus her duty was to maintain a good household and cover her face on the rare occasions she went out in public. Covering the face became standard practice among upper-class women in the seventeenth century and among most Korean women by the nineteenth century.

Shin Saimdang, who lived in the sixteenth century and was a devoted mother to her son Yulgok (a leading Confucian scholar and government official), is still seen by some today as an ideal Confucian woman: in 2007, the Bank of Korea chose to place her portrait on the 50,000 won bill—the highest value bank note—due to her "mothering skills and filial piety," according to a *Los Angeles Times* article. (Yulgok himself appears on the 5,000 won bill, and another Confucian thinker, Toegye, features on the 1,000 won bill.) A bank official referred to her as "the best example of motherhood in Korean history." More than twelve Korean feminist groups protested, arguing that it reinforced stereotypes of women as subservient and worthy of recognition only for their ability to serve their children or husbands. If Korea can legitimately be accused of sexism, then Confucianism is the culprit.

How Old Are You?

The relationship between older and younger is also of great importance. When two people meet for the first time in Korea, one of the first questions that will be asked is, "How old are you?" Once it has been determined who is older, the younger person will be expected to act with a degree of deference. Special titles emphasize this hierarchy: a younger man will call an older male friend *Hyung*, and a younger woman will call an older female friend *Eonni*. In the case of a friendship between people of different sexes, an older man will be *Oppa*, and an older woman *Nuna*. The younger person in the relationship will simply be called *Dongsaeng*.

Traditionally, if a young man went out to eat and drink with an older man, he would be expected as a matter of courtesy to turn his head away when taking a sip from his glass. He would listen attentively to (and agree with) whatever the older man said, regardless of his true opinions. Today, such behavior may seem excessively deferential, as the power of Confucianism is in fact weakening, to some extent. Still, the young owe the old a certain amount of respect—and in return, the oldest person at the table pays for the meal.

Language reflects the age hierarchy in other ways. Korean has different levels of speech, based on the degree of respect required for different situations. *Banmal*, the most basic, exists for friends and social equals. After *banmal*, there are then six degrees of honorific speech, classified as *jondaemal*. In the most commonly-heard form of *jondaemal*, *haeyoche*, sentences ending with verbs conclude with the suffix *haeyo*. Another form, *haerache*, ends with *handa* and is used a great deal in newspapers and books. *Hapsyoche* is more deferential and ends in *hamnida*; this is typically used with customers, and on television news programs. With one's *Hyung*, one may use *haeyo* endings or perhaps even *banmal* these days; with an elderly, respected person, *hamnida* may be necessary. The chairman of one's company would probably require "hamnida" as well. With children speaking to parents, *haeyo* is standard, though there are many these days who use *banmal* when talking to their mother or father.

Family and Ancestry

Confucianism holds family bonds to be the most important of all. Not only are one's living relatives deserving of respect, but a sense of duty and devotion also exists for deceased family members. *Jesa*, a ceremony to commemorate a departed relative on the anniversary of their death, and *charye*, a special type of *jesa* that takes place on the two national holidays of Chuseok and Lunar New Year, are held to remind people of the importance of their family and lineage. These are Confucian rites in which food is offered at a shrine set up for the occasion, and family members bow in front of it. Traditional *jesa* foods include rice cakes known as *songpyeon*, which are offered alongside an elaborate spread of vegetables, fish, and soup dishes. There is room for variation, though, as it is also customary to lay out the favorite dish of the deceased person. In 2011, photographs of a *jesa* table containing pizza were run by the national press; when the family was asked why they laid out such a non-traditional food, their response was simply, "Our father liked pizza."

Jesa suggests to many that Koreans practice ancestor worship or that Confucianism is a religion with special rites of its own. Indeed, some early Korean Christians were martyred for refusing to perform it. These days, some Christians do not do *jesa*, and Protestants may even follow their own "*jesa* replacement" ceremony, *chudo yebae*. However, Zhu Xi did not believe that the souls of the dead actually exist, but rather viewed such rites as the opportunity to demonstrate respect and remember. In this way, the act of commemoration serves the purpose of upholding one's filial piety, as well as promoting *li*.

To one's ancestors, one owes respect. To one's parents, one owes a lifelong debt. This debt can never be truly repaid, since without one's parents one would not exist. For this reason, the debt must be acknowledged throughout one's life, and one must strive to come as close to repaying it as one can. A child should not marry whomever he or she wants, but rather the person his or her parents approve of. The same applies to the child's choice of studies in school and career; rather than follow one's dreams and become an artist or a musician, for instance, one ought to select the most highly paid and stable job available in order to provide for one's parents in their old age and create a secure environment in which to raise children—since there is also an imperative to continue the family line.

Today much of the influence of Confucianism on the parent-child relationship is being eroded. Children exert more free choice and are more likely than before to marry whom they please, and argue with their parents. Many see *jesa* as a burden. Furthermore, with regard to Confucian gender hierarchy, over the past generation women have gained equal access to education, as well as a dramatically increased role in public life, albeit one that is still far from equal. Traditional respect for elders is also in decline. Tourists in Seoul who have read about Korea's Confucian culture sometimes express surprise when riding the subway and seeing an infirm old person waiting in vain for a youngster to give up a seat.

Education

It would be a mistake, however, to assume that South Korea is ever going to truly rid itself of Confucianism. Aside from its enduring influence on this country's hierarchical corporate culture and language, Confucianism's power can be felt in the realm of the national obsession, education. South Korea is famous for its unhealthy preoccupation with exam results and the pursuit of admission to the best universities. This is a legacy of Confucianism's injunction to self-improvement through education, and of the civil service examination system that existed for over a thousand years. From the beginning the Joseon dynasty to the Japanese invasions of 1592–1598, passing such exams were virtually the only means of social advancement. In reality, the odds of success were heavily rigged in favor of those from families who were already of high status, but still, there remained a slight possibility for a brilliant member of a poor family to make something of himself by taking the exam. Those who passed were given *yangban* (aristocratic) status and land, for three generations. Passing meant glory and security, not merely for oneself but also for one's descendents (until three successive generations failed to pass, an unlikely outcome after *yangban* status was acquired).

Though the *yangban* system was consigned to history following the royal court's weakening and eventual surrender to Japan in 1910, the belief in the power of education and examinations as a way of improving one's lot remained. Following the partition of Korea, and the resulting civil war of 1950–1953, South Korea briefly became a very egalitarian society. Apart from those who were closely allied with the corrupt regime of President Syngman Rhee, South Koreans were united in poverty. The country had only bombed-out infrastructure and precious few natural resources and suffered from one of the lowest GDP per capita figures on the planet.

Once again, the main way of getting ahead was via education. South Korea's desperate state led to the realization that the only true resource the country had was the brains of its people—which, as Confucianism taught, could, and should, be improved via education. Successive governments pursued a policy of making schooling available to all, regardless of parentage, relative wealth, or gender. Until the 1980s, the way for a poor young person from a small village to improve his lot was to grasp that educational lifeline and study around the clock to gain entrance to institutions like Seoul National University, Korea University, or Yonsei University (collectively, "SKY") and graduate with a degree in a subject like medicine. Such an individual could become a well-paid doctor in Seoul and support not just himself, but his parents, and siblings too. In a country as poor as South Korea was then, this would have been no less of an achievement than passing the civil service exam in the Joseon era.

Even today, a SKY degree is considered a ticket to the best job opportunities, the best human networks, and the best marriage prospects. SKY schools are similar in stature to the Ivy League in the United States or Oxbridge in the United Kingdom, but even more powerful: seven out of ten CEOs of the largest Korean firms are SKY graduates, as are eight out of ten appointees to the judiciary. To enter SKY, one needs to pass a grueling examination, the *suneung*, a day-long test given to third-year high school students. Tales of excessive pressure on *suneung* takers by parents and teachers are legion. It is common for those preparing for the test to wake before six a.m., spend the whole day studying, with breaks only for food, and collapse into bed at around midnight. Some parents start putting such pressure on their children years prior to the *suneung* period. The Gangnam area of Seoul is famous for its private institutes, which provide extra after-school instruction at exorbitant cost. The stereotypical Gangnam mother is renowned for forcing her children to attend such institutes until well after dark, no matter what their age.

Those who teach lucky SKY entrants are near the very top of the social ladder. In South Korea, professors from elite universities are easily able to enter politics or business or become public intellectuals whose voice is welcomed by the media, regardless of whether or not their comments relate to their area of specialization. Consequently, the title "Professor" is much sought-after, and cases of bribes in the hundreds of thousands of dollars being paid to secure tenure are not unheard of.

Today, the top-level civil service exam is the *godeung goshi*. Though the existence of better-paid jobs in business means a civil service career is relatively less attractive than it used to be, working in the higher ranks of the government still confers excellent social status and near-bulletproof job security. Open to all since its creation in 1949, the exam is a playing-field leveler for those with the fortitude to sacrifice all of their time studying to be the one student in forty-one who gains a passing grade. There are special private halls of residence called *goshiwon*, which are located near preparatory institutes and offer cheap accommodation and cooked meals for those preparing for the *godeung goshi* or other tests like the bar exam. Living near the institute saves commuting time and thus allows more time for study. Districts with large numbers of *goshiwon* are known as *goshi-chon*, "*goshi* villages." Life in a *goshi-chon* is bleak, but success on the *goshi* exam brings a lifetime of stability, and respect.

Chapter 4

Christianity

The view from the hills above any South Korean town, particularly at night, will reveal a striking sight: red neon crosses dominate the landscape. The crosses are so commonplace there are popular songs about the phenomenon. Christianity has had a relatively short period of contact with this country, but what it lacks in history, it has made up for by the force of its appeal. Apart from the Philippines and East Timor—both ex-colonies of Christian Western countries—South Korea is now the most Christian country in Asia by percentage of the population who subscribe to it. In achieving this level of adherence, Christianity has been transformed from outlaw sect to establishment faith.

The Arrival of Catholicism

Today Christianity edges out Buddhism as the most popular religion in Korea, but it got off to a slow and difficult start. The first known Korean Christian was the wife of Konishi Yukinaga, a Japanese commander who came to Korea in the 1590s during the *Imjin Waeran* invasions. The young woman, who took the name Julia, eventually accompanied her husband to Japan. Further attempts to introduce Christianity to Korea during the period were not successful; one missionary, Gregorious de Cespedes, preached to Japanese invaders but was not permitted to do the same to Koreans.

In 1603, a diplomat named Yi Gwang-jeong returned from Beijing with texts written by Matteo Ricci, a Catholic missionary to China. These texts began to attract the attention of intellectuals, but conversions did not result. Ricci's works were read largely by Confucian scholars, who were curious for knowledge but ultimately rejected the Christian worldview.

It was not until the late eighteenth century that Catholicism began to gain a serious foothold. The religion had been outlawed in 1758 by King Yeongjo, a strict Confucian, in response to the discovery of believers in provinces such as Gangwon and Hwanghae. Nevertheless, in 1784, a young man named Lee Sung-hoon, who had traveled to Beijing with his father, returned to Seoul and began actively proselytizing in defiance of the ban. He created the first organized community of Catholics in Korea, who called themselves the "believing friends." Unlike in other Asian countries, the early growth of Catholicism happened not via missionaries (who had reached China and Japan but not Korea, despite several attempts throughout the 1600s and 1700s) but from Koreans who had come into contact with the religion in China and returned to preach it to fellow Koreans. It was a grass-roots movement, with very little involvement from foreigners.

Kim Beom-woo, the owner of the house used by Lee as a makeshift church, became the first Korean Catholic martyr, after he was arrested by government officials and tortured to death in 1786. Members of Lee's group, which included prominent scholar and philosopher Dasan Jeong Yak-yong (1762–1836), began acting as unordained priests against the wishes of the bishop in Beijing. In 1795, the bishop finally sent a real priest from China, Zhou Wenmo, to administer to the group, which by then had four thousand members. Zhou slipped into the country secretly and was provided with safehouses by Korean Catholics. He was the first foreign priest in Korea.

Lee and Zhou were later beheaded in the 1801 Sinyu Persecution, a purge that reportedly would also have claimed the life of Dasan, had he not renounced his faith. In total, over three hundred were executed. Catholicism was perceived as a threat by the regime for several reasons. This foreign religion held that all people were created equal in the eyes of God, clearly threatening the social order and contravening the tenets of neo-Confucianism, which called for absolute obedience to social superiors, particularly the monarch. Many Catholics also refused to perform the ancestor ritual of *jesa*, out of a belief that it was ancestor worship and therefore idolatry.

The interception of a letter sent by Hwang Sa-yeong, a member of Lee's church, advocating the invitation of Western troops to Korea to aid Catholics revealed another threat and led Queen Jeongsun, regent from 1800 to 1805, to order the 1801 persecution.

There were around ten thousand Korean Catholics by then. Further purges committed by the authorities in 1815, 1827, and from 1866 to 1871 fostered an insular, fearful mentality among believers that still has some degree of influence on Korean Catholicism today. The religion remained underground until the 1870s and 1880s, when the Korean government began to seek better relations with Western powers and therefore curbed its policy of repression. In 1882, there were 12,500 believers—barely higher than in 1800—but by 1910, when Korea lost its independence to Japan, the number had grown to 73,000.

Protestants from America, Colonizers from Japan

Korea saw its first Protestant missionaries with the arrival from the United States of the Methodist Horace Allen in 1884 and Presbyterians Henry Appenzeller and Horace Underwood in 1885. There were already Korean Protestants when they arrived, though: a Scottish Presbyterian named John Ross living in Manchuria managed to produce a Korean translation of the New Testament in 1882, and this text had inspired some living in the northwest of Korea to convert.

This book was printed in *Hangul*, the Korean alphabet developed by King Sejong the Great in the mid-fifteenth century. *Hangul* is composed of twenty-four characters, and was envisioned as a very simple writing system that ordinary people could learn, in contrast to the complex *hanja* (Chinese characters) that Koreans had used exclusively until then, and of which only the social elite had a good command. Confucian and Buddhist texts were written in *hanja* but Western missionaries ensured that, when Christianity texts were translated into Korean, they were written in a script that everyone could understand. This was a very important factor in the spread of Christianity among the lower classes.

Soon after their arrival, Allen, Underwood, and Appenzeller established hospitals, schools, and universities, contributing materially to the development of the country. By 1890, the three had between them founded Baejae Boys High School and Ewha Girls School, among other schools, and later came Yonsei University. At one time, the Protestant church was the greatest provider of education in Korea. These institutions proved instrumental in spreading Protestantism and also gave rise to the notion that the new form of Christianity of the Americans was progressive, modern, and beneficial to the country. Thus, while Protestantism arrived in Korea much later than Catholicism, it quickly became the most popular form of Christianity: by 1910, it had 100,000 adherents.

1910 saw the beginning of one of the most bitter periods in Korean history. The Joseon state had been weak throughout the preceding century, because of persistent palace infighting and the maneuverings later in the century of foreign powers like Japan and Russia, which had designs on its territory. This left Korea vulnerable, and following several years of increasing Japanese influence over the peninsula Prime Minister Lee Wan-yong (in the absence of Emperor Sunjong, who refused to sign) stamped the national seal of Korea on the Japan-Korea Annexation Treaty on August 22, 1910. Thus began thirty-five years of brutal colonial rule, which ended only with the defeat of Imperial Japan in 1945.

The period of Japanese rule was harsh for almost all Koreans, but it proved to be Korean Christianity's finest hour. Almost from the beginning, the new religion was seen as part of the struggle against Japan. In 1912, 124 people were accused of being part of a plot to assassinate the Japanese governor general Terauchi Masatake; of them, 98 were Christian. The fact that only six were convicted may suggest that the Japanese authorities were looking for ways to clamp down on the Western faith. This incident helped create the impression that Japanese rule and Christianity were in opposition, a belief enhanced by the Japanese policy of instituting schools that competed with the Christian ones. These new schools taught in the language of the invader and forbade religious instruction.

On the first of March of 1919, a group of thirty-three activists convened at Taehwagwan, a restaurant in Seoul, to adopt a declaration of Korean independence drafted by Manhae, a poet, and Choi

Nam-seon, an historian. They were encouraged in this in part by U.S. president Woodrow Wilson's speech on self-determination, which had inspired them and gave them hope that the United States might come to Korea's assistance against the Japanese occupiers. The activists signed the document, sent a copy to the Japanese governor general, and contacted the police, informing them of their actions. This immensely brave act stirred a protest movement that brought two million Koreans out onto the streets. The crackdown that ensued resulted in the deaths of 7,500 people and showed the world the true nature of Japanese rule in Korea.

Sixteen of the thirty-three signatories were Protestant, although Protestants made up no more than 2 percent of the population. In the aftermath of the declaration and protests, more than 20 percent of the people arrested were Protestant. Japanese reprisals were swift and bloody. Forty-seven churches were burned down, and thousands of Christians were killed, or imprisoned and tortured. The independence activists did not act completely in vain though: the repercussions eventually forced the governor general to resign, and his successor replaced military police with a civilian force and allowed a small amount of press freedom.

Most of the anti-Japanese resistance among Christians came from Protestants rather than Catholics. This was arguably due to the harsh history of Catholicism in Korea, which had bred a cautious, insular mentality. Some Protestants also did not see the value in fighting the oppressor. During the 1920s and '30s, two camps emerged in Korean Protestantism: one was a theologically liberal bloc that tended to be activist in opposing Japan, while the other was a conservative bloc that focused more on purely church-related matters and less on political activism. Likely due to the difficulty of striving against a harsh oppressor, the latter group made the greater gain in numbers during the period.

American Influence and the Boom Years

Imperial Japan was wary not only of the commitment of the Korean Christians but also of the fact that their religion was so deeply part of Western culture. Following liberation, division, and the birth of

South Korea, Christian sects, particularly Protestant ones, benefited from their Western origins. Protestantism was seen as the religion of the Americans, the people whom elite Koreans came to believe they should emulate in order to be successful. The first president of the Republic, Syngman Rhee, was a Harvard-educated Americanophile English speaker who gave his name in Western fashion—given name first and surname second. He himself was a Methodist, and 39 percent of politicians in his Liberal Party were Christian.

Americans were considered modern, progressive, and rich. Their religion was also seen in that light. Forty-two percent of Koreans believe Protestantism the faith that was "most instrumental in the country's modernization," according to a 2004 study. After the end of World War Two and the Korean War, the United States provided a military backstop and plenty of aid, and the Korean government put up no impediment to the continued spread of the American religion. Indeed, the army was one of the main instruments for conversions. In addition, during its rebuilding after the Korean War, South Korea received plenty of Christian charity, which bolstered the positive image of this Western faith.

Throughout the 1960s, '70s, and '80s, there was a boom in conversions. It is common today to hear people say, "My grandparents were Buddhist, but I am a Christian." In 1958, Protestants in South Korea numbered around eight hundred thousand; in 1968, there were just under two million; in 1978, there were just over five million; and today there are eleven million. Korean Protestants also tend to be fervent: a 1995 government survey found that 80 percent of Korean Protestants attend church at least once a week, with 40 percent going two or more times. There are also now three million Catholics, bringing the total proportion of the population who are Christian to well over a quarter.

Korean Protestantism has a mostly conservative orientation, though there are some liberal preachers. In the 1980s, groups like the Federation of Christian Youth for the Defense of Democracy campaigned vigorously against right-wing military dictator Chun Doo-hwan, and today, there are some prominent left-of-center preachers, like former government minister and Anglican priest Lee

Jae-joung. There are far more right-of-center Protestants, however. There exists a Christian Council of Korea, presided over by leaders of conservative Protestant churches that sometimes campaigns for a tough policy against North Korea, or free market policies. Right-wing President Lee Myung-bak was strongly aided by the so-called Protestant lobby during his election campaign in 2007, with some megachurch pastors openly asking their congregations to pray for his election.

The political left accuses the Protestant right of being an over-politicized, socially conservative bloc. In 2004, a group of conservative church leaders to set up a Christian political party modeled on American televangelist Pat Robertson's Christian Coalition, with an agenda of opposing same-sex marriage and abortion. During the 2011 Seoul mayoral election campaign period, Kim Hong-do, pastor of Keumran United Methodist Church, asked this question in a sermon, with reference to left-of-center candidate Park Won-soon: "What are we to do if someone who belongs to Satan and demons becomes mayor of Seoul?" In 2011 another group, led by pastor Jeon Gwang-hoon of Sarangjeil Presbyterian Church, announced plans to form a political party that would oppose the separation of church and state. Jeon later lost credibility when he stated that he would combat the nation's low birth rate by sending people with less than five children to prison.

Protestantism is seen as the pro-capitalist religion. This may be due in part to its history of association with the United States, as the opponent of Communist North Korea. But also, 42 percent of CEOs of large Korean firms are Protestant. Large Protestant churches are criticized by some as places where business networking and deal-making take place. Somang Presbyterian Church in the affluent Gangnam area of Seoul is popular among executives and conservative politicians. Competition to become a church elder there is very intense, as it offers excellent opportunities to make connections. President Lee Myung-bak himself is an attendee of the church. Despite being a member of the National Assembly and former CEO of Hyundai Engineering and Construction at the time he sought this office, he failed to be elected as an elder in 1994. After volunteering as a car park attendant while his wife cooked meals in the church kitchens, he finally won election the second time around.

This association has not always guaranteed President Lee a free ride by the Protestant right. Cho Yong-gi, the powerful founder of Yoido Full Gospel Church, a Pentecostal church, intervened in 2011 when the government introduced an Islamic Finance Bill, aimed at allowing the development of a Sukuk bond market in Korea, chided the president for failing to remember that the Protestant lobby elected him. Cho Yong-gi warned that Islamic finance would provide funding for "terrorists." He followed this up just weeks later with the claim that the Japanese earthquake and tsunami of 2011 was a result of that country's lack of Christian faith.

Aspects of Korean Christianity
Protestantism in Korea has adapted to native cultural ways. This is evidenced in one respect by the size of certain churches. According to the *Guinness Book of Records*, Yoido Church in Seoul has the world's largest congregation. Around 150,000 people are believed to attend services in the main church complex, but the membership the church claims reaches one million, and the reason for this is that Yoido has created a network of affiliated churches that may be likened to franchises. Pastor Mark Cho (not his real name) of a Seoul-based church with the relatively small membership base of 75,000 attributes this collectivization and franchising of belief at least partly to the Korean people's fondness for group bonding and uniformity.

Pastor Mark goes on to state that the culture of uniformity in religion has other consequences. Korean Christianity has a tendency toward "finger-pointing," that is, a dogmatic intolerance, toward those who practice their religion in a different way: "If you have a slightly different perspective, they'll use it and say you're a heretic," he comments. His own church has ironically faced criticism for being too "Bible-centric."

Despite the general distaste Korean Christians have for *Musok*, Korea's deeply ingrained animist shamanism has affected Christian worship in several ways. Some churches are markedly materialistic, just as shamanism is. Yoido Church admonishes believers to reject "misguided thoughts considering material wealth as being equated with sin." Furthermore, "a poor Christian is not a good Christian" was the message delivered in one famous Yoido sermon, for example. Not surprisingly, some Korean Christians—Protestants in particular—hold that their Christian beliefs will somehow help them become wealthy. The history of Protestantism in Korea as the "modernizing religion" and the religion of the business and political elite may well contribute to this feeling.

Shamanism may have helped pave the way for Christianity to be so successful in Korea, according to Pastor Mark. The shamanic association of spirituality with peaks like Inwang-san, Jiri-san, and Baekdu-san resonates with the spiritual significance of mountains like Mount Sinai, at which Moses received the Ten Commandments in the Book of Exodus. Around Korea, there are hundreds of *gidoweon*, small "prayer houses" located in the mountains, where church members can go for extended periods of concentrated prayer. The founder of Pastor Mark's church spent three and a half years in a cave at Jiri-san, where he read the Bible over a thousand times. His text was from an imported religion, but his choice of location was the most traditional one possible for a Korean.

Fervor

Perhaps what is most striking about Protestantism in Korea is its fervor. Pastor Mark observes that, "Koreans have had a difficult history, so many people believed that praying harder would help them." Unlike Buddhism or Confucianism, Christianity offers salvation. During the time Protestantism has been present in Korea, this country has suffered from poverty, war, colonialism, and division into two separate states. During Japanese rule, Protestants were among the most determined rebels. And following the creation of South Korea, Protestantism became associated with the new American-inspired capitalist order, which was seen to be the people's road out of poverty. Given all this, it is perhaps unsurprising that believers have clung to Protestantism so strongly.

The rate of Protestant church attendance, with 80 percent of believers attending at least once per week in 1995—dwarfs the rate at which Catholics attend church and Buddhists attend temples. Every day, around 10 percent of practicing Korean Protestants attend early-morning devotional prayers. There are also many thousands of cells, small groups of Protestants who gather, often on Fridays, for extra prayer sessions. Most members tithe as well, giving on average ten percent of their income to the church; "if you're getting married to a Protestant here, the tithe is definitely something you'll need to discuss before you tie the knot", says one Korean Protestant.

Research firm Gallup conducted a survey on the fervency of Korean Protestants in 1997. It found that 52 percent had "experienced the Holy Spirit"; 68 percent were "certain of their salvation"; and, 69 percent believed in "the imminent end of the world." Of all the various Protestant denominations in Korea, only the Episcopalians, the Lutherans, and one sect of theologically liberal Presbyterians are non-evangelical, according to Timothy S. Lee, author of *Born Again: Evangelicalism in Korea*. According to him, in the late 1990s at least 75 percent of all Korean Protestants were "solidly evangelical."

Korea is now the world's second-largest exporter of missionaries after the United States. In 2006, some 15,000 Protestants from South Korea engaged in mission work. Protestant missionaries have been abducted while preaching in places like Afghanistan and Iraq. Despite the missionaries' obvious risks to themselves and the liability for South Korea's image and defense policy, the government has not been able to stop groups from going to such danger zones. On July 19, 2007, twenty-three missionaries were kidnapped on the road between Kandahar and Kabul. The twenty-one who survived the ordeal were eventually released for a reported ransom of twenty million U.S. dollars, paid directly to the Taliban by the South Korean government.

This fervor is much less pronounced among Catholics. In the same year that 15,000 Protestants went abroad for missionary work, only 634 Catholics did so, according to the Catholic Bishops' Conference of Korea. Even within Korea, Catholics generally do not proselytize, but rather wait until someone expresses interest in joining their church. In contrast, it is very common for Protestant Koreans to exhort their non-Protestant friends to attend church with them. Some evangelical groups even stop people on the street. Seoul abounds with public preachers, usually old men and women, who sometimes employ megaphones to harangue passersby and bear placards with the message "Yesu, Cheonguk—Bulshin, Jiok" ("Jesus, heaven—No belief, hell").

Protestantism and Catholicism also differ in how their adherents relate to other faiths. Buddhists sometimes complain that their religion is under attack from Protestants. During the 1980s and 1990s, groups of fervent Protestants entered Buddhist temples and destroyed property, even committing arson. In one case, at Muryangsa Temple on Samgak Mountain in Seoul in 1984, crosses were daubed on Buddhist paintings, and Buddha statues attacked with axes.

Social Network

Korean society traditionally emphasizes the group over the individual. A church provides for the spiritual needs of its followers, but it also provides an affiliation and a network that responds to the need to belong. Even people who are not especially religious may attend a church because their friends go there, and for many middle-aged women it is a meeting place and support group. As Korea has been a society in which women were mostly excluded from public life until the most recent generation of adults, church gave them a sense of involvement in something wider than the bounds of the family home.

Koreans abroad, including those who never went to church back in their own country, often find friends of their own nationality by attending Korean services. Over 70 percent of Korean-Americans attend church regularly, according to Min Pyong-gap and Kim Jung-ha in their book, *Religions in Asian America*. This is several times higher than the rate of church attendance in Korea itself, and the main reason for that is the social role the church plays—that of the community center for people of Korean origin living in the midst of a non-Korean culture.

Some miss out on the collective setting furnished by churches, though. It is well known that South Korea has one of the world's highest rates of Internet usage (and the fastest broadband speeds). Perhaps incongruously, Web culture impacts upon church attendance, for it is possible to "attend" many churches virtually, sitting in front of one's computer screen and singing along to hymns via live-streaming video. With Koreans working the longest hours in the OECD and church membership among young people now actually in decline, even the strongest religion in Korea must adapt to social change and embrace new methods.

Chapter 5

Capitalism with a Korean Face

Anyone can tell you that North Korea is communist and South Korea capitalist, but what do these words mean? Authorities in the North frequently turn a blind eye to street markets and encourage investment from prospective foreign partners seeking to make a profit out of cheap labor. And in the South, capitalism is still evolving, but has some very distinctive characteristics based both on old influences like Confucianism and the unique means of industrial development known as the *chaebol* system.

Park Chung-hee

During the 1950s, South Korea was "the poorest, most impossible country on this planet," according to a long-time advisor to President Park Chung-hee, Kim Dong-jin (not his real name). The Korean War had made a third of the population homeless; orphaned children roamed the streets looking for food; GDP per capita was far below $100; and, the government was utterly dependent upon foreign aid, principally from the United States. Politically, things were no better. President Syngman Rhee presided over a regime as bloody and repressive as it was corrupt.

When student protests sent Syngman Rhee fleeing to Hawaii in 1960, South Korea engaged in a brief experiment with democracy under the government of Prime Minister Chang Myon and President Yoon Po-seon. Unfortunately, the country was in turmoil—with severe factionalism, a currency crisis, and Communist agitation—and these leaders could not hold things together. Han Seung-joo, an anti-Rhee demonstrator who dodged the bullets that killed over a hundred of his comrades and eventually went on to become a cabinet minister in the 1990s, recalls, "There was a sense that we weren't going to make it as a country."

In this circumstance, army general Park Chung-hee took his chance. On May 16, 1961, he seized power, and he soon started putting in place the changes that would make South Korea a wealthy country. General Park—later President Park—is the one person who undoubtedly had the greatest influence on this country, for both better and worse. He remains a divisive figure due to his autocratic rule, but credit for his contribution to the economy should never be overlooked.

General Park was no Ayn Rand–style free-marketeer. In fact, long before he came to power, he was nearly executed for being part of a Communist cell. Immediately following his takeover in 1961, he rounded up businessmen and subjected them to public humiliations, such as being forced to march through the streets carrying placards proclaiming, "I am a corrupt swine." He was not being unreasonable: during the 1950s, entrepreneurs close to the Rhee government were able to grow quickly by purchasing assets abandoned by Japanese colonialists, such as factories, at knock-down prices. Once a firm began producing a certain product, the government would block importation of competing goods from overseas. Firms that benefited from this protectionism included Samsung—still the largest business group in Korea today.

Samsung founder Lee Byung-chul, the most successful entrepreneur of 1950s South Korea, was in Japan at the time of General Park's coup. The new regime alleged that Lee held one-fifth of the nation's illicitly acquired wealth, had given illegal political donations, and had evaded taxes. He was somehow persuaded to return to Korea and was immediately jailed. Yet the talented and persuasive Lee managed to make a deal with General Park, offering to "donate" most of his wealth to the state and use his influence to persuade other entrepreneurs to follow the economic plans General Park was then drawing up. This offer was accepted, and Lee was made head of the new Federation of Korean Industries, an organization that to this day represents the interests of the largest Korean firms. General

Park's objective was to pursue industrial development, in order to make the country more powerful than North Korea and dig South Korean people out of poverty. In negotiating with Lee he realized that the "corrupt swine" could be instrumental in achieving this goal if their organizational expertise could be put to work in the ways he wanted.

With that in mind, General Park offered eighteen leading entrepreneurs a deal they could not refuse: participate in his development plans or go to jail. These business leaders included the founders of companies like flour miller and cement-maker Daehan and cotton-spinner Samho, who, along with Lee Byung-chul, had been heavily fined for tax evasion and the paying of kickbacks. The fines they paid were reinvested by the government in projects that General Park had asked the chosen companies to develop. As part of the government's first Five Year Economic Plan laying the foundations for industrial development for 1962 to 1967, the focus was set on areas like fertilizer production, cement, chemicals, oil refining, and textiles,

Later, the number of firms able to participate in the club was expanded: Kim Woo-choong, who was still in school during the Rhee era, founded Daewoo in 1967 and, perhaps owing to the fact that his father used to teach President Park, was able to join. Daewoo was originally a textile firm but also ended up making electronic goods, cars, and ships, in accordance with subsequent government economic plans. In fact, Kim entered the shipbuilding business against his will—Park forced him to do it. Daewoo Shipbuilding & Marine Engineering Ltd. now generates annual revenues of over U.S. $10 billion.

Though these were the largest firms in Korea, at the time they lacked the resources required to enter such capital-intensive industries as shipbuilding and car manufacturing. However, the government was relatively flush with infusions of cash from U.S. government loans and later from payments for participation in the Vietnam War, as well as soft loans and compensation from Japan for its depredations during the colonial period. The state could therefore fund favored firms through its national banks, at rates of interest much lower than the 25 to 30 percent interest rates offered on the open market at the time. In 1964, 40 percent of all money loaned by Korean banks was shared between just nine business groups.

Corruption still existed, owing to the close relationship between government and business. It was typical for kickbacks of up to 10 percent to be paid to high-ranking officials when loans were made. Thus Lee Hu-rak, the president's chief of staff, was able to garner an illicit fortune of a reported U.S. $40 million. A mutually beneficial relationship between the political and economic elites developed: companies received cheap loans and were able to expand, and officials got their cut. The incentives were lined up then for firms to take on as much debt as possible, and use it to expand. Throughout the 1960s, the capital structure of a Korean manufacturing firm employing more than 200 people was on average 17.3 percent equity, and 82.7 percent debt.

Despite this, President Park himself was not personally corrupt. His strong leadership and integrity ensured that the system did not dissolve into chaos. Furthermore, he encouraged an important shift that resulted in Korean firms developing into world-beaters. During the 1950s, large Korean companies were engaged in import substitution. This is when the government blocks imports and allows domestic firms to make the blocked products (usually very inefficiently) and sell them in the local market. President Park's shift was to instruct the companies to export as well, and thus Korean firms had to learn to compete on the international stage. High import tariffs remained, ensuring that Korean products kept their advantage at home, but the necessity to compete abroad meant that groups like Samsung and LG became highly efficient operations.

Not all could make it. Though it is true that Korea's economic miracle was a result of partnership between the state and industry, one aspect of proper capitalism did remain: it was still possible to fail. Especially in the early days, bankruptcies were more likely than may be imagined. Gaepung, one of Korea's five largest firms during the 1960s, had disappeared by the mid-1970s; Dongmyung, which was the world's largest seller of plywood in the early 1970s, went under in 1980. Since the mid-1980s, though, the top ranks of the largest Korean firms have been more stable. Between 1983 and 2000, only two business groups lost their place in the top ten. This could be due to the fact that large Korean firms and the Korean economy as a whole are both more stable now; it could also be due to reduced political interference.

The sprawling conglomerates that grew under Park's auspices became known simply as *daegieop* (big business), or *chaebol*. The word *chaebol* comes from the same (originally Chinese) characters that make up the Japanese word *zaibatsu*, which means a kind of "financial clique." The model for the *chaebol* was the vertically integrated *zaibatsu* conglomerate from nineteenth-century Meiji Japan, only more centralized and without the ability to own banks. The state controlled the banks, allowing President Park to keep hold of the purse strings.

Lotte is probably the most ubiquitous *chaebol* from the perspective of the Korean consumer. Founded in Tokyo in 1948 by Shin Kyuk-ho, a Korean living in Japan, Lotte first entered Korea in 1967 with a confectionery business, before spreading out with President Park's blessing. One can still buy a Lotte chocolate bar today. In fact, Lotte is Korea's dominant maker of chocolate, cookies, and other snacks. But one might also purchase the chocolate in one of the many large Lotte Department Stores. Within a Lotte Department Store or Lotte Cinema, one will likely find a café named Angel-in-us or a fast food restaurant named Lotteria. Both are owned by Lotte. One may live in a Lotte apartment and protect it with Lotte insurance. One's weekly shopping may be done at a LotteMart. Lotte Group has over sixty subsidiaries, employing over 60,000 people. It has a credit card company, too—but no bank.

The *Chaebol* Approach

Chaebol-style capitalism was, and to some extent still is, very different from the dictionary definition of capitalism. Not only was industry directed by the state, but the *chaebol* corporations were rigidly hierarchical and bureaucratic, influenced by Confucian culture. Firms were expected to treat workers as sons, and workers were expected to respond in kind by thinking of their chairmen as father figures and offering absolute loyalty. It was a paternalistic style of management reminiscent of the father-son relationship in Confucianism. Companies would give employees gifts on their birthdays and national holidays, much as a parent would do for a child. When the close family member of a worker died, the firm would also assist with funeral expenses. Leadership of *chaebol* was also a family concern—literally. Sons of chairmen were accelerated through the ranks, and given subsidiaries to run; the one who did the best job would eventually inherit the chairmanship of the whole group from his father. All the major *chaebol* today are run by descendents or in-laws of founders. In that respect, it is scarce wonder that foreign journalists often jokingly compare *chaebols* with North Korea, the supposedly socialist state that is now on its third generation of monarchical rule.

From the 1960s, *chaebol* wages were kept low and unions banned—but headcounts were higher than they would naturally have been. The corporate philosophy was of "growth together," everyone working for the same goal of national economic development. The state supported this with poster campaigns exhorting people to work hard and hit government-set export targets. *Chaebol* bosses typically owned just a small percentage of their companies, with much of the rest belonging to banks or the state. Import tariffs on critical industries were kept high, in order to protect nascent domestic firms.

The economy was so dominated by these *muneo kyeongyeong* ("octopus businesses," each with a battery of subsidiaries) that true competition—a cornerstone of capitalism—simply did not exist in the domestic market. *Chaebol* had to be competitive on an international scale, a feat they accomplished extremely well. However, if you were a Korean consumer, the only choice was usually a *chaebol*-made product. It was also often a reverse-engineered, intellectual property rights–busting product copied from elsewhere.

Furthermore, the power of these companies, supported by the state, meant that there was no real culture of entrepreneurship in South Korea. For a talented young person, the most attractive jobs other than in the professions of doctor or lawyer were either in the civil service or entry-level positions with the likes of Samsung or Hyundai. The possibility of having a truly self-made Korean Bill Gates was little more than zero. If one looks at the Kospi-100 index of the largest Korean firms (the equivalent of the Dow Jones or FTSE indices) even now, one still finds that the vast majority of them are *chaebol*. The largest conglomerate, Samsung, accounts for a full 20 percent of South Korean exports.

Less than ten non-*chaebol* companies in Korea have ever managed to generate annual revenues of 1 trillion won (around US $900 million). This small club is tech- and Internet-firm- heavy, containing Humax, the digital TV set top-box manufacturer; NHN, the operator of search portal naver.com; and online game-maker NCSoft. The Internet in particular is proving to be a leveler, as it provides a realm of business where, according to one young entrepreneur, "some kid with a smartphone" is not necessarily at a disadvantage relative to the *chaebol*.

It is still the case though that one should not compete with the *chaebol*. *Chaebol* are no longer supported financially by the government, but their sheer size due to their past advantage makes taking them on a foolish endeavor. For an ambitious entrepreneur, one's goal should be either to sell to a *chaebol*, or find a blue ocean—unexplored or unexploited territory—in the way NCSoft and NHN did. If one cannot do that, then the international market offers possibilities: Humax, a company started by a group of Seoul National University engineering students following a conversation in a bar, managed to join the trillion won club by selling their products mostly overseas.

Jeong Ju-young

President Park rewarded the companies that most fulfilled his wishes—those who would build a particular road, hospital, or bridge, for example, in time and on budget. According to one insider, the two that did this best were Lee Byung-chul's Samsung, and Hyundai, which explains at least in part why they are still the most dominant *chaebols* today. They were naturally more able, and their reward for this was a better head start.

Today's business students may know plenty about Samsung, but the story of Hyundai is more revealing. The founder, Jeong Ju-young—born into rural poverty in Tongchon, Gangwon Province (in present-day North Korea)—is a model of resilience, unshakeable self-belief, and determination. His story is the story of South Korea: he started with nothing, and, relying on his capacity to overcome any problem, he took on the world—albeit with some help from Park Chung-hee, with whom he shared a strong bond over their shared belief in national development. His autobiography, available for free online in English as well as Korean, is to be recommended for anyone interested in learning more about the development of South Korea.

According to General Park's advisor Kim Dong-jin, Jeong had a singular lack of self-doubt. The two would have meetings in which Park would detail some long, complicated project and ask, "So, can you do it?"—to which Jeong always responded, "Yes, of course I can do it." Later, Kim Dong-jin would ask Jeong, "Do you really understand what the president wants you to do?" Jeong would say, "No, but I'm sure I can do it anyway." That response tells you almost everything you need to know about why South Korea was able to develop so quickly after the war. One could relate it to the Buddhist capacity for overcoming and refusing to accept one's lot; one could also relate it to the Confucian ethic of merit and constant hard work.

Kim Dong-jin tells another very illuminating story concerning Jeong. In an interview, he asked rhetorically, "Why do you think he built six, seven, and eight dry docks at his Ulsan shipyard, when other shipyards only have one or two?" The answer was not because he thought he would need them. It was that President Park believed in shipbuilding so much that he would always give Jeong money to build another dry dock, even when one was not needed. Jeong of course wanted the money for something else, so he learned how to build dry docks more cheaply and divert the remainder into the real project.

A System That Suited Its Time

This tells us plenty about Jeong's character, but it also reveals some of the negatives of government-mandated *chaebol* development. Imagine if, in your country, a privileged insider was being lent government money—and then not even spending it on the intended purpose. It sounds outrageous, and the stuff that leads to scandal and resignations.

Yet Jeong was capable enough to use these resources to great effect. Today, companies bearing the name Hyundai employ hundreds of thousands of people globally. His firm and others, like Samsung, LG, and Lotte, were at least partly responsible for South Korea's urbanization, attracting farm laborers from the countryside to the cities. Seoul had a population of around 2.4 million in 1960 and today stands as one of the world's true megacities, home to 10 million within the bounds of the city proper and 24 million within its metropolitan area—half the population of the country. The *chaebol* have changed the landscape and the way people live. There are even entire *chaebol* cities: the city of Ulsan developed as a place for Hyundai employees to live and work, and now has a population of over a million.

The *chaebol*-government compact of the 1960s and 1970s suited its time. It is not a system suited to a large, modern economy, but it did, despite its faults, enable South Korea to generate enormous economic growth and dig itself out of poverty. Exports rose from $100 million in 1964 to $10 billion in 1977, and GDP per capita went from around $120 to $1,040 in the same period. The arrangement was characterized by favoritism and "lent itself to a certain amount of corruption," in the words of Mr. Kim, but it was also a practical solution that combined the power of the state with the profit incentive and harnessed Confucianism's ability to bring everyone in line under their chairmen, who in turn fell in line under President Park.

After Park Chung-hee

How much has changed since the 1960s and 1970s? In legal terms, virtually everything. In the 1980s, the military dictator Chun Doo-hwan set a course of economic liberalization. A group of U.S.-trained, neo-liberal advisors in the government's Economic Planning Board (who had been virtually ignored by President Park) were given great influence over economic policy. They dropped the kind of quantitative targets set by Park's government (for instance, the export of a certain dollar value of products) and began reducing import tariffs, and selling off stakes in banks to private investors.

Chun was not completely above intervention, though, at least for his own ends. In 1984, according to the New York Times (March 25, 1998), Cho Bong-gu, chairman of top-ten *chaebol* Samho, refused to bribe Chun beyond his usual U.S.$700,000, despite being advised that a golf course or hotel would be necessary. Chun retaliated by simply handing Samho over to a rival company named Daelim (with whom he had excellent relations) and confiscating Cho's personal assets too. Cho ended up fleeing the country.

In 1997, the Asian economic crisis broke, resulting in twenty-five *chaebol* bankruptcies in just one year, including that of carmaker Kia (Kia was eventually taken over by Hyundai Motor). This crisis was largely the result of decades of corporate debt addiction, which began in the 1960s, finally coming to a head. Heavily indebted Daewoo, which had once been responsible for 10 percent of South Korea's GDP, finally went under in 1999, despite the best efforts of founder Kim Woo-choong to keep it alive by cooking the books. The reform-minded Kim Dae-jung administration, which came into power in January 1998, used the opportunity to pass laws geared towards improving corporate governance, protecting minority shareholder rights, and cracking down on corruption between politicians and the *chaebol*.

In recent years, Korea has continued to reduce import tariffs and protectionist legal hurdles, especially for those countries with which free-trade agreements have been signed. This means that *chaebol* now have to compete against foreign firms in their own backyard: Apple, for instance, sold almost two million iPhones in Korea in 2010, despite Samsung Electronics making a very similar product. Thankfully for Samsung, though, its own Galaxy S phone is so competitive that it has become a worldwide success, more than making up for Apple's encroachment on Korean soil.

Despite liberalization, the weakening of Confucian top-down thinking, and legal changes, the *chaebol* chairmen still have a gigantic head start over anyone else in Korea. Groups like Samsung, Hyundai, Lotte, and LG have so much money, political influence, and sway over the media that their power is still overwhelming. Their dominance of the industrial landscape is also intact: of the top fifty companies listed on the Korean Stock Exchange, only three are not *chaebol* (or former state-owned firms): NHN, NCSoft, and Shinhan Bank, an old bank that was reorganized by Japanese-Koreans and brought to Korea in 1982.

Chaebols often use their dominant market power to squeeze both suppliers and consumers. Small firms that sell to *chaebol* complain they are simply told what price to sell at. That price will inevitably be one that enables the supplier to survive, but not actually earn enough of a profit that it can expand. For shoppers, *chaebol* price-fixing acts as a kind of extra sales tax. Since markets for most consumer goods are dominated by a tiny handful of companies, it is very easy for collusion to occur. In January 2012, Samsung Electronics and LG Electronics were fined for a long-running operation in which they colluded to drive up the price of computers and home appliances. Unfortunately, the total fine levied—the equivalent of US$42 million—was only a fraction of their illicitly earned profit.

Perhaps one vestige of the old system is the power of *chaebol* chairmen to get away with almost anything. On occasions like Liberation Day (August 15), there is a tradition of presidential pardons. In a spirit of forgiveness, thousands of convictions—usually traffic offenses—are expunged. Rarely does such an occasion pass without a *chaebol* chairman being forgiven for bribery, tax evasion, or even violent crime. Kim Seung-yeon of Hanwha Group was convicted of abducting and beating bar workers with an iron bar (with the help of a group of henchmen) in revenge for an assault on his son. He was forgiven on Liberation Day 2008, as was Chey Tae-won of SK Group, who had been found guilty of accounting fraud worth over a billion U.S. dollars.

The justification for such pardons is always that the economy needs these men, and that it is not good for Korean businesses that are competing internationally to be living under a cloud of perceived criminality. Of course, the best way to improve the image of Korean business would be for those convicted of crimes to serve their full sentences, in order to deter further criminality. South Korea has improved immensely in recent years as an economy, a democracy, and a rule-governed society. Yet many investors around the world do not seem to be aware of this, and part of the reason is the perception of unfairness that comes from practices like the pardoning of corporate criminals simply because of who they are.

It is to be hoped that this culture changes at some point, and that more is done to encourage real entrepreneurship in Korean society. No one should wish for the weakening of the likes of Samsung Electronics—South Korea's flagship firm and biggest export earner as a world leader in semiconductors, mobile phones, and computers—but a more advanced economy requires a freer exchange of ideas, more competition, stronger creativity, and above all, the opportunity for those with talent to build up new businesses that can take on world markets.

For the most part, the large *chaebol* firms today are highly efficient companies that produce products the whole world buys: Samsung televisions, Hyundai cars, and LG refrigerators. In the long run, South Korea needs to find ways to encourage a new generation of entrepreneurs to rise up and join them rather than bow before their almighty presence.

Chapter 6

Democracy:
Beyond Asian Values

The phrase "miracle on the Han River" describes the feverish economic development that took place in South Korea from the 1960s onwards, yet this country has achieved two miracles. The second is the political transformation that occurred in the past quarter-century. In a very short time, South Korea has graduated from military dictatorship to the twentieth most democratic country in the world, and the most democratic in Asia, according to the Economist Intelligence Unit.

Overshadowed by the North Korean problem, Chinese growth, and Japan's cultural power, South Korea never gets the credit it deserves. However, in a political sense, this country is becoming a model for Asia. Around the region, there are countries with successful economies but authoritarian politics, such as Singapore and China. Only Japan presents a serious challenge to South Korea in terms of democratic development, but Japan's free and fair elections belie a rigid, bureaucratic system in which genuine change is very difficult to achieve.

During the 1990s, a debate took place over so-called Asian values, in which Singaporean leader Lee Kuan Yew argued that democracy is a Western concept not suited to Asian people, who have grown up in Confucian-influenced, authoritarian cultures. The idea of Asian values has its origin in Lee's Singapore and Mahatir Mohamad's Malaysia, where it was seen as an approach that could unite the ethnic Chinese and the Muslim Malays as well as justify continued one-party rule. One of their opponents in the debate was Kim Dae-jung, the long-time democratization campaigner and eventual president of South Korea, who lost no time in replying that "culture is not our destiny. Democracy is."

Given the general lack of democracy in Asia, it is appropriate to ask why South Korea has embraced democracy so strongly. A number of factors in the Korean character and Korean history may provide the explanation. Among them are Koreans' desire for education; the creation of the Korean *Hangul* alphabet, which dramatically improved literacy, giving ordinary people the opportunity to express themselves; and the country's deep tradition of revolt and protest.

Education and Literacy

Following the creation of South Korea, there was a great push towards expanding education for all. In 1945, only 5 percent of people had graduated with secondary school or higher-level qualifications; by the early 1990s, this figure stood at above 90 percent. Successive governments saw education as key to national development and pursued a policy of educational egalitarianism, dramatically increasing the number of schools throughout the country. Parents were only too happy to sign on. Korean society is in some ways very elitist, with well-established "old-boy" networks that run business and politics. However, it also despises ignorance and prizes literacy and basic knowledge among the general population.

Respect for learning goes back to Confucianism, of course, but literacy in Korea has a founding hero. In the early Joseon period, King Sejong the Great (r. 1418–1450) mandated the creation of *Hangul*, the Korean alphabet, thereby committing one of the most empowering acts of egalitarianism in Korean history. Sejong is considered the greatest Korean ruler and was a man of many achievements, but none was more significant than this.

Foreign visitors are always surprised by how easy it is to learn to read Korean words. The reason for this is that Sejong deliberately made it so. Prior to *Hangul*, Koreans used Chinese characters (*hanja*), which were so complex and numerous that only the *yangban*, who lived a "gentleman-scholar" existence on the back of peasant labor, had the opportunity to properly learn them. Sejong, against the wishes of many of the elite, wanted to create a writing system that enabled ordinary people to become literate. The characters his scholars came up with were so straightforward that it was said at the time, "A wise man can acquaint himself with them before the morning is over; a stupid man can learn them in the space of ten days."

Hangul was such a powerful tool that a subsequent king, Yeonsangun, tried to ban its use when propaganda posters against his rule began to appear in the invented script. Crucially, he couldn't; the cat was already out of the bag. Later on, the use of *Hangul* to produce religious texts helped spread Christianity, which proclaimed that all were equal in the eyes of God—unlike Confucianism, which required everyone to know their rightful place. Nowadays, the level of illiteracy in Korea is virtually zero. Unlike many other places in the world, all people with an interest in politics have the ability to communicate their views. They also benefit from access to an open educational system that can provide them with knowledge of the fundamentals of civics as well as political theory, political history, and public administration, for instance.

Culture of Protest

Korea has a vibrant tradition of protest. Sometimes this can go too far, as when farmers in the town of Icheon, protesting against the location of a military base in their area, ripped the limbs off a live pig and beheaded it outside the Ministry of Defense in May 2007. Such excesses aside, it remains true that people in Korea express their views more openly, more noisily, and in greater number, than in most other Asian countries. Park Won-soon, the mayor of Seoul, a former human rights lawyer, and the founder of Beautiful Store (Areumdaun Gagye), Korea's first chain of charity thrift shops, proudly points out that, in years gone by, scholars angry with the king would throw caution to the wind and engage in "ax protests," so named because taking part in one was a guaranteed way to have one's head removed with said implement. "And if you look at Chinese protestors after Tiananmen Square," he notes, "they just gave up... Korean democracy campaigners kept on going" until the military government threw in the towel.

The American writer P. J. O'Rourke visited Korea in 1987 to report on the democratization movement. After witnessing various protests first hand, he expressed shock at the sheer persistence and resilience of Korean protestors. In his essay, "Seoul Brothers," he writes that during the Guro-gu district office building riot, police "were firing salvos of gas grenades, twenty at a time, into the fifth floor windows... That the students could even stand in this maelstrom was a testament of Korean-ness. But they were not only standing; they were fighting like sons of bitches."

Even today, this tradition is as strong as ever. Though South Koreans have relatively much less to complain about, you can go to Gwanghwamun or Yeouido (the center of government and the parliament, respectively) now and see people protesting against or advocating for just about anything. From trade unionists to anti–North Korea army veterans, they will be out in force, holding banners, shouting, and singing oddly cheerful songs. Though many people complain about this culture of protest, South Korea's young democracy benefits from having citizens who make whoever is in government realize that they cannot act with impunity.

The Rebels of Later Joseon

The stereoptypical characterization of Joseon dynasty Korea is as "the land of the morning calm." By the nineteenth century, it was anything but. Persistent infighting between various powerful families and palace insiders rendered Korea restive and vulnerable. The state grew weak and divided, and ordinary citizens were wearying of the rigors of Confucian hierarchy. While Europe was undergoing its own period of revolutionary changes, Korea contended with a series of peasant uprisings, brought on by the excessive taxation of poor farmers and popular rejection the *yangban* class's entitlement to live well off peasant labor.

As early as 1811, Hong Gyeong-nae, a poor man from Pyeongan Province (in today's North Korea) believed to have been either a "fallen *yangban*" or a common soldier, gathered a peasant army and took control of much of the north of the country. The Joseon forces were not able to kill him and put down his revolt until April of the following year, by which time he had inspired similar movements in other areas of the country. In 1862, farmers led by a scholar named Yu Gye-chun from Jinju, Gyeongsang Province, rebelled in response to the rule of Baek Nak-shin, the military commander who held jurisdiction over their region. Baek had stolen farmers' incomes with the help of corrupt civil servants. The rebels burned government buildings to the ground and killed local officials. The authorities in Seoul were forced to make reforms to military, land, and grain policy, to reduce the fraud by local civil servants that so angered the peasantry.

Towards the end of the century, similar small-scale rebellions occurred throughout the country, in the provinces of Jeolla, Gyeongsang, Jeju, Hamgyeong, and Pyeongan. Then, in 1894, came the Donghak Peasant Revolution. Donghak means "Eastern learning," and was a movement that began in the 1860s as a kind of indigenous semi-religion preached by Choi Je-woo. Choi promulgated a mixture of Confucian and Buddhist philosophy, combined with what today might be termed democratic socialism; he advocated the equality of all human beings, democracy, and human rights. Unlike socialism in Europe though, it was not a matter of political theory. Choi believed in a god, or state of perfection, but it was one that exists within all people rather than in some unearthly realm. Since all humans possessed this, all men and women were equal, whether farmer or *yangban*. Choi was also extremely nationalistic and anti-foreign. He had become alarmed with the spread of Christianity in Asia, and wanted to restrict outside influence to stop this Western religion from taking over Korea.

Choi's philosophy was not necessarily consistent, but his movement was popular among farmers, who saw him as offering a message of hope. Though Choi was apprehended and executed in 1864, Donghak lived on as an underground movement through the efforts of his successor, Choi Si-hyeong. By 1892, its followers had grouped themselves into a guerrilla army, and its fighters began to conduct raids on traders, landlords, government officials, and foreigners, seizing their assets and distributing them to the poor.

Throughout the first half of 1894, this force, comprised mostly of farmers, grew in power. By May, Donghak fighters had taken control of Jeonju, the capital of the historically rebellious Jeolla Province in the southwest of the country, provoked initially by the actions of a corrupt local official. They also had designs on Seoul, overrunning garrisons on the road to the capital and setting as one of their main objectives to "march to Seoul and clean the government."

One faction of the Joseon government appealed to China for help, since the government itself was too weak to handle the rebels. The three thousand troops sent by Qing authorities were enough to halt the Donghak army's progress and bring about a ceasefire and negotiations, but this Chinese incursion angered the Japanese, who were already asserting their influence in Korea with the intention of eventual annexation. Japan sent 8,000 troops to Korea in retaliation, seized the royal palace, and replaced top government officials with pro-Japanese Koreans. The resulting standoff between China and Japan in Korea was a major cause of the First Sino-Japanese War of 1894–1895.

By October 1894, the Donghak army again began to march northwards from its base in Jeolla towards Seoul and was met at Ugeumchi, near the city of Gongju (around 80 miles from the capital), by Japanese troops. The foreign force had cannons, giving them a great advantage over Donghak fighters, who possessed swords, bows and arrows, and occasionally, muskets. By November 10, 1894, the Donghak forces had suffered a resounding defeat.

The Donghak army had not fought entirely in vain, though. The government, which had by then fallen under Japanese influence, began instituting the Gabo Reforms (1894–1896), which ended the class system, mandated the appointment of government officials on the basis of merit alone, and allowed widows to remarry, among other reforms. The extent to which Donghak influenced these reforms is a matter of debate but that it had some impact is certain.

In 1905, under the direction of its third leader, Son Byeong-hui—who would later become a hero of the Korean people for his involvement in the March 1, 1919, declaration of independence from Japan—Donghak evolved into a proper religion, called Cheondogyo.

Cheondogyo is even more philosophically diverse than Donghak, for it is influenced by Christianity on top of Donghak's traditional influences. At its heart, though, is the fundamental belief that all human beings are equal. Cheondogyo still exists today and is believed to have around one million adherents. The story of Korean religion is one of syncretism, and Cheondogyo is probably the most syncretic of all religions practiced in Korea.

Early South Korea

With the defeat of Imperial Japan in 1945, Korea recovered its independence. However, by 1948, it also found itself divided, into a pro-Soviet Union north and a pro-U.S. south. The regimes that coalesced in both were authoritarian but different in important ways. In the North, Kim Il-sung became a dictator in all senses, aided by Joseph Stalin. In the South, which was under U.S. military administration until 1948, democratic institutions were established and elections were held, and the first authoritarian South Korean presidents had to maintain the trappings of democracy. Even in the darkest days of South Korean dictatorship, there were always strong, identifiable opposition figures. Democracy-era presidents Kim Young-sam and Kim Dae-jung were themselves former opposition leaders. In North Korea, by contrast, no dissent has ever been tolerated, and no figure outside of the Kim family has been allowed to build a support base.

Syngman Rhee, a descendent of the royal Yi clan, had been a leader of the provisional government of Korea based in Shanghai, from 1919 to 1925. In the immediate postwar period, he was the most powerful of a number of figures competing to lead the South. As a Harvard graduate who wrote his name in the Western manner (family name last, rather than first) and who detested Communism, he attracted the support of the U.S. military administration. He won a seat as a member of parliament in elections held under UN supervision in May of that year. Parliament in turn elected him first president of the new republic. On August 15, Rhee formally assumed executive powers from the U.S. military in a handover ceremony.

The parliament elected in 1948 drafted and ratified a new constitution, which combined the American system (including the separation of executive and legislative powers, an independent judiciary, and the vesting of the executive power in a president, albeit a president elected by parliament rather than through direct elections) with a unicameral legislature, which featured a cabinet and prime minister. The legislature, the National Assembly, was to be elected by the people, who enjoyed universal suffrage. This system was new to Koreans: they had grown up under either absolute monarchy, or rule by Japanese governor-generals. However, the initial openness of the period and the gap left by the pullout of Japan resulted in a political awakening. By 1947, ahead of elections, there were more than 340 registered political parties.

Nevertheless, President Rhee managed to subvert South Korea's untested democratic system and eventually rule as a de facto dictator. His National Security Law of 1948 made praise for Communism or North Korea illegal and was used to execute, imprison, or simply deter, political opponents. By 1949, 30,000 people had been arrested under the new law. North Korea's decision to invade the South on June 25, 1950, which precipitated the Korean War of 1950–1953, firmly entrenched anti-Communism as a defining ideology of South Korea. Rhee's forces also indiscriminately massacred thousands of people on Jeju island, including women and children, in the name of anti-Communism. Both Rhee and later presidents like Park Chung-hee and Chun Doo-hwan were able to use the threat of Communism as a justification for clamping down on political opponents.

In 1952, President Rhee lost the support of parliament over his proposal to have the president elected by popular vote rather than by parliament. Members voted 143 to 19 to block his move, and with the end of his four-year term approaching, Rhee's days as leader looked numbered. He responded by declaring martial law and threatening to execute those who did not support him. Unsurprisingly, his proposal then passed. He used bullying tactics again in 1954 to remove the limit on the number of terms a president could serve, effectively allowing him to be president for life.

Throughout the 1950s, President Rhee's Liberal Party was able to win successive parliamentary elections through vote buying and the use of hired thugs to coerce voters. This activity was funded by the proceeds of corruption. Any businessman hoping to prosper had to pay off the party. Having navigated the confusion of the immediate post-colonial period as well as the Korean War, the president firmly entrenched his autocratic rule. Yet the parliamentary system—and the need to avoid alienating the United States, which provided most of the South Korean government's budget in the form of aid—forced him to play the part of a quasi-democrat, allowing opposition, albeit in small doses.

Some of Rhee's opponents were to pay the ultimate price. In 1949, former presidential candidate Kim Gu—a man considered a hero for his long opposition to Japanese rule—was assassinated by military officer Ahn Doo-hee. Ahn stated in court that he acted alone, but the fact that he only served one year in jail and rejoined the army after his release, later becoming a colonel, suggests rather strongly that he acted on orders from above. It is suspected that the killing was ordered by Kim Chang-ryong, President Rhee's chief enforcer.

Cho Bong-am, Rhee's rival in the mid- and late 1950s, was another victim. Though Rhee needed opponents in order to maintain the pretense of being a democratic politician, Cho had become too popular: he received 30 percent of votes cast in the 1956 presidential election on a platform reminiscent of European-style social democracy. Put on trial in 1958 for allegedly being in league with North Korea, he was acquitted but, following governmental pressure on the judiciary, was retried and found guilty, then executed in July 1959.

Democracy Denied: The April Revolution and Park Chung-hee
President Rhee's rule was not to last much longer. Following the obvious vote rigging of the March 1960 presidential election, students began to protest. After a demonstration in the southern city of Masan, a young protestor named Kim Ju-yeol was found dead, his head split open by a tear gas canister. This event shocked the nation and served as the spark for the April Revolution: on April 19, students marched from Korea University to Cheong Wa Dae, the presidential mansion. Soldiers opened fire, killing two hundred of them. The ranks of protestors grew in response, and by April 25, the police

and military began disobeying orders to shoot. Rhee fled to Hawaii, where he died five years later.

The era of dictatorship was not over, though. There followed a brief flirtation with democracy under the elected government of Prime Minister Chang Myon, but in May 1961, General Park Chung-hee took power via a coup. General Park, like President Rhee, was subject to American restrictions: the Kennedy administration pressured him to renounce his military role and become a civilian leader. This he did, and in 1963 he won his first presidential election. This was believed to have been a reasonably fair vote, and due to his highly successful economic policies, Park was able to narrowly win another in 1967.

In 1969, President Park managed to push through a constitutional amendment to allow himself to serve a third term. By this point, however, his popularity was declining, and in the 1971 election, he was able to defeat rival Kim Dae-jung by a margin of only 8 percent, 53 to 45 percent, with the aid of vote fraud. No doubt fearful of losing control, he decided to suspend the constitution, dissolve parliament, and declare martial law in October 1972. He promulgated a new constitution, the so-called Yushin Constitution, which gave the president theoretically unlimited six-year terms; replaced presidential elections with an electoral college fixed in his favor; and awarded the president the power to appoint one-third of members of parliament, which allowed him to virtually guarantee a majority in the assembly. These reforms were approved via a rigged public referendum.

In response to this, a protest movement began to build, particularly among students at the elite Seoul National, Korea, and Yonsei Universities. According to former protestor and current mayor of Seoul, Park Won-soon, anti-regime students formed cells or "under-circles," which used elaborate code-word systems to communicate with similar groups in order to arrange flash protests in which they would make their point and beat a hasty retreat.

Between 1974 and 1975, President Park issued a series of extremely repressive decrees that targeted students in particular. Criticizing the Yushin Constitution was made illegal; the army was given the power to enter universities; and political activity by students was banned. Those found to be involved in political activity—like Park Won-soon—were thrown in jail and stripped of their university places. Those who attended Korean universities or worked on Korean campuses at the time will talk of becoming accustomed to the smell of tear gas or the sight of tanks by the university gates.

Unlike in the case of President Rhee, it was not students who brought down President Park. Park was shot at a private drinking session by trusted comrade and former military academy classmate Kim Jae-gyu, the head of the Korean equivalent of the CIA, on October 26, 1979. There is some debate as to whether Kim had planned this act or not. Some claim it was a spur-of-the-moment reaction to criticism from Park and chief presidential bodyguard Cha Ji-cheol over his lack of willingness to crack down on protestors. Others claim that it was a premeditated act with the intention of bringing an end to dictatorship in South Korea. In 2011, a tape recording of a conversation between Kim and a lawyer at a military prison after his arrest came to light; the recording appeared to confirm that Kim had been planning the assassination for some time, for he had been disillusioned with President Park ever since the Yushin Constitution had been installed.

From Dictatorship to Democracy

In testimony during the trial that saw him sentenced to death, Kim stated that he shot Park "for the democracy of this country." If instituting democracy was his intention, he would have been disappointed with what came next. Following the assassination of Park Chung-hee, Prime Minister Choi Kyu-ha became acting president. However, Chun Doo-hwan, an ambitious and opportunistic army officer, maneuvered himself into a position of de facto command. He forced the most senior officers of the Korean CIA to report to him twice daily, effectively putting himself in control of intelligence, and then on December 12, 1979, with the aid of Hanahoe, a secret group of elite officers that he led, he began putting into place a coup. He arrested the army's chief of staff without President Choi's approval. In early 1980, he had himself promoted to lieutenant general, and formally took over the Korean CIA. He declared martial law in May and dissolved parliament in June, effectively becoming leader of the country in the process. Choi resigned, and Chun, via the electoral-college method, had himself declared president on September 1. As president, he replaced Park's constitution with a new one, which, although less authoritarian, still gave him broad powers.

Lacking any legitimacy, Chun Doo-hwan maintained his rule initially through violence. In May 1980, he declared martial law. Citizens of Gwangju, the largest city in Jeolla Province, revolted, and he responded by sending in the army and killing hundreds. Later, his attempts at control were more subtle. Through the "3S policy"—the s's relating to "sex, screen, and sports"—he reduced the censorship of sexual content in films, introduced nationwide color TV broadcasts, and attempted to focus the nation's attention on the 1988 Seoul Olympics. Unlike Park Chung-hee, he was extremely corrupt, and he enriched himself to the tune of many hundreds of millions of dollars. For the Gwangju massacre and his unrivaled graft, he stands out as the president people love to hate. During the course of interviews, one businessman who described Park Chung-hee as "the best leader we ever had" referred to Chun simply as "that bastard."

Parliamentary elections in 1985 saw Chun's party receive only 35 percent of the vote but claim a majority of seats. The blatant electoral fraud increased demands for genuine democracy, but it became apparent that Chun, who had constitutionally given himself just one presidential term of seven years, wanted to hand over power to a chosen successor, fellow Hanahoe member, Roh Tae-woo, rather than hold a fair presidential election in 1987. During this period, opposition to President Chun's rule widened. Chun could handle continuing protests by university students, but, when the students were joined by church members and ordinary workers, the tide started to turn.

In May 1987, it was revealed that Park Jong-chul, a student activist, had been tortured to death four months previously. This revelation inflamed public sentiment, and by June, demonstrations against Chun's rule were attracting millions of people. On June 19, the president issued orders to mobilize the army but apparently changed his mind three hours later. On the 29th, his protégé Roh Tae-woo made the historic declaration that free and fair elections, and a new constitution, would be instituted. As Park Won-soon states, "the best thing they [Chun and Roh] ever did was to know when their time was up." The promise of democracy was finally to be realized.

A Happy Ending

Anticlimactically, the winner of the presidential election of December 1987 was Roh Tae-woo, Chun Doo-hwan's friend and military comrade. Long-time democracy campaigners Kim Dae-jung and Kim Young-sam both ran, splitting the pro-reform vote with 27 and 28 percent respectively, enabling Roh to triumph with just 36 percent. It was a fair vote, with no electoral college or other manipulation: Roh's win was simply a reflection of the choice of the people between three main candidates. Roh himself respected the new system during his period in office, and when Kim Young-sam won in December 1992, power was handed over without incident. Five years later, when Kim Dae-jung won, the transfer from one civilian president to another was seen as a defining moment by former activists. This precedent has remained in place, with all subsequent transfers of power taking place smoothly, and all sides respecting the process.

Showing just how far democracy had come, both Roh and Chun Doo-hwan were convicted of treason, mutiny, and corruption in August 1996. They were fined hundreds of millions of dollars, and sentenced to death. Following consultation between President Kim Young-sam and by-then president-elect Kim Dae-jung in December 1997, both military men were pardoned as a gesture of national unity. Chun and Roh are living out their remaining days in heavily guarded seclusion, close by each other in the Yeonhee-dong area of Seoul. Ironically, they live just a short distance from the place chosen by Kim Dae-jung—the man whom Chun once sentenced to death—as the site of his retirement home in nearby Donggyo-dong. The idea of Kim Dae-jung having been their neighbor seems strange, but it is somehow fitting for the era of peaceful politics that he helped to usher in.

PART TWO

Cultural Codes

Chapter 7

Jeong—The Invisible Hug

In the Korean language, there is a word that elicits instant feelings of warmth, belonging, and even frustration as soon as it is heard. That word is *jeong*, and it represents one of the most potent, if diffuse, concepts in Korean culture. Regardless of what one makes of it, anyone coming to Korea ought to be aware of its power and implications. But what is *jeong*?

There are about as many definitions of the concept as there are people, but according to UCLA psychiatrists Christopher K. Chung and Samson J. Cho, *jeong* refers to "feelings of fondness, caring, bonding, and attachment that develop within interpersonal relationships." It is not felt purely within the heart or mind of an individual but is a connection that exists "between" two or more people, with the psychiatrists likening it to a cord linking people to each other.

Another interviewee sums it up as being like "an invisible hug that brings people together." In fact, *jeong* could be said to bind them together. A critical aspect of *jeong* is deep interdependence, for the cord is both tie and bond. Two people who share *jeong* should have a relationship of mutual give and take, assisting each other when needed. *Jeong* demands loyalty and sacrifice between those who share it. It also requires forgiveness: "There is no 'sorry' between friends," runs one Korean maxim.

Jeong is not a matter of choice. When Koreans talk about the beginning of a *jeong*-filled relationship, the expression "jeong deul-eott-da" is used: "*Jeong* has permeated me." It is even possible to have *jeong* with a person one does not like. For example, the expression "miun jeong" (hateful *jeong*) describes the bitter interdependence of an old married couple, or of co-workers who cannot stand one another but would feel bereft if one of them were to leave the firm. One acquaintance of the author confided that the reason he married was that he felt this kind of *jeong*—in contrast to what we might term romantic love—with his partner, despite their constant rows and apparent unsuitability to each other.

By its very nature, *jeong* is hard to describe: "You just have to feel it," says one interviewee. Some foreign residents of Korea, particularly those from more individualistic cultures such as the United Kingdom or United States, react to the mention of the word with scorn. Because it is considered a feeling that exists between people—rather than within the heart or mind of one individual, according to Chung and Cho—it requires a very strong sense of "we," which other cultures may not feel can exist. "Among Koreans, 'we' (or *woori*, in Korean) is not just a plural pronoun. Rather . . . it is a collective 'I,'" say these two academics. When a Korean talks about a person close to her, she will precede their name or title with "our" rather than "my." "My mother" becomes "our mother" in this perspective.

Koreans attach enormous importance to *jeong* and consider it one of their country's defining qualities. So, if a person is told he or she has a large capacity for *jeong*, it will be taken as a compliment. By the same token, one may hear the lament that "people complain that I have no *jeong*," and one sometimes sees recruitment advertisements looking for "jeong mahneun bundeul" ("people with a lot of *jeong*"). Though the Chinese character used for *jeong* exists in China and Japan, the thing it represents is accorded high social value only in Korea.

Skeptics may contend that *jeong* sounds very similar to love or friendship. To an extent, this is true, but unlike love or friendship it may exist between members of a group as large as a geographical region or an association or society: people from the same hometown, soldiers from the same regiment, and graduates from the same university or school can feel a sense of strong mutual support and obligation based on *jeong*. School alumni associations and church groups that harness this fellow feeling can develop significant influence: Seoul-based Somang Church gained notoriety as a recruiting ground for political office and top corporate positions after one of its elders, Lee Myung-bak, became president in 2008. It was already powerful before then, for over sixty Somang members have served as government ministers since its foundation in 1977.

While this example may seem like classic "old-boy network" behavior, it is in fact different and more powerful. The perceived imperative to help one's friends is stronger than in other cultures. *Jeong* is "unreasonable," according to one Korean company executive, and "makes it necessary to do things one otherwise would not do. It is the opposite of logic." Foreign visitors to Korea sometimes remark on the extreme displays of assistance to others that can be observed: for example, the lending of large sums of money to uncreditworthy friends or relatives in spite of spousal opposition. *Jeong* creates a kind of unwritten contract, promising help whenever it is needed.

The Power of *Jeong*

Between those who share it, *jeong* is "beautiful" and "makes us human," says a manager at POSCO, Korea's largest steel-making firm. It inspires people to do more for each other than they know makes rational sense. This is in large part why Westerners, and even Chinese, for whom *guanxi* (connections) are all-important, may find interpersonal behavior among Koreans—particularly when financial decisions come into play—mystifying, as one British executive puts it. Peter Underwood, an American businessman in Seoul, talks of a foreign businessman complaining of being "cheated" out of a deal, after offering a better price than a local competitor who had a relationship with his prospective partner. The businessman no doubt felt that nationalism or prejudice was to blame, but it was probably more a matter of *jeong*. If one has a *jeong* connection to another person, one may feel obliged to make the deal with them, rather than with the stranger—even if the stranger is offering a better deal. As Mr. Underwood wryly states, "if Adam Smith had been Korean, *The Wealth of Nations* would have been a completely different book." The idea of always making one's business decisions in the rational, self-interested, reward-maximizing way prescribed by classical economics is not truly in accordance with Korean culture.

While, to the average person, *jeong* is positive, heartwarming, and a triumph of humanity over cold rationalism, it can lead those with political power to act in ways detrimental to society. South Korea is a fully advanced country by all measures of economic development, except one: corruption. It ranks just forty-third in the world on Transparency International's Corruption Perceptions Index (North Korea is the world's most corrupt nation, according to this ranking). This low ranking is due mainly to the culture of doing favors, even when common sense, legality, and social justice say one should not. When one reads of a corruption case involving a businessman and a politician, usually a hometown, school, or military connection lies behind it. It should therefore come as no surprise that the word for favoritism, *jeongshil*, is derived from *jeong*.

The old-boy style of awarding top jobs exists everywhere, but its pervasiveness in Korea is astonishing. Key appointments in the governments of Presidents Park Chung-hee, Chun Doo-hwan, and Roh Tae-woo went so often to men from the same hometown that people spoke of a "TK Mafia": TK stands for Taegu (Daegu), Kyongsang (Gyeongsang)—the old English-language spellings of the city and region from which they came. And in December 1988, every single member of Roh's senior staff was a graduate of the same high school as him. His successor, Kim Young-sam, likewise surrounded himself with his own regional "mafia" when he was in power, drawn from his home city of Busan. Later, Kim Young-sam was succeeded by Kim Dae-jung, who began replacing the Busanites with people from his home region of Jeolla. Though this practice is heavily criticized, it would be surprising if a Korean president did not elevate those with whom he shared such connections.

Woori and *Nam*—In and Out

Jeong requires a sense of "we," or "woori," in Korean. "We" cannot include everyone in the world; if one is to extend one's greatest warmth and kindness to certain people with whom one shares *jeong*, then there must also be a larger, outside group of people whom one treats less well. The word for such unknowns is *nam*. During his presidential campaign, candidate Kim Young-sam made successful use of the rhetorical question "Woori-ga nam-iga?"—which means "Are we *nam*?"—when courting voters. The answer hoped for was of course "No, so we'll support you!"

Throughout the years of military rule, when South Korea was governed by elites drawn mainly from the Gyeongsang region (such as the T-K Mafia), Gyeongsang received disproportionately high funding for development, while its historical rival region, Jeolla, was relatively overlooked. The Gyeongsang city of Pohang was chosen by the government as the site of South Korea's now world-leading steel company POSCO, and the first highway linking Seoul to another major city was the Seoul-Busan Expressway (Busan is in Gyeongsang on the southeast coast). This regional favoritism has contributed greatly to regionalized splits in Korean politics, with voters in each region calculating which party is likely to give them the most assistance and then voting accordingly.

Woori is also one of the most commonly used words in marketing in Korea. One of the largest Korean banks is Woori Bank. The bank's appropriation of *woori* became a matter of controversy when the rest of the nation's major banks took legal action to stop Woori Bank from trademarking the word's use in advertising materials. President Roh Moo-hyun's political party was the Woori Party. A brand of rice is called Woori Ssal ("Our Rice"), and one beer company's slogan is "Woori nara, woori maekju" ("Our country, our beer").

Woori Nara, "Our Country"

In fact, *woori* and *jeong* are elastic in application and can extend to the whole country. In the context of one's neighborhood, family is *woori* and a person living down the street *nam*. In the context of the country, someone from one's own region is *woori*, and someone from another region *nam*. But if two Koreans with absolutely nothing else in common met in France, they could still develop *jeong* and feel the need to help each other out in times of difficulty. At international universities, Koreans are famous for sticking together and sometimes even shunning students of other nationalities.

Koreans feel such a strong connection to those within their in-groups that the sense of pride or shame felt by the group about one

Seoul's financial district, Yeouido, in 2012.

Top: Seoul in 1945. (Don O'Brien)

Below: Sejong the Great, the most admired Korean king and creator of the *Hangeul* writing system.

Top: A *musok-in* at Gangneung Danoje, a thousand-year-old festival. Despite South Korea's cutting-edge sophistication, many still turn to shamanism in times of trouble.

Below: Bukchon *hanok* district, a rich-turned-poor-turned-rich-again neighborhood where modernists and traditionalists now fight over the soul of Korean architecture.

South Korea has a very strong tradition of protest; sometimes it is excessive, but at other times, it is necessary. Here, it is merely amusing.

Fortune-tellers, like *musok-in*, are still very popular. This fellow is one of many who ply their trade in the downtown Jongro district of Seoul.

Top: With over a million members, Yoido Full Gospel Church is the largest in the world. Christianity is now the most popular religion in South Korea.

Below: Buddhism has a 1,700-year history in Korea. This temple, Yonggungsa in Gijang, near Busan, is notable for its location by the sea.

Top: Park Chung-hee (third from left in this 1966 photograph) ruled South Korea from 1961 to 1979. In many ways, the country is still under his influence, for better and worse. (LYNDON B. JOHNSON LIBRARY)

Below: The man in the hat is Hyundai founder Jeong Ju-young, Korea's most legendary entrepreneur. (U.S. DEPARTMENT OF DEFENSE)

Top: A Seoul street scene from 1945. The "Off Limits" sign warns American soldiers to stay away, owing to the presence of brothels in the area. (Don O'Brien)

Below: Less than fifty years ago, South Korea was an extraordinarily poor country. This 1966 photograph was likely taken near Cheonggyechon, a stream in downtown Seoul. (Michael Russo)

Top: A scale model of Jeong's Ulsan Shipyard, which is now the largest in the world. (U.S. Navy)

Below: Riot police stand guard at Seoul's City Hall in 2010. Sadly, this is a common sight in the capital. (Antti Hellgren)

Top: Myeongryundang at Sungkyunkwan, the greatest educational institution during the Joseon era and a renowned center of Confucian scholarship.

Below: Jeju Island's Cheonjeyeon Waterfall. Korea is famed for heavy industry and economic development, but that does not mean that natural beauty cannot be found.

Top: An old lady works preparing food at her pojang macha, a kind of makeshift street restaurant. Note the green bottle of *soju* in the middle. (MARK ZASTROW)

Below: At the heart of the Korean dining experience is *banchan*, a seemingly endless array of side dishes. (PATRICK LEE)

Top: Urban sprawl: Due to rapid industrialization, "cookie-cutter" apartment blocks were erected with little concern for urban planning or aesthetics. (ANTTI HELLGREN)

Below: Korea does not close down after dark. A night scene, complete with copious amounts of neon, at the Seomyeon district of Busan.

Top: The first sight that greets most new arrivals to South Korea: Incheon International Airport, regularly voted the best airport in the world. (Antti Hellgren)

Below: Seoul, 1966: the militarism, contemporary look in fashion, and beginnings of economic development and consumerism that mark the period can all be seen in this image. (Michael Russo)

Top: Tapgol Park, Seoul. The statue on the left is of independence movement leader Son Byeong-hui. Today, the park is a meeting place for elderly citizens of Seoul.

Below: Work life in South Korea is tough. Hours are long, and stress levels are high. These workers relax with a cigarette on their all-too-short break.

Korean Christians are known for their fervor. This preacher's slogan reads, "Jesus, heaven—No faith, hell."

Top: Third Line Butterfly: they don't make K-pop, but they are the best Korean band around, in the humble opinion of this author.

Below: A DJ entertains the crowds at the open-air "playground" in Hongdae, Seoul's heartland of youth culture.

member may seem excessive to people from other countries. When Time magazine held an online poll to determine the "world's most influential" person of 2011, the winner was not Hu Jintao, Vladimir Putin, or Barack Obama. It was Rain, a Korean pop star—his victory the fruit of endless re-clicking by proud Korean netizens. Rain had previously won the poll in 2006 and 2007. By the same token, a Korean who causes outrage overseas is considered to bring shame upon the nation, rather than merely himself. When Cho Seung-hui committed the Virginia Tech massacre in 2007, killing more than thirty students, President Roo Moo-hyun issued an apology on behalf of the country.

The expression "woori nara," or "our country," rather than the country's actual name is commonly used in television news bulletins and weather forecasts to refer to Korea. Foreigners in the country sometimes feel a sense of alienation because of "woori nara," since clearly the expression does not include them. They are perceived to be unconnected to Koreans via *jeong*. In that sense, *woori* and *jeong* can have nationalistic overtones. Indeed, some Koreans claim that no foreigner could possibly understand *jeong*. With South Korea now engaged in a full-on rush to internationalization, and the foreign population having jumped sevenfold between 2000 and 2010, it will be interesting to see whether "woori nara" can ever open fully up to include residents who are not ethnically Korean.

Why Korea?

Forming in- and out-groups, going out of one's way to help a friend, and favoritism are of course not unique to Korea. Neither is *jeong* inaccessible to non-Koreans. However, there are certain aspects of Korean culture and history that provide possible explanations as to why the concept of *jeong* would arise here and become such an important part of the nation's psyche.

Cho and Chung of UCLA locate the source of *jeong* in the intensely "collective nature of Korean society." South Korea scores 18 points out of 100 on Professor Geert Hofstede's Individualism Index in comparison to the United States' ranking of 91 and Japan's of 46, making it one of the world's most collective or group-oriented nations. This collective orientation is manifested in many ways. When eating in Korea, for instance, dishes of food are communal. Everyone may dip his or her spoon in a bowl of soup in the middle of the table. This can shock guests, even some from other Asian countries. Co-workers from the same department at a Korean company will go to lunch together as a matter of course, rather than going their separate ways at noon.

It also happens that groups of university students, for example, from the same academic department, will head out to the countryside for so-called "Membership Training" or "MT." This is not really training but rather group bonding through the consumption of large amounts of alcohol. They will rent the biggest room in a guest house, eat instant noodles, and drink beer and *soju* (an alcoholic spirit) until everyone finally collapses. The next day, participants wake up with pounding heads, surrounded by the strewn, clothed bodies of their friends. The MT is an important part of university life, and to show no enthusiasm for it would be considered poor form.

Since the Koryo dynasty, mutual aid societies called *gye* have existed here: members of a community, (typically a village) contribute regular sums of money, and when one experiences financial difficulty, he or she receives a large lump sum from the *gye*. People sometimes cheat—joining, feigning trouble, collecting the payout, and then disappearing—but the fact that the system has existed for so long indicates that the vast majority play by the rules.

Why does this group orientation exist? Arguably, it stems from Korean village life. For much of the country's long history, the majority of Koreans were poor, oppressed village folk who earned their livelihoods from farming. Cooperation and mutual assistance were practical necessities and sometime a matter of survival. A *yangban* lord could impose taxes at will, and crops would fail periodically. People found assisting each other useful—sharing labor or farm produce, or by operating *gye* to educate their brightest young men in the hope that they could pass the civil service exams, join the government, and then perhaps protect the community from the depredations of other officials. On Jeju Island, divers formed cooperatives, sharing their catch equally. There are still versions of these, called *eochongye*, in existence today. The fact that most Koreans lived in villages rather than towns or cities also meant there was naturally more closeness between people and greater opportunity to organize the sharing of resources and labor.

There are other reasons why Koreans favor collectivity. As a small country in a geopolitically strategic location, Korea has always been a target for invasion and dominance by foreign powers. This country has been a victim, but, more importantly, over the years victimhood has been deeply woven into the national narrative by politicians, writers, and historians. The way Koreans are instructed to avoid being victimized again is through unity and avoiding the pursuit of individual interests over those of society. In his 2006 Memorial Day speech, President Roh Moo-hyun declared that Japanese colonial rule over Korea was the result of "infighting among ruling factions." Referring to the Korean War of 1950–1953, he then added, "Had our nation confronted the situation united, we could have averted this horrible misfortune."

Confucianism also played a role. This ethical system imported from China, which provided the ideological foundation of Korea for centuries, emphasizes loyalty and subservience of the self to social harmony, and the notion of duty to the people with whom one has relationships. Buddhism, too, with its concept of the Sangha—the community of believers who help each other on the path to greater understanding—could be said to encourage Korea's collective orientation, in the same way it has given Korean corporate culture more of a team style.

The Decline of *Jeong*?

Other nations that rank near South Korea on Hofstede's Individualism Index are either poor—like Pakistan or Ecuador—or newly wealthy—like Taiwan, or Korea itself. Established rich countries like Germany or France are much more individualistic. But South Korea's young adults have grown up in material comfort like the youth of Japan and the West. They do not live in tight-knit villages but rather in multistory apartment blocks in metropolises. Between 1945 and 2010, the percentage of South Koreans living in urban areas rose from 14.5 to 83 percent. Most people today do not even know their next-door neighbors. All this means that there is less need, and less inclination, for people to provide mutual support to each other.

One would therefore expect the culture of *jeong* to be weakening, and indeed that is the case. With increased wealth and more bank lending, participation in *gye* and the lending of large sums of money between friends, for instance, is less prevalent than before. If one were to ask an older Korean about the younger generation—particularly those living in Seoul—he or she would probably describe them as cold or individualistic, or even Westernized. One area of Seoul, the nouveau-riche district of Gangnam, is sometimes jokingly labeled *Gangnam-guk* ("Gangnam nation," i.e. a foreign country) by other Koreans because of its perceived lack of *jeong* and Korean-ness in general. Yet Gangnam is a place where very many Koreans aspire to live.

"*Jeong* is the scariest thing" is a common expression in South Korea, because of the lengths people will sometimes go to in the name of *jeong*. Yet, despite the socially harmful behavior it can occasionally inspire, *jeong* is also the most attractive aspect of Korean culture, for it encourages warmth and generosity. Though foreign visitors still feel the power of *jeong* when they observe how Koreans behave around each other, there may well come a day when that is no longer the case. And that will be a sad day indeed.

Chapter 8

Competition

To live in South Korea is to be a competitor: one must fight intensely to win one's university place, job, marriage partner, and many other things besides. The pressure to compete against others begins in early childhood and does not let up even following retirement. It can be no coincidence that one of the most popular Korean expressions—an equivalent of "You can do it!"—is the English loanword "fighting!"

Confucianism puts a premium on educational success and the provision of a stable life for one's family. This emphasis encourages people to strive for at least a baseline level of achievement and respectability. However, the baseline never seems enough in South Korea. So why are the people of this country so driven—for better or worse—to be the best they can be? And why have South Korean leaders from General Park onwards been so keen to make their country into number one?

Between Nations: Korea, Number One

From the 1950s onwards, South Korea offered perfect conditions for the development of a mindset that encouraged competition with other nations. South Korea emerged from the Korean War with a third of its population homeless, due to the massive destruction of housing that occurred during that conflict. Average GDP was less than US$100 per capita. The country was unable to feed itself, as there was no money to import food, and only 21 percent of South Korean land was fit to grow crops on. To make matters worse, the country had virtually no natural resources. To this day, only the tiniest fraction of South Korea's energy needs is met from domestic fuel sources.

Crushing poverty—and the lack of resource wealth to remedy it—led to a crucial realization. To dig themselves out of their terrible situation, South Koreans needed to focus on developing human skills and then put them to unceasing use. As Kim Dong-jin, advisor to President Park Chung-hee, recalls, "All we had was the hard work and brain power of our people." South Korea's Confucian legacy dictated that the starting point was the education of the populace: the nation's young had to be educated as well as possible, and after they became adults, they had to work as hard as possible.

In 1945, only 5 percent of South Koreans had received secondary or higher education. By 1960, the Syngman Rhee government—though a violent, corrupt dictatorship—had increased primary school enrollment eight times and secondary school enrollment ten times. Up to 19 percent of the government's budget was spent on education. From then until the 1980s, South Koreans enjoyed greater access to education than did the people of any other country of a similar GDP level, according to Michael J. Seth of James Madison University, in his book *Educational Fever*.

After General Park took power in 1961, the people were exhorted to work around the clock in order to improve South Korea and help it do better than others—particularly Japan, the former colonizer. Koreans who remember this period can recall posters encouraging them to "Beat Japan" (through industrialization) and spurring them on to break ever-increasing national export targets. The people were transformed into "industrial soldiers" who could help overcome the nation's poverty, tragic history, and the North Korean threat through long days at shipyards, factories, and industrial plants. Six-day workweeks were the norm; Saturday was just another weekday.

From a young age, children were told that they would become such industrial soldiers: A professor of economics who was in grade school then speaks of a childhood in which teachers "drilled it into our heads that we were on a historic mission to revive the nation." In school, Korean children were to be diligent students, and then when they grew up and joined the workforce, they were to participate in the quest for economic power, by working for the companies that were pushing relentlessly to make South Korea into a top export nation.

The Park government focused on numerical targets, and inculcated the need to make Korea's numbers better than those of other countries. General Park had a personal obsession with statistics, and he forced his underlings to have similar awareness of export volume and inflation data, for instance. This orientation dies hard: even today, journalists, politicians, and business leaders make constant reference to the position of South Korea in world GDP ranking tables and the industries in which Korean firms hold "world number-one" status. When Lee Myung-bak ran in the December 2007 presidential election, he made the so-called "747 Pledge": 7 percent economic growth, US$40,000 GDP per capita, and the seventh largest economy in the world. Though his pledge was frankly impossible, it was electorally very successful. And in 2011, when South Korea had its first year of trade with other countries in excess of US$1 trillion, large firms responded by draping huge celebratory banners across the front of their headquarters, and newspaper editorials eulogized the achievement.

No doubt a deep sense of national insecurity is also at play in South Korea's headlong pursuit of economic power. As a small country born in poverty, divided from the more industrialized North, and surrounded by more powerful and aggressive states, South Korea's leaders have always felt the need to make their country as economically competitive as possible, to become a top trading partner for the larger powers that affect Korea's destiny—such as the United States and, more recently, China. Countries that conduct significant trade with each other have an obvious incentive to support each other politically, or at least, avoid conflict. Trade not only made South Korea a wealthy country, but also helped secure its continued existence.

This idea doubtless increased the drive to make Korea into the top-ranking exporter in any industry deemed important. As Park Chung-hee's advisor Kim Dong-jin recalls, he was ordered by the new dictator in 1961 to "make Korea into the number one shipbuilding country in the world." Despite South Korea at the time having virtually no shipbuilding industry at all, General Park was intent on becoming the leader in this strategically valuable industry. He eventually got his wish, posthumously, in the 1980s.

Naturally, South Korea's unrelenting focus on building world-beating economic prowess had its costs. All other goals considered worthwhile by a nation—a clean environment, a happy populace, freedom of expression, and a rich cultural life, for instance—were sacrificed completely. In evaluating Park Chung-hee, it is important to weigh these sacrifices against the economic miracle he created. Park remains the most popular South Korean leader to this day, but there are also those who feel his project was not worth it. Kim Dong-jin, a close associate of Park, offers the following analogy in defense of his former boss: "When the plane is on the ground, ready to take off, the pilot tells you to fasten your seat belt and sit still. Then, when you're in the air, you can take off the belt and relax, and a beautiful stewardess brings you something to drink." The question for South Korea is, now that prosperity has been achieved, will its people finally learn to unbuckle their belt, and sit back with a glass of champagne?

Competition Between Individuals: Education Is Everything

During the days of Syngman Rhee and the early years of General Park, South Korean society was surprisingly level and meritocratic. The Korean War of 1950–1953 had resulted in a state of almost universal poverty in both Koreas. Apart from those closely allied to the corrupt Rhee administration, South Koreans were on an equal footing: almost no one had any money or major social advantage over the rest. Even when owners of large *chaebol* firms started to become extremely wealthy, the distribution of income in the greater part of society remained fairly even. Between 1957 and 1969, South Korea had a Gini income inequality coefficient—which measures income distribution (essentially, a measure of the gap between rich and poor)—of 26.3 on average. This is comparable to the most egalitarian of European states, like Sweden.

Equality of need went hand in hand with equality of opportunity, particularly with respect to education. Now almost half of new Seoul National University undergraduates come from the rich areas of southern Seoul (Gangnam, Seocho, and Songpa), but as one much older graduate recalls, "Even when I attended—in the early 1980s—two-thirds of the students there were from poor circumstances. It seemed like everyone was from some village I'd never heard of. Being from Seoul, I actually stood out."

The combination of a level playing field, equal access to education, and the desire of individuals to escape from poverty, together with a natural limit to the best opportunities, heightened competition between individuals. Careers in the civil service, law, medicine, and at the best large companies could pull a young man out of poverty and enable him to provide comfort and stability for his family, but the available positions were few, especially at the outset of a renascent economy. It therefore became essential to outdo others, first at school, then in professional exams, and later in the workplace. And when a young man and his wife had children of their own, they would inculcate their sons and daughters with the same values. It is hardly surprising, therefore, that this mentality of having to outdo peers remains, even though South Korea no longer needs to dig itself out of poverty. The stereotypical Korean mother is not satisfied when her child receives 99 percent on a test, if five other children in the class received 100.

When the first generation of elite graduates started having children, in the 1970s and 1980s, they were eager to pass their hard-won advantages on to their own sons and daughters. Their own experience and the Confucian legacy of civil service exams directed their focus to education, and they used *hakwons* (private after-school academies), private lessons, and overseas schooling to move their children to the front of the pack. Between school and expensive private tutors, their children might study for fifteen or sixteen hours per day, in order to enter elite universities and gain the best jobs. When their hard work and advantages paid off, a new elite was born, one that may be termed "neo-*yangban*."

The original *yangban* maintained their status through their ability to excel in the test that provided by far the best opportunities for social advancement in Joseon society, the civil service examination. Disadvantaged in study time, money to pay for tuition, and influence among officials, the average citizen was effectively precluded from passing the exam. The current elite similarly maintains their position through their ability to outspend other parents on private tuition, in order that their children gain top marks in the university entrance exams that determine a South Korean's social status today.

The rest of society did not simply give up following the emergence of the neo-*yangban*, though. Seeing the new educational upper class beginning to pull away from them, they responded as they had learned—by competing even harder, sacrificing more of their income to send their children to academies and private tutors. Since the 1980s, the nation's children have been taking extra afternoon and evening classes in English, mathematics, and other subjects and then doing homework both for these supplemental classes and for school. The financial cost of this makes parents less likely to have another child, which in turn contributes to South Korea's dangerously low birth rate.

Because almost everyone tries so hard to be educationally successful, there are far more graduates with very high test scores than there are good jobs available. This creates a vicious cycle of competition, as people are forced to strive to distinguish themselves even further. Thus, for many, it is no longer enough to go to Seoul National University; Korea is now the third largest supplier of foreign undergraduates to Harvard University. Undergraduates majoring in economics or finance will also simultaneously study for professional accounting qualifications. English test scores are considered of extreme importance too, and for this reason, parents who can afford it will send their children to an English-speaking country for at least some part of their education. All this is so their child will eventually be able to get ahead of others in the race for jobs.

The Widening of Competition

As a country, South Korea has pursued a policy of achieving economic power. The South Korean people have been driven to achieve financial success, but with achievement in education as the starting point. One might have expected that, when the country joined the ranks of the world's wealthier nations from the 1990s on, the competitive spirit would have declined, but that did not happen. In fact, the competitive urge spread to other areas.

People vie as hard as ever to gain the best jobs and places at the best universities, but now they also feel obliged to look as attractive as possible. Between 1987 and 1996, spending on cosmetics quadrupled. Most of this spending comes from women, but in the 2000s there was also a boom in male cosmetics and male spending on fashion and hair styling in general. In 2010, Korea accounted for 18 percent of male skincare spending worldwide. Korean men now spend more than women on clothes: they spent 7.27 trillion won (around US$7 billion) on clothes in 2010 compared to 7.1 trillion won by women. In 2005, men spent only 4.5 trillion won on clothes; the growth rate in just five years has been more than 60 percent.

South Korea has become notorious for its love of plastic surgery. Usually, when foreign commentators give their opinion on this phenomenon, they express disdain for the apparent superficiality of the women who have nose jobs, breast enlargements, or the painful and dangerous procedure of jaw-line reshaping—but this is to miss the point. A winning combination of physical appearance and background—in career, education, or family—puts a woman ahead of her peers in the search for the best jobs and the most eligible men, who themselves are expected to have money, a superior education, and good looks. Surgically enhanced attractiveness confers other advantages too. When applying for a job in Korea, it is customary to affix a passport-type photograph to the application form. Needless to say, this practice can turn recruitment into something of a beauty contest, particularly where female applicants are concerned.

Plastic surgery is so common now that, as in a sprint race in which half of the field is on steroids, even those who do not want to resort to it feel they have to. A BBC News article reported that: "By conservative estimates, 50 percent of South Korean women in their twenties have had some form of cosmetic surgery." It is so completely normal and stigma-free that many parents encourage their daughters to have something done—the highly routine double eyelid procedure, for instance.

Advertisements for plastic surgery are everywhere. On Line 3 of the Seoul Metro, posters for it are affixed in every carriage of the train and can be found throughout stations as well, particularly in wealthy, youth-oriented districts such as Sinsa and Apgujong. One ad takes the classic "before and after" approach, but with the twist that the "before" picture shows a small diamond wedding ring and the "after" picture shows a huge one.

The Cost of Competition—Childhood

For the youth of South Korea, competition results in, "a lack of a childhood," in the words of one recent university entrant. Children enjoy relatively few opportunities to play and socialize with their peers. According to research undertaken by the International Association for the Evaluation of Educational Achievement, Korean children are among the worst in the world at social interaction (thirty-fifth out of thirty-six countries surveyed). In school, children are constantly tested and ranked, rather than taught to work with one another. After the final bell, most are sent to *hakwons* that teach English, mathematics, music, and so on. When school vacations come, children are not free to relax but instead spend more time in *hakwons*.

Many also receive private lessons from expert tutors. President Chun Doo-hwan banned private tuition in 1980, because it puts children from poor backgrounds at a disadvantage. The desire of parents to gain any possible advantage for their children though rendered his efforts futile. Private lessons were re-legalized, and by 1997, 70 percent of elementary school students and 50 percent of middle and high school students, were receiving some form of private tuition. Some tutors, particularly Korean graduates of elite American universities, can make well over ten million Korean won per month (almost US $10,000) giving private lessons in subjects like English or mathematics.

Relentless study can be hard on Korean children, as well as unhealthy: 96 percent of high school students do not get enough sleep (they average around six and a half hours per night), with 8.8 percent of them even taking private lessons after 11 p.m. In 2011, a survey of high school students showed 87.9 percent had felt under stress "in the past week," and 70 percent blamed school for this. Less than half of Japanese, American, and Chinese high school students felt under such stress. Also in 2011, the Institute for Social Development Studies at Yonsei University published a survey showing that Korean teenagers are the unhappiest in the OECD. Suicide is the leading cause of death among Korean youths, and given the country's educational culture and the pressure to excel, that fact should not be surprising.

The Cost of Competition—Adulthood

Though General Park's industrial soldiers no longer exist, companies still push their employees to work long hours, and workers are compliant. Every year, South Korean workers put in 2,193 hours of work on average, the highest figure in the OECD. This figure will underestimate the real hours put in though, due to the large amounts of unrecorded, unpaid overtime done by the majority of workers. Foreign businesspeople may remark at the diligence of Korean workers, but they may not recognize the cost: 74.4 percent of South Korean workers feel that their jobs have driven them to depression, accordingly to a survey conducted by, ironically, the economic research arm of Samsung. Labor productivity (i.e. the economic result of each hour worked) is extremely disappointing, with South Korea coming 28th out of the 30 OECD countries: only Mexico and Poland produce less economic value per hour of work. The lack of adequate breaks, holidays, and sleep takes a heavy toll on the amount of work that people can actually produce in a given time.

Yet even finding such a stressful job is difficult. Koreans are over-educated—because of the perceived necessity of possessing academic credentials, over 98 percent of South Koreans between the ages of 25 and 34 have graduated from either a junior college or university, the highest rate in the world —so there is always a large pool of well-qualified applicants for every position. As a result, companies create extra criteria, such as English test scores, by which to judge candidates. The new criteria in turn force people to put more effort and money into studying English or taking additional higher degrees, and the vicious circle continues to turn. Every year 500,000 Koreans graduate from universities, but large firms, the government, and public corporations only create 100,000 openings. Some of the remaining 400,000 end up at small or medium-sized firms, which are typically unstable and cannot compete against the market power of the *chaebol*. Only 51 percent of graduates overall find "steady work," according to a report in the Chosun Ilbo newspaper in December 2011.

When people reach their late twenties, the race is on to find a good partner for marriage. Parents pressure their children to get married by their early thirties, out of fear that they will be left behind in the quest for the husband or wife with the best "back" (a loan-word derived from "background," which refers to job, education, and family circumstances) and the best appearance. When a partner is found, one set of parents may still veto the match: for families that view themselves as having high status, a would-be in-law without the right degree, family background, and work history may prove unacceptable.

All this makes life for South Koreans stressful. Competition is undoubtedly a factor in the country's high suicide rate. Many parents no doubt wish to raise their children to grow up happier and more balanced. Yet, for mothers in particular, the sight of a single B on a report card can provoke anguish. Groups of Korean mothers—particularly those who do not work, and have time on their hands—compare their children's educational performance and, even with friends, feel a strong sense of vicarious competition over their son's or daughter's grades. Though their own days of competing may be over, they still feel the need to compete through their children.

A More Valuable Philosophy?

When asked the question of what makes success, Seoul Mayor Park Won-soon states that "GDP is very important, but we also need to be guided by a more valuable philosophy." He was referring to the quality of people's lives—the amount of leisure time they have and their overall happiness. As South Korea is now a wealthy country and people can feel more secure with their own financial status, more Koreans are now starting to come around to the mayor's way of thinking. They are well aware that the lack of sleep and constant need to do better and better are counterproductive and cause illness, stress, and general unhappiness—and that this works against the efficient output and innovation that are crucial for South Korea's next stage of economic development.

For now though, actual change seems far away. The Satisfaction with Life Index, a measure developed by Adrian G. White, a social psychologist at Leicester University, that is based on asking people directly, "Are you satisfied with x?," places South Korea as the 102nd happiest place in the world out of 178 countries surveyed. This unfortunate showing is in stark contrast to the country's impressive scores on quantitative measures like the UN Human Development Index (12th) and overall GDP ranking on Purchasing Power Parity (also 12th). Competitiveness has driven South Korea to success after success, but with a paradoxically negative impact on its people's emotional well-being. To top such a list as this, people may well have to give up on trying to be number one.

Chapter 9

Chemyon, or Face

In South Korea, people are usually careful not to publicly criticize others. Harsh words, when needed, should be either delivered in private, or cloaked in a veil of respectfulness. It is common for investment analysts in the financial district of Yeouido to point out companies' weaknesses between the lines of their reports while still labeling them a "buy." Advertisers call attention only to the merits of their own products rather than the negatives of rivals. The realm of politics—for instance, the National Assembly, in which insults, and occasionally punches, are traded—is virtually the only exception to this rule.

The reason for this discretion toward and respectfulness of others' public image is the importance of preserving face, or *chemyon*, in Korean society. *Chemyon* is considered something of an old-fashioned word, and one that encourages stereotypes. Part of the classic image Westerners have of East Asian society is the notion of people doing anything to avoid a loss of face. In Korea though, a person's, family's, or company's public image is of utmost importance, and there is still plenty of truth in the stereotype. Very often, such a public image is the product of a great deal of work and refinement.

The Nature of *Chemyon*
Chemyon is essentially a product of Confucianism. Under Confucianism, conforming to society's expectations, especially as related to duty, was extremely important. The perception of others that one did not meet expectations was grounds for deep shame—a loss of face. In a paper on the influence of *chemyon* on Korean consumer

culture, Yoosun Hann of the University of Illinois wrote that it was important "not to stand out, but to fit in" with society. Confucianism values harmony, and this meant all members of society must play their proper role and fulfill the duties that came with that role. For example, a married woman was supposed to be a devoted wife and mother. During the later Joseon era, it would have been a source of shame to a respectable man were his wife to be constantly seen around town, spending time with friends, contrary to the expectations of her role.

According to Dr. Hann, "for Koreans, high social status implies a high moral level." Because of this, members of the *yangban* class were more influenced by *chemyon* than were members of the general peasantry. For a *yangban* family, it was important that the sons be educated, the daughters chaste, the father a pillar of his community, and the mother a devoted servant of the household. Society demanded less of a family of poor tenant farmers.

Chemyon was something to be defended. Preserving face used to mean not falling below expected standards. However, the wave of competition unleashed in South Korea since the economic take-off in the 1960s has brought about a crucial change. Now, according to Hwang Sang-min, a professor of psychology at Yonsei University, Koreans feel impelled to achieve an image of perfection rather than mere respectability and to be seen as doing not just well but better than others. A kind of "face inflation" has taken place. According to Professor Hwang, face in Korea today is "not simply [about] what one is but rather what one wants to be." It relates to an idealized version of one's true self. People construct about themselves the public image of a perfect person and then somehow they must live up to it. A word that has great currency in Korea today is *jalnancheok*, or "pretending to do well." It applies to anyone considered guilty of exaggerating his or her social value.

The perfect person is no longer just a good mother, a devoted student, or a father who provides a stable income for his family. As with other countries that have experienced high economic growth, such as China from the 1980s on and Russia in the 2000s, the materialistic side of Korean society has become exaggerated. People establish face in South Korea not just by having a good education or being an excellent parent; they also achieve it through wealth displayed conspicuously by means of the purchase of visible status symbols, such as expensive cars or designer clothes.

Face still applies most to those of high social status. The *yangban* no longer exist, but there are families whose elevated social rank is based on relative wealth and educational credentials. For such people the pressure to preserve their image in society is great. The average person in a rural South Korean town may merely dream of graduating from Seoul National University and consider a Gucci handbag a ridiculous waste of money, but for the denizen of a nouveau riche area of Seoul such as Gangnam or Seocho, these things may seem like necessities.

Creating the Image
South Koreans of high social status, or those who aspire to it, may seek to enhance their image in a number of ways. Department stores in the major cities of South Korea dedicate a large percentage of floor space to *myeongpum*, luxury products, and huge amounts of money are spent on designer bags and clothes. One example is the Galleria Department Store in the new-money Cheongdam-dong neighborhood in the Gangnam area of Seoul, where the most immaculately dressed, beautiful, and yet curiously unhappy-looking women in Korea can be seen.

According to McKinsey Consulting in their 2010 Luxury Goods Survey, "Korea is different." Despite the global economic downturn, South Korea saw a 16.7 percent increase in luxury goods sales between 2008 and 2009, driven by what they label as "the pressure to conform," i.e. to preserve face in front of peers ("keeping up with neighbors"), as well as Korea's overall "luxury-friendly culture." As of 2010, only booming China had higher growth in luxury spending than South Korea. Koreans spend 5 percent of their income on luxury goods, on average—the absolute highest rate in the world.

Similarly, when one is offered a drink at an important meeting, one will probably be served a very old whiskey, perhaps Ballantine's, the most popular imported luxury whisky brand in Korea. Whether or not this is objectively the best whiskey, it is an expensive one, and that is what counts in this circumstance. Bringing out the thirty-year-old Ballantine's or Johnnie Walker Blue Label signals that you respect the other person—you would not want to insult him by offering a glass of Jack Daniel's—and underscores that you have the wherewithal to afford it.

Housing, too, has such power to convey social status or value. The district of Seocho in Seoul, south of the Han River, looks little different from other parts of the city. However, the quality of schools in Seocho is high, and this has led education-obsessed parents to seek out apartments there, resulting inevitably in inflated apartment prices. Today, many people without school-age children want to live there too, simply because a Seocho address confers status on them. According to the Yahoo! Korea property website, an apartment that would cost 1.33 billion won (around US$1.3 million) in the immediately adjacent district of Dongjak would cost 2.45 billion won in Seocho, other things being equal. The excess amount spent on an apartment in Seocho by a childless person could be called an investment in face.

The most important way in which face is gained or lost is in education. A degree from Seoul National University has brand value in the same way that owning a $3,000 handbag or a big Seocho apartment does. In addition, though, it also reflects a person's intellectual capacity and academic achievement, and because of the legacy of the Confucian exam culture, this is especially prized. The prime means of social advancement for centuries, academic success meant entry into the prestige class. Advancing to a prestigious university is valued for that reason as well as for what it means in potential earning power. Education plays a large part in a family's face, and not only an individual's. If a child has been to excellent schools and has received endless hours of after-school tuition from private tutors, as is very often the case, but ends up only being accepted by a mid-ranked university, his or her family will feel gravely disappointed. The child will feel an acute sense of shame. Where the family can afford it, youngsters in this situation are often shipped off to mid-ranked universities in the United States, since an American education is generally prized, and does allow for some degree of status rebuilding.

This aspirational kind of face is no doubt a recipe for personal disappointment and unhappiness. However, the power it has over attitudes to education has probably done a world of good for South Korea's GDP. "I don't mind what you do as long as you are happy," is not a philosophy that many Korean parents adhere to. Instead, they spur their children relentlessly to achieve top grades, admissions to the world's best universities, and jobs with the highest salaries. Far less than one percent of the world's people are South Korean, but in 2007, a full 10.7 percent of foreign students at American universities came from South Korea. In the same year, Harvard had 37 South Korean undergraduate students, a figure exceeded only by students from Canada and Britain, two countries culturally and linguistically far closer to the United States.

The Face of Tragedy

What happens when you cannot make it, though? What if your standard of education is a letdown to your family, your apparently perfect marriage breaks down, or your business goes bankrupt? Unfortunately, the combination of the event itself and the sense of shame it brings from the loss of face creates an unbearable amount of pressure for some—and may result in tragedy.

Every year there are suicides of third-year high school students at the time of suneung, the university entrance exam. For the students, their entire lives—and social value—will seemingly be determined by that single day, and, unable to tolerate the pressure, some choose to end it all. They are not the only suicides, though. South Korea has the second-highest suicide rate among all nations of the world, at 31 per 100,000 people per year. By comparison, Japan, also well known for its suicide problem, has a figure of 24. Korea's high suicide rate is due at least in part to the perceived necessity to vault the impossibly high bar of success and honor, according to Professor Hwang Sangmin. "Koreans always want to show their best image to other people," he notes, but when that proves impossible, it can lead to a final "desertion" of the self and a desire to simply give up on life.

Celebrity suicide is also common in South Korea. The year 2009 was an especially tragic one, with no less than nine famous people taking their own lives. It is natural to imagine actors and singers having enviable existences, but in Korea celebrity brings a special burden. When they lose face, the whole country sees it, which can make the pressure of celebrity unbearable. Internet bulletin boards embolden "anti-fans," who benefit from anonymity, to break the taboo of public criticism and spread malicious stories about their unfortunate targets. According to a masters-degree paper written by actress Park Jin-hee in 2010, 40 percent of 260 actors she surveyed had contemplated suicide at some point in their lives.

Unfortunately, suicide can have a cleansing effect on a person's image. When former president Roh Moo-hyun took his life in 2009 in response to the corruption investigation targeting him and his family, the family image (which had been under attack) was restored. Despite having very low opinion poll ratings upon leaving the presidency in 2008, by 2011 Roh emerged in a public opinion survey as the second most popular South Korean president of all time, behind Park Chung-hee. His suicide also rendered continuing the investigation against his family a political impossibility. Roh saved them by sacrificing himself, in an act that was both his apology and his redemption. His death was immensely tragic. He was an extremely accomplished man, who rose from rural poverty to become a self-taught human rights lawyer and later president of the country. No doubt there was much more he could have done in this world.

The Public-Private Gap

Because of face inflation, the gap between public image and private reality is unusually high in South Korea, and people defend the gap with vigor. It can be no coincidence that in South Korea libel laws are the strictest in the democratic world. Myeongye hweson—defamation—may occur, according to Korean law, even if the original allegation was true. Defamation can also be tried as a criminal offense. This has serious negative implications for free speech in Korea. In December 2011, Jeong Bong-ju, a former Democratic Party politician and regular guest on Nakkomsu, the world's most popular podcast, was sentenced to a year in prison for accusing President Lee Myung-bak of complicity in a notorious fraud scheme. In another democratic country, the greatest punishment Jeong would have faced would have been the payment of damages. Yet in South Korea, "many criminal defamation suits are filed for statements that are true and are in the public interest, and are used to penalize individuals who express criticisms of the government," the special rapporteur on the freedom of opinion and expression at the United Nations, Frank La Rue, told the New York Times in December 2011.

The Internet poses unique new problems for the preservation of public face, for it blurs the boundaries between public and private. An online critic is able to remain private while making public criticism. Theoretically, any individual may destroy the honor of a well-known person without ever having to face the consequences that would come from being identified. "Anti-fans" are a prime example. The popular rap artist Tablo came under repeated attack in the late 2000s by Internet users, who alleged that he had not graduated from Stanford University, as he had publicly stated. He even received death threats. The choice of educational record as avenue of attack is of course very Korean. Tablo's career suffered, and even after he was vindicated, many continue to believe him a liar. "Since my attackers were all anonymous, there was no way for me to know who was after me," Tablo is quoted as saying.

South Korea's response to this sort of vulnerability has been to enact a "real name" law, by which Internet users must enter their national ID numbers when registering for forums. This requirement leaves users open to being exposed and possibly sued. For celebrities terrified of having their honor attacked, it is a godsend. However, like the defamation law, the real name law can also be used for political purposes, restricting free speech and criticism of those in power. In 2008, an Internet forum poster going by the name of Minerva began making a series of gloomy predictions about the Korean economy on an online forum. After being proven correct a few times in succession, he attracted a following that ran to millions of other Internet users. The fearful government unmasked him as the unemployed thirty-year old Park Dae-sung and prosecuted him on charges of "spreading false information." He was later acquitted, but the fact that he was tried means that free speech is not at all guaranteed in South Korea.

When the Lee Myung-bak administration finally announced in 2012 that the real name law would be scrapped, it was seen by government critics and free speech campaigners as an overdue step in the right direction. However, it is hard not to sympathize with celebrity victims of anonymous attacks, because the price they pay in Korea is so much higher than in other societies. The comparison between American celebrity heiress Paris Hilton and Korean pop star Baek Ji-young is instructive in this regard. Both were featured in private sex tapes that were leaked into the public domain (in 2003 and 2000 respectively). While Paris Hilton's career actually benefited from the public airing, Ms. Baek's was ruined. She had the misfortune to be filmed without her knowledge doing something that every other adult does, and in her country that was enough to destroy her image and keep her out of the mainstream media for almost six years. She finally made a comeback in 2006, but to this day her public reputation still suffers from the effects of a scandal that should not have been considered scandalous.

Chapter 10

Han and *Heung*: The Deep Sadness and Pure Joy in the Korean Mind

Koreans are known to be an emotional people. This perception relates in part to *jeong*, the "invisible hug" discussed in chapter 7, but more frequently Koreans' emotionality is thought to stem from *han*, a kind of deep-rooted melancholic pain that has been called a uniquely Korean emotion. Han culture permeates both life and art, leading some to refer, as *Time* magazine once did, to "the unbearable sadness of being Korean."

Yet *Time's* formulation captures only half the picture. While a tendency toward negative extremes of emotion is beyond doubt, Korean culture is also given to almost manic displays of joy and pure abandon. The manic side might be termed the spirit of *heung*, or "joy." While not cited as frequently as *han* by those who take an interest in Korean culture, *heung* is just as important and perhaps more evident—as those who witnessed how the entire nation celebrated during the 2002 World Cup could testify.

Because of *han* and *heung*, such classic East Asian stereotypes as inscrutability and extreme self-control are rendered absolutely false when applied to Korea. This is a country where people wear their heart on their sleeve.

Han
Han, like *jeong*, is a well-known concept in discussions of Korean

culture. It has been the subject of all manner of analysis by psychologists and cultural critics, and generates much debate. Typically, it is defined as an unresolved resentment or emotional pain that is carried by a person, a kind of grudge but an internalized one. It is accompanied by an inward sense of despair and injustice, to the point where it may become a physical feeling in one's gut. The causes of *han* can be many: disability, the death of a child, or abusive treatment from someone in a position of power, for example. The link between all of these instances is the powerlessness of the sufferer to remedy the situation. The greatest example of such a situation in recent Korean history must surely be the separation of families that came with the division of Korea. There can be few greater traumas than separation from one's loved ones, especially when there is absolutely nothing one can do about it.

The response to such a burden is not to seek revenge, since there is either no person to target, or the person responsible is untouchable. In cases where it is possible to target someone, the feeling is called *won*, a more violent and wrathful emotion. *Han* is different because the victim is unable to obtain satisfaction through some form of revenge or payback, and must seek an alternative outlet for his or her feelings.

Some claim *han* to be a uniquely Korean emotion. However, the poet Ko Un, Korea's greatest living literary figure and a man who has written extensively about *han*, believes it is part of a wider Asian tradition. He points out that, going back to ancient India, a kind of resentment similar to *han* has been ingrained in many other cultures. He traces a lineage of *han* from the old Indian word *upahana*, which also relates to the Chinese word *hen* and Japanese *kon*, all of which are similar to *han* but considered more aggressive. Given Korea's history of invasion, division, and war—and long status as a pawn in the game of larger powers—it is not surprising that Korean *han* would contain an aspect of resignation rather than aggression. Historically, Koreans never really had the chance to fight back, so had to internalize their pain.

On the other hand, the novelist Jang Yong-won (not his real name) argues that "Korean han is a colonialist invention," inculcated in the

Korean people during the period of Japanese rule and designed to keep them oppressed through the belief that there was nothing they could do about their political situation other than find a way to accept it. He believes that *han* is no more essentially Korean than it is essential to any other culture. Instead, according to him, it was inserted as a cultural code in the early twentieth century so successfully that Koreans became convinced they possessed an emotion special to them.

This is a controversial and non-mainstream view, especially Jang Yong-won's assertion that Japan is the source of *han*. However, regardless of *han's* provenance and how "real" or "purely Korean" it may or may not be, *han* has become a part of the psychological landscape of Korea in that it affects people's behavior as well as the music, art, and drama they produce.

The peculiarly Korean aspect of *han* is the manner in which the emotion is stored up and even cherished. Long-term foreign residents here note a tendency of people to wallow in or enjoy their sadness, in an almost romantic way. There is a deep strain of melancholy in Korean culture, and this is expressed in the modern age through sad songs, films, and TV dramas that offer an unrelenting stream of tragic heroes, unrequited love, and bittersweet memories—most likely contributing to the appeal of Korean pop culture abroad. To illuminate *han*, Master Ko provides an image that will be instantly recognizable by anyone familiar with Korean television: the woman, standing alone at night waiting for her lover, a man who never arrives. In such a story, the heroine will no doubt carry the burden of loss and rejection forever.

Many of the Korean films most popular among international audiences have *han*-filled plots. The war film *Taegukgi* (2004), for instance, features two brothers, fighting in the Korean War, amid a backdrop of massacres and unrelenting conflict. At the climax, one brother dies, while saving the other. The end of the film shows the surviving brother discovering the remains of his sibling at a war excavation site, lamenting over the loss and begging vainly to speak to him, repeating the words they had exchanged on the battlefield. It is a scene that speaks of a lifetime of unresolved torment.

Overcoming

According to Professor Kim Ui-cheol, *han* is not an unchanging condition but can be resolved through *han-puli*, the "untying" of *han*. This is done via acts of joyful catharsis. Professor Kim cites the famed masked dance of Korean folklore in which a handicapped beggar—a figure who is usually the object of pity or ridicule for the rest of society—stands up before an audience and, through song and dance, celebrates his suffering, transcending his tragedy. The result for the beggar is a sense of joyfulness and ecstasy, as though his pain has been untied from his body and released, like a weight lifted off.

Traditionally, such performances also mocked the *yangban*, the unassailable source of the ordinary people's woes. The beggar's performance brought *han-puli* to the peasant audience as well as the performer. Here, there are parallels with the idea of the "carnivalesque" in the thought of Russian philosopher and critic Mikhail Bakhtin, and to the "Feast of Fools" found in many medieval European countries, in which the roles of peasant and king were temporarily reversed. For a brief moment, social order is cast aside, and the lowborn and unfortunate are able to feel joyful freedom from the oppressive social hierarchy that holds them down.

In this way, the Korean approach to sorrow can paradoxically involve amusement and laughter. What *han* calls forth is not an Anglo-Saxon "stiff upper lip" but rather a strong opposite reaction. A well-known story from World War Two illustrates this. In it, a group of young men waiting for a train that will take them to a forced labor camp in Hokkaido, Japan, were seen laughing and enthusiastically playing *jaeki-chagi* (a game similar to hacky-sack, in which an object is passed by foot from player to player without touching the ground) on the platform, despite facing what for some of them would have been a death sentence. The Japanese soldiers guarding them were astonished at the Koreans' levity.

In a similar vein, an old Korean funeral was in some senses a festival. It included singing, plenty of alcohol, and even the playing of games, amid an atmosphere of surprising raucousness. Lim Jae-hae, professor of folklore at Andong University, is quoted in an article on Korean funeral culture in the Chosun Ilbo newspaper as stating that

"Koreans used to see funerals as a chance to overcome sorrow with laughter," and to "sublimate the grief and darkness of death into the happiness and brightness of life." This might remind American readers of the spirit animating funeral processions in old New Orleans. In the English language, the funeral of a loved one is perhaps euphemistically referred to as a "celebration of life"; a funeral in the old Korean way was a hearty, genuine celebration of both life and death.

Knowing that tragedy cannot be overturned or undone, people see no alternative but to celebrate it, and in doing so, they transcend it. The word *shinparam*, "elation" or "high spirits," describes the feeling of such release. Shamanistic *gut* can be seen in this light: people commission *gut* often out of tragic reasons, and the ceremony contains a great deal of dancing, singing, and the release of energy. Though to some the *gut* ceremony may seem a kind of "voodoo," with no basis in reality, it is psychologically rewarding for the catharsis it brings to the troubled person. One interviewee who commissioned a *gut* claims that, even though she did not truly believe in the power of the ceremony to exorcise malign spirits, the experience was very emotional and ultimately uplifting. *Shinparam* may have a Buddhist underpinning as well as a shamanist one, since it involves the acceptance of suffering (or the fact that "life is pain") and seeing that the way around this is through transcendence rather than the pursuit of revenge or correction.

Pure Joy

Though the image of Korea conveyed by its most successful TV and film exports like *Taegukgi* is one of tragic melancholy, this country is also the home of a devil-may-care, "for its own sake" kind of joy. For Master Ko, the mention of the word *heung* ('joy') is enough to bring a smile to his face and a kind of breezy animation to his frame. He leans forward, moving his shoulders up and down, to express the energy and satisfaction the word gives him and to convey its meaning physically. "Imagine there is an Earth God, and you pour alcohol on the ground in offering—he is so happy that the ground shakes": this is the feeling of *heung*, he says.

Though the urban reality of today and the long hours of office work do not lend themselves to *heung*, there remains nevertheless a love of pure amusement, especially among older people. For instance, if one goes to Tapgol Park in central Seoul, one sees retired people drinking and dancing their afternoons away. Country festivals in great variety still take place and are occasions for abundant *eumju-ga-mu*—drinking, singing, and dancing. The most famous of these is the annual Danoje celebration, which grew out of shamanistic ritual commemoration of the sowing season. At a Danoje, one can witness *ssireum* (a kind of wrestling), *nol-twigi* (a game in which participants perform back flips and other aerial stunts while jumping on see-saws), and shamanistic *gut* as well as singing, dancing, and the consumption of large amounts of alcohol. Similarly, older Koreans have a practice of forming excursion groups, renting a bus, and going on long journeys to some site—the special feature being that the bus will be stocked with beer, rice wine, and Korean spirits like soju and have a karaoke machine. The excursion is transformed into a party on wheels.

Eumju-ga-mu is really never far away in Korea. Drinking (and drunkenness) is more socially acceptable here than in neighboring countries like Japan, as well as most of the rest of the world. According to the World Health Organization, South Koreans drink slightly more alcohol than the Irish and the British and almost double the amount drunk by the Japanese, on average. Very often, drinking will be accompanied by song and dance. It is in fact socially useful, even in business, to be considered skilled in at least one of the three (especially drinking). *Eumju-ga-mu* is enjoyed by both young and old and people of all social classes and regional backgrounds. Official tourist literature tends to downplay the significance of *eumju-ga-mu*, since it may not look sophisticated or appealing to outsiders. However, visitors to Korea often remark that their most lasting memories involve experiences like drinking in a *pojang macha* (tent bar), followed by singing and dancing in a *noraebang* (karaoke-type room), rather than visiting one of the "Kimchi Museums" or "Folk Villages" that they are forever being encouraged to attend. Quite simply, *eumju-ga-mu* is one of the most attractive aspects of this country's culture.

Even political protests can have a joyful side. While joy may seem completely at odds with the serious purpose of such events, stages may be erected upon which protest leaders sing upbeat songs in between the usual speeches and demands for the righting of whatever injustice they seek to overturn. Another instance of the pursuit of sheer joy is *samulnori*, drumming based on old shamanistic ceremonial practice, which is performed in groups. University students form clubs to practice *samulnori* and will gather in circles to hammer out rough, noisy rhythms for hours on end.

The boisterousness of this country's culture of enjoyment often surprises visitors, for it runs completely contrary to the rather inappropriate "Land of the Morning Calm" image, as well as the stereotype of East Asian people in general being placid and contemplative or overly business-like and serious. Surely, this was never truer than during the 2002 World Cup, when South Korea managed to reach the semi-finals, on home turf. For the entire World Cup period, the whole country converted to carnival mode, with impromptu parties, informal football (soccer) matches, and of course, *eumju-ga-mu* taking place on streets, in parks and public squares, and even on trains. All it took was one person in a busy place to shout "Daehan-Minguk!" ("Republic of Korea") and seemingly everyone would stop what they were doing and start singing and dancing. As then-president Kim Dae-jung declared, it was the happiest moment for the nation since the mythical Dangun founded Korea five thousand years before.

The Balance

Master Ko, who has published well over a hundred volumes of work, adduces *heung* as one of the reasons his output has been so prodigious. For him, poetry is a celebration: he cites the words of Borges, who "drank poetry." Master Ko says his work is not truly "work" but rather, play, and thus even in his late seventies, he has no desire to stop. When he speaks about his latest project, a collection of love poems, it is with obvious enthusiasm.

But *heung* is not in constant, steady supply. *Han* and *heung* are opposites, and, in his view, when one is high, the other is low. He sees Korea as having continually gone through times where either one or the other was in the ascendancy. Even in times of *heung*—such as the current era, in which he notes an abundance of it in people's behavior and the music they listen to—*han* is always there, "buried down in the feet," but present.

However, in times of *han*, there is also hope—as there always remains the possibility of release and celebration. This is part of the nature of this culture: happiness tinged with the bittersweet, and sadness accented with hope. This is why Korea can seem so raw and emotional; it is also one of the reasons for the success of its television shows and films abroad. *Han* and *heung* make for a volatile, yet attractive mixture.

Chapter 11

From Clan to Nuclear Family

The Korean equivalent of "looking for a needle in a haystack" is "looking for Mr. Kim in Seoul." Indeed, more than 21 percent of the population bears that family name. A further 15 percent bears the name Lee, and around 9 percent goes by Park. However, there is much more to Korean family names than meets the eye. Kim identifies more than 300 separate and unrelated clans that descend from different ancestral hometowns. These clans, known in Korean as *bon-gwan*, were of great importance historically. During the Joseon period, one's position in society was at least partly dictated by which *bon-gwan* one belonged to. Families who could afford to bought their way into highly regarded ones.

Today, clans in Korea have very little influence. The network and security provided by the *bon-gwan* in the past no longer exists. Even within the smallest sub-groups of the *bon-gwan*, where members genuinely are family, there is much less closeness or cohesion than before. South Korea in the twenty-first century is embracing the nuclear family model and turning away from the notion of the extended family. And though some label the new Korean family "Westernized," that is an over-simplification. Koreans are proving that the nuclear family can take varying forms.

The *Bon-gwan*

A family name was once a rarity. During the Three Kingdoms period, only royals and top aristocratic families possessed them. The kingdom of Shilla, which brought the Three Kingdoms period to an end by unifying Korea in 668, initially had just six families considered worthy of naming: Lee, Choi, Son, Jeong, Bae, and Seol. These names were bestowed by King Yuri on the leaders of six districts of Gyeongju, the city from which the Shilla kingdom emerged. The leaders and their descendents would enjoy special privileges and the glory of being part of an exclusive clan. The rest of the population had no family name at all.

By the end of the Shilla period, most of the aristocracy had come to possess surnames granted by the monarch. Following the fall of Shilla and the rise of the Koryo dynasty, Koryo founding king Wang Geon also pursued a policy of granting family names to loyal followers. One former Shilla aristocrat named Kim Haeng so pleased Wang Geon that he was given the new surname of Kwon (Kwon means "authority," a powerful compliment coming from a king). Andong in Gyeongsang Province was designated the hometown of this new *bon-gwan*, and thus the lineage of the Andong Kwon came into being.

In handing out surnames, Wang Geon was far more liberal than Shilla kings. He even gave names as punishment, forcibly burdening enemies with ugly monikers like Don and Oo, which mean "Pig" and "Cow," respectively. He also encouraged his government officials to choose their own family names and establish new *bon-gwan*. These officials often copied noble-sounding Chinese names like Yi (Lee), which was the family name of the philosopher Laozi; overall more than 130 Korean family names were imported from China. It was also sometimes possible for naturalized foreigners to take Korean names and start their own clan, as was the case with Samga, a Muslim Uighur who took the family name Jang and founded the Deoksu Jang *bon-gwan*. A Jurchen named Tung Duran took the family name Yi and started the Cheonghae Yi *bon-gwan*. Both clans began in the fourteenth century, and as of the 2000 census, they had 21,000 and 12,000 living members respectively.

A man who either received a new name from the king or chose his own became *sijo*: the father of a clan. Future generations would come to look upon *sijo* almost as kings in their own right. Myths were created about them. For instance, the *sijo* Jin Hwon of the Hwanggan Jin *bon-gwan* (the Jin clan, from the town of Hwanggan) was said to have been raised by a tiger. Families began keeping books, *jokbo*, that listed all the descendents of their particular *sijo*. The oldest extant book of this kind was made by the Andong Kwon in 1476. Family history books were also written by subsequent generations of clans, and in them the achievements of notable ancestors, such as government ministers or generals, were recorded in detail.

Today, over a thousand years after Wang Geon's great expansion of family names, Korean families still possess *jokbo* and family histories. However, with the number of generations that have passed since most *bon-gwan* were founded, a process of splintering has also occurred. Clans have divided out into sub-clans and further. One member of the Andong Kwon states that he belongs to one of thirteen branches; these thirteen branches themselves form just one of fifteen sub-clans of the overall Andong Kwon clan today.

While originally family names were only for the *yangban* aristocracy, during the Joseon dynasty it became possible for anyone to own a family name (although not until Japan forced all Koreans to list a family name in 1909 was absolutely everyone required to have one). Common people rushed to start a *bon-gwan* or join an existing one, motivated by Neo-Confucianism's emphasis on filial piety and ancestry combined with a desire to improve their lot and status. As early as the reign of the early Joseon king Sejong (r. 1418–1450), there were already 250 surnames in Korea. *Yangban* clans such as Kwon of course continued, but lines descending from poor commoners also started: the name Pi, for instance, became regarded as a poor man's surname.

The desire of the middle and lower classes to improve their status also motivated the practice of "name trading," in other words, trading up to a more prestigious name by purchasing the right to use it, as opposed, for example, to marrying into it. For a person with no family name, the poor man's surname of Pi was an improvement, but a Pi would have rather been a Kwon, and there were pragmatic reasons for this. Joseon Korea exercised *bon-gwan* snobbery to a great degree. Opportunities to work in the higher ranks of the government, for instance, were effectively limited to those from highly regarded *bon-gwan*. The Joseon scholar Yu Su-won lamented that "the government prevents [those from humbler *bon-gwan*] from having any chance of success in society and forces them to live their lives as if they were sinners." A good family name provided opportunities that came with status, so it was natural for those without opportunities or status to see the advantages in a "better" clan affiliation.

Name trading was especially pronounced in the aftermath of the Japanese invasions of 1592 to 1598. The violence and destruction of the invasions brought about a decline in fortunes for many *yangban* families and created a more level social playing field. The weakened *yangban* hold on economic activity allowed the rise of the merchant middle class (*jungin*) and even brought wealth to some members of the *cheonmin* peasant class. The result of all this was that *yangban* families had reason to sell faked entry into their *jokbo* to commoners who had acquired enough money to pay for it. This is why, today, a common reply to a person's supercilious boast of noble lineage is "Yes, but nobody really knows their origin for sure, do they?"

Certain *bon-gwan*, such as the Kim clan from the town of Kimhae and the Park clan from the town of Miryang, saw a large expansion in membership through this practice. Common people rushed to trade in their "low-born" surnames (such as Pi) for a more respected Kim or Park. This explains why such family names are so common, as noted at the outset. Today, over four million people in South Korea are members of the Kimhae Kim clan. The preponderance of this one clan name created some unexpected social problems: until 1997, it was illegal for a man and a woman of the same clan to marry. The law forbidding it was abolished that year, but, before it was, there were reportedly well over a hundred thousand Kimhae Kim couples living together as common-law husband and wife, unable to enjoy the legal benefits of marriage.

Naturally, name trading and the swelling of clan ranks tended to reduce the clan's prestige and the value of belonging to it. As a *bon-gwan* like the Kimhae Kim expanded, there would have been less and less advantage to being a member of it. However, even as late as the nineteenth century, certain clans enjoyed great unity and power. During much of the 1800s, the smaller and tighter-knit Andong Kim clan effectively controlled the country by having made puppets out of successive Yi family kings beginning with Soon-jo, who came to the throne in 1800 as a boy. His father-in-law, an Andong Kim named Kim Jo-soon, acted as a regent to the boy-king, and appointed many other Andong Kims to powerful positions. Their only competition for the next sixty years came from another clan, the Pungyang Cho, when Soon-jo's son took a wife who was a Cho. Between them, the two clans vied for power and the state's wealth during a period known as "sedo jeongchi" (in-law politics). Their depredations both weakened the government and destabilized society, making it easier for Japan to colonize Korea in 1910.

Are Clans Still Important?

During the period of "in-law politics," the Andong Kim and Pung-yang Cho put clan above country, illustrating how important *bongwan* membership once was. Particularly for elite clans—such as the Andong Kwon—membership was a great source of pride. Yet today, pride in clan membership is disappearing. The power that came with such a lineage no longer exists. One's boss at the office may have any surname at all, as may the president of the country. By the 1950s, after the leveling caused by Japanese rule and war, South Korea had become a very equal society. And from the 1960s onwards, a completely new top social tier began to emerge. Their success had nothing to do with family names.

The wealthiest and most powerful Korean families today are almost all from *chaebol* backgrounds. These families began to distinguish themselves only in the mid and late twentieth century. At the top is Samsung Group chairman Lee Kun-hee. It is common to hear Koreans talk of him as a king, and his family as though royalty. "A Korean president lasts for five years, but Samsung's power is forever," says one local journalist. TV drama series frequently employ storylines in which a beautiful girl from a poor family marries a *chaebol* heir, as though she were marrying a prince.

The second-biggest *chaebol*, Hyundai, was founded by Jeong Ju-young. Jeong came from an extremely poor family of peasant farmers, but today his descendents too are quasi-royalty in Korean society. By contrast, Yi Seok (1941–), a grandson of King Gojong, spent much of the 1960s singing to American soldiers on military bases and later emigrated to the United States, where he ran a liquor store. He returned to Korea in 1989 but ended up homeless. He was eventually saved by the city of Jeonju, where he is employed to promote tourism. The current leader of the Yi Imperial Household is Yi Won (1962–), the adopted son of Yi Gu, who would have been king had Japan not colonized Korea. Yi Won worked as a manager for Hyundai Home Shopping. In present-day Korea, there is very little connection between a person's ancestral origins and their social status.

The elderly still generally value clan origin, but they will probably be the last generation who do. The major change in attitude towards clans has come from the current generation of young and middle-aged adults. This divide in opinion is illustrated well by the comments of Kwon Ji-hoon (not his real name), an Andong Kwon in his thirties. Ji-hoon relates that his seventy-year-old father remains extremely proud of the Kwon lineage and even wrote and bound his own book on the subject for Ji-hoon and his sister. The book contains details of the achievements of various Kwon ancestors who served as high government officials in the Joseon dynasty. For Ji-hoon's traditionalist father, it is important that his children know about this and try to live up to that legacy. When asked what the clan means to him, though, Ji-hoon replies simply, "I don't care about it at all."

Another man in his thirties, with the surname Jeong, argues that concern over *jokbo* and clan origin is "pointless" and can "put pressure on you to live up to something...without giving you the advantage it used to." He declared that he wouldn't be teaching his children to value their clan origin. In contrast, a young male member of the Gyeongju Lee clan, the one that President Lee Myung-bak comes from, said, "I'm proud of my name, but then, I'm more conservative than most."

Another Jeong, a young mother from a smaller Jeong clan (the same one as Jeong Yak-yong, the famed Joseon scholar mentioned in chapter four) reported that "When I was a little girl, my dentist, who was quite an old man, found out that we were from the same Jeong, so he gave my parents a discount. But that was the only time it [*bon-gwan*] ever made any difference in my life." She says that *bon-gwan* means very little to her and that "it's mostly old people" now who care about *jokbo* and ancestry.

Traditional Kinship Structure

There are three important levels of Korean kinship structure, with the *bon-gwan* the largest. Every descendent of the original *sijo* is part of this *bon-gwan* group. As we have seen, membership of a highly regarded *bon-gwan* could traditionally provide opportunities and status. However, such groupings are too large, particularly in the case of *bon-gwan* like Kimhae Kim, for close-knit ties and familial feelings to exist between members. As clans grew, it was natural for sub-division to occur.

The next level down from the *bon-gwan* is known as the *pa*. A *pa* is a sub-clan, and its size may range from a handful of households, to over a thousand, depending on the total number of *pa* and the size of the *bon-gwan*. *Pas* tend to have deep roots in one particular village or town and own land and houses as well as gravesites for deceased members of the *pa*. They would also operate schools for the children of the *pa*, and provide financial assistance for members in need. The growth of the state has mostly removed the need for such a role now. The *pa* would also administer rites to commemorate ancestors going five or more generations back.

Then there is the *jipan* (household), comprised of a *keunjip* (big house) and potentially several *jageunjip* (small houses). In the *keunjip* live a husband and wife, with their children, plus the husband's parents. The husband will be the oldest among his brothers; younger brothers live with their own wives and children in *jageunjip*. A sister, upon marriage, joins the household of her new husband and from then on is considered a member of that family. Traditionally, a female relative ceased to be considered one's relative once she married.

As with the *bon-gwan*, *pa* and *jipan* have lost much of their relevance. The division of Korea contributed to this to some extent, and in Seoul today it is easy to meet people whose parents came from North Korea either before or during the Korean War and were completely separated from the rest of their family. However, the main reason for the breakdown of kin-based ties must surely be urbanization.

Even up to *pa* level, kinship structures were firmly rooted in individual towns and villages, so the mass movement of people to Seoul and its environs in the mid and late twentieth century made it more difficult for ties to be maintained.

Another factor is lifestyle. Today's South Koreans live busy lives. They work the longest hours in the OECD, and most women—who were expected to stay at home until perhaps one generation ago—are now part of the work force. Competition makes adults toil away in offices all day long and forces their children to study around the clock. Most people simply lack the time to visit relatives often.

Even close relations like cousins will now typically gather only at weddings and funerals and the annual holidays of Chuseok (the autumnal harvest) and Seollal (lunar new year). At Chuseok and Seollal, all family members are supposed to return to their ancestral hometown and honor their forebears in Confucian-influenced commemoration ceremonies. However, even these two traditions are now under attack. Increasingly, restaurants and bars in Seoul stay open throughout Chuseok and Seollal, as more and more people choose to remain in the city. Though the roads out of Seoul are still very busy on these occasions, outbound traffic from Incheon Airport at Chuseok and Seollal—taking people away from Korea altogether—has boomed in recent years. In 2011, 506,000 people took foreign holidays from Incheon Airport on Chuseok, a 15.7 percent rise over 2010.

The Nuclear Family

For the 83 percent of South Koreans who live in urban areas, the traditional family structure has essentially been replaced by the simple nuclear family. Only 4.8 percent of Korean households now have three or more generations living together in the manner of the *keunjip*. Many older Koreans lament the decline of the extended family and its replacement with the household merely comprised of two parents and one or two children. It is a development they see as part of the general decline of social unity and *jeong* in today's urban South Korea. Old people arguably lost the most from the rise of the nuclear family: between 1975 and 1996, the percentage of the elderly living in an "elderly-only household" rose from 7 percent to 53 percent, according to government statistics.

The picture is not all negative, though. For one, the lot of women has changed dramatically. Previously, a wife's role was not just to cook, clean, and raise the children, but also to deal with the constant demands of her mother-in-law—especially if they were living together in a *keunjip*. These days, most Korean wives only have to spend Chuseok and Seollal slaving away for their in-laws. Those who go away on holiday do not even have to do that. Korean women may not yet have equality, but they have a much better deal than their mothers and grandmothers ever did.

Furthermore, the Korean nuclear family has changed the dynamic of a family's relation to in-laws. Under traditional family structure, the wife's family was considered much less important than the husband's. In 2011, however, surveys in the Korean press showed that middle and high school children now feel closer to their mother's relatives than their father's. One married interviewee, who lives near her parents in the Jamsil area of Seoul, is "worried about the feelings" of her husband's parents, since she, her husband, and their young son see much more of her parents than of his. In 2004, almost 47 percent of men in their twenties said that they would not even mind living with their wife's parents.

Some believe the new nuclear family model to be an instance of Westernization. Westernization is an often-used word in Korea, and can be applied to something considered cold, lacking in *jeong*, and going against traditional Korean values. To suggest that Korean households are now "Westernized," whatever that may mean exactly, would be a gross oversimplification. There is still much more mutual dependence between members of the nuclear family in Korea than in the West. Most grown-up children still live with their parents until they marry, unlike in Western Europe or North America. Parents have much more involvement in the choice of their child's degree and university, and eventual career. They also have plenty of say in their child's choice of marriage partner; 70 percent of young Koreans still say they would not marry someone without parental approval.

Koreans in their twenties and thirties typically continue to rely on their parents financially. Fees for advanced degrees such as MBAs and PhDs and costly *jeonse* (deposits on houses) for newlyweds are usually paid for by parents. A survey by online shopping site GMarket in 2010 revealed that 47 percent of married Korean women "often go shopping with their mothers," and the reason for this is financial. Most women in that 47 percent do not pay anything when they shop with their mothers.

Traditional in Other Ways

One other classically Korean practice remains popular. Kwon Ji-hoon, a secular, well-educated urbanite working in the financial sector, chose his son's name with the help of a specialist in *jakmyeong*, the art of making names in accordance with astrological and shamanic principles. Ji-hoon does not truly believe in *Musok* or in any kind of spirituality, he claims, but does not regret the decision to spend 300,000 won (about US$270) on the service. Traditionally, names are supposed to influence the child's fortune, and it is important that the chosen name match the astrological characteristics of the baby's time and date of birth (known as *saju*). For Ji-hoon, in deference to his father, it was also necessary to satisfy *dollimja*, the *bon-gwan* tradition in selecting the first syllable of the boy's given name. Finally of course, the name also had to be one that both he and his wife liked.

A list of fifty names was drawn up by Ji-hoon and his wife and then handed to the consultant, who culled them one by one with admonitions like: "if you choose this name, he will die young. If you choose that name, he will have an eventful but miserable life." Finally, a shortlist came back—with just two names on it. Only two names in the whole world would have suited all the criteria.

Had their child been a girl, the process would have been less complicated. Ji-hoon's father is of a generation that values sons more highly than daughters, so he would not have involved himself in the naming process if the child were female. This is a Confucian hold-over from the old days. In the Joseon era, the focus in raising children was on the sons—eldest sons in particular—in order to groom them to be successful men. Daughters were mostly deemed unworthy even of basic education. While something has been lost in the changes to family life that have occurred in South Korea over the past six decades, plenty has been gained. Today's parents love and value daughters as much as sons.

Chapter 12

Neophilia

For every statement about South Korea, there will always be one major caveat. The usual disclaimers for generalizations hold true, of course: everyone is different, and not every South Korean thinks in one particular way or another. But beyond that, a fundamental fact about this country is that it has an immense capacity for change. Because of this, a statement about life in Korea that is true at a particular moment may become completely false far sooner than can be predicted.

This capacity for change can be positive, especially when it enables people to overcome horrific misfortune and build a country they can be proud of. That Seoul is absolutely unrecognizable from the city shown in photographs taken fifty years ago is testament to the benefits of openness to change, and a reminder of how much has happened so quickly in Korean society.

The rapid pace of development seems to have created a desire in the Korean people to always seek out the next thing—and no doubt issues of face and the spirit of competitiveness that has grown acute during the boom years contribute to this. The latest gadget, idea, or trend is much more compelling than what came before, often simply because it is newer than what preceded it. In a society driven by the perceived need for economic and technological progress and impatient to move forward—one of the first phrases visitors learn is "bballi bballi," which means "quickly, quickly"—nobody wants to be considered old-fashioned or slow to catch on.

Your Phone Is Old in Korea

The rate at which things become obsolete in Korea is remarkable. Songs are "old" that were hits the year before, as if they were from the 1970s or '80s. The same is true of celebrities who reach the age of around thirty. For the celebrity whom the public now finds boring, the best recourse is to disappear for a time before making a comeback with a revamped image. A mobile phone that was top of the line just two or three years earlier will almost certainly be considered backward, especially by young people. According to SK Telecom, Korean consumers replace their phones every 26.9 months on average. By contrast, the Japanese take 46.3 months.

While considered very quality-conscious and unaccepting of defects, Korean consumers are also consummate early adopters. This makes South Korea the ideal test market for any new device. Local and foreign manufacturers who have recognized this imperative to always own the next thing introduce their newest gadgets or latest models in the Korean market before anywhere else. Japanese camera manufacturers such as Olympus are known for doing this. They will monitor the Korean consumer reaction, make adaptations to the product if necessary, and then roll out sales to the rest of the world. The purpose-built city of Songdo near Incheon Airport is being used as a test bed by Cisco Systems of the United States for a whole range of new wireless Internet technologies.

The introduction of the smartphone in 2009 was greeted with near-hysteria in South Korea. In the eighteen months that followed, Koreans bought more than seven million of the devices, discarding their old cell phones, which, in being able only to make calls, send text messages, and take photographs, suddenly seemed old-fashioned. Millions of people will know the exact release date of the next version of the Apple iPhone. If the launch is delayed, millions will share the disappointment. Apple's biggest competitor in the smartphone market is Korea's own Samsung Electronics, which has sold around 100 million of its own Galaxy S and Nexus smartphones worldwide, and over five million in Korea in 2011 alone. In typical fashion for Korean business, the Galaxy S is a classic "follower" product, but it was brought out with amazing speed, allowing Samsung to overtake

Apple and become the world's number one seller of smartphones in terms of units sold.

It is common to see people in their fifties and sixties making use of smartphone apps that Westerners young enough to be their children have never heard of. Koreans are positively addicted to these gadgets. A joint report from the Korea Communications Commission and the Korea Information Security Agency notes that, among consumers overall, the average owner uses his or her smartphone for 4.9 hours per day.

In the context of certain foreign places, such as China or Europe, old is acceptable: Korean tourists enjoy visiting the Forbidden City or Venice as much as anyone else. But old within a Korean context usually carries negative connotations. Old reminds people of the past, when times were not as good as they are now. It is probably not overstepping the mark too much to say that old things can bring about a sense of shame.

Korean has a word, *chonseureopda* ("country style"), to denote something considered old-fashioned or tacky. A hairstyle, a jacket, a particular singer, or even a person's name may be deemed "country style" and subject to scorn or mockery. During the period of rapid economic development, anything that belonged to the countryside was seen as backward or out of fashion and in need of replacement, while Seoul was its opposite. That the countryside is so completely equated with "old" is a testament to the overwhelming influence that urbanization and the glamour of city life have had over people.

One rarely sees truly old cars on the streets of Seoul. Indeed, if one comes across a twenty-year-old car and peers through the windshield, often one will see a foreign face behind the wheel. Thirty-year-old blocks of apartments are considered due for thorough renovation or outright demolition, though this may also have to do with the poor quality of construction in days gone by. Because of where South Korea came from—and where it was until recently—society prefers to remove the traces of the past.

There are slight signs of change, though: even neophilia may not last forever. From the 2000s onwards, some wealthy and artistically inclined Koreans have begun to rediscover traditional Korean houses (*hanok*), and are now prepared to pay handsomely for beautifully renovated ones. And from around 2010, bars that play genuinely old Korean music from the 1960s and '70s, such as Gopchang Jeongol in the Hongdae art school area of Seoul, have become popular. Ironically, this trend for nostalgia is still a cutting-edge pursuit, enjoyed by the cultural elite.

A Nation of Gadget-lovers
Korean neophilia manifests itself most obviously in the realm of technology, as we have touched on, but mobile phones are merely a small part of the phenomenon. Virtually any new type of device will reach mass-market status here much earlier than in other wealthy countries, with the possible exception of Japan. In-car navigation, DSLR cameras, and MP3 players were all taken up here long before Europeans or Americans converted to them.

People are selective, however. Popular adoption of a product can be all or nothing, which is why Samsung Electronics' Galaxy S was such a huge hit and LG Electronics' rival Optimus One a complete disaster that plunged the firm into losses and resulted in CEO Nam Yong losing his job. When a new product vaults the hurdle of acceptance, the face-driven, consumerist reality of South Korea takes over and millions are ready to pull out their wallets.

Of course, it helps that the largest Korean firms are among the chief manufacturers of such products. With their big marketing budgets and influence within the domestic market, the likes of Samsung Electronics have a strong likelihood of convincing people that without their very latest gadget, life would be meaningless. Long before anyone else felt them necessary, flat-screen TVs were a standard in South Korean homes. 3D TV was similarly available in Korea before anywhere else.

Contrary to received notion that the country's business culture lacks of creativity—a perception encouraged by the "fast follower" strategy of Samsung and LG Electronics—high-tech leadership is now a hallmark of South Korean business. There are TV-phones that work on the Seoul Metro, since one can find a signal even down there; millions of people own such devices. The Seoul Metro also offers WiFi access. Broadband speed in Korea is the fastest in the world. Long before Facebook or even Myspace existed, Korea had Cyworld, a social networking site that virtually everyone under the age of forty made use of. And in 1998, five years before the launch of Skype, a Korean company named Saerom was running a huge VoIP (Voice over Internet Protocol) phone service named DialPad.

Koreans were also pioneers of citizen journalism, in which non-professionals write articles for websites such as Ohmynews.com, which mushroomed in popularity in the early 2000s. This left-leaning website, which acts as a counterbalance to the mostly right-leaning mainstream press, is one of a number of Internet-based news out-lets that blur the distinction between journalist and reader. Far more people now access news online than through traditional print media: in 2009, 53 percent of South Koreans used Internet media on a daily basis, while only 32 percent picked up a paper, according to Korea Broadcast Advertising Corp.

Online media has even influenced the outcome of elections. Roh Moo-hyun won the 2002 presidential election against all expecta-tions after a last-minute Internet campaign won him support among young voters. Furthermore, the 2010 regional elections saw the rul-ing Hannara-dang (Grand National Party) receive a shocking defeat that analysts credit in part to the combined impact of Twitter and smartphone use, since young people were receiving messages on election morning reminding them to go out and punish the govern-ment for its various failings.

As mentioned in chapter five, the only way to achieve serious busi-ness success in South Korea is to work with a *chaebol* partner, or dis-cover a rare "blue ocean." Generally, blue oceans in Korea are found in high tech. This is virtually the only area in which a small business-person can sufficiently narrow the capital and influence gap. Thus, former startups like NHN—owner of search engine Naver.com (one of the only search portals to succeed in resisting Google in its home territory)—and NCSoft, a developer of online games, have become successes, unlike e-Hyundai or the equivalent thereof. The top fifty companies by market value on the Korean stock exchange are domi-nated by formerly government-supported *chaebols* and privatized utilities, and NHN and NCSoft are the only two truly independent entrepreneurial firms to rank among them.

Inspired by the likes of NHN, a second wave of high tech entrepreneurs is now emerging. Many of these produce apps for smart phones, owing to the popularity of iPhones and Android devices in South Korea. There is also a large community of indie video game developers. The growth of the venture capital industry in Korea is making it increasingly possible for young people with good ideas to pitch to potential investors and attract capital. Many founders and investors are Korean-American ex-Silicon Valley workers, but increasingly, more and more young Koreans are opting out of the *chaebol* track and trying their luck with start-ups.

Faddishness

The negative side of South Korea's neophilia is the extent to which fads influence people. Koreans who leave the country for a couple of years are always disappointed to find that half of the restaurants, bars or cafés they used to go to have disappeared. Everything has a shelf life and will inevitably be replaced by something newer and more fashionable in relatively short order. A smart businessperson will ride the trends, for example by closing down his or her restaurant, rebranding it, and selling a different type of food—then repeating this process with every change in the public mood.

In the mid-2000s, an immensely popular (and immensely spicy) dish called *buldak*—"fire chicken"—became known as a "yuhaeng," or "mania," food. Restaurants dedicated to serving it sprang up everywhere. Not long after, though, the mania subsided and the restaurants almost completely disappeared. Nowadays, anyone seeking a *buldak* eatery has to search in advance, as the dish has returned to the realm of specialty.

Slang vocabulary changes with dizzying rapidity. In 2007 and 2008, the popular TV show *Muhan Dojeon* ("Infinite Challenge") caused an explosion in young people's use of the word "jimotmi," which is an abbreviation for the Korean words that mean "I'm sorry I couldn't save you." If one lost a drinking game or suffered some other mild misfortune, "jimotmi" would chorus from the mouths of one's friends. However, *jimotmi's* popularity died quickly, and one never hears the word now.

Much of slang comes from advertising, as it does in other countries. The difference in South Korea is the extent to which such memes almost immediately capture the whole country's attention. Talented marketers are constantly working to come up with the next hit concept. Some of the most successful in recent years have utilized the English word "well-being," which was applied to a vast array of products. The mere use of the word denoted that the item in question was healthy—even when it was served up by the manufacturer of Choco-pie. Another catchphrase was the "S-line," a description of the shape of a curvy woman's body—which a woman could obtain ostensibly via the purchase of certain foods or exercise equipment. The media joined in, looking for the celebrity with the best S-line, and soon, "S-line mania" took hold, until a newer concept came along.

A similar fickleness occurs in politics, with perhaps more worrisome overtones. A politician caught up in scandal will be held in disgrace for a while, but chances are good that the public will soon forget his misbehavior, allowing him to resurface later. There is an expression that can be applied to such phenomena. "Naembi geun-seong," or "boiling-pot disposition," means that people are quick to boil over into anger but equally quick to simmer down and forget that anything happened.

Roh Moo-hyun won the 2002 presidential election through a last-minute Internet-led surge, but a great deal of support ebbed away early on in his term. Sensing an opportunity, opponents tried to impeach him for expressing support for his party in subsequent National Assembly elections, since the constitution states that the president must show impartiality. The impeachment effort brought a million people into the streets, leading to a dramatic resurgence in the president's popularity. Subsequently, his ratings declined yet again. The point is not that Roh was a good or bad president but rather the public's volatility: many people thought he was good, then bad, then good again, then bad again. And as of 2012, Roh Moo-hyun is the second most popular South Korean president ever, behind only Park Chung-hee.

PART THREE

Hyun-shil: Cold Reality

Chapter 13

North Korea: Friend, Foe, or Foreigner

How does South Korea feel about North Korea? If one believes the international press, one may be forgiven for thinking that the Democratic People's Republic is an ever-present source of fear south of the border. Images of old men in Seoul burning photographs of Kim Jong-il and Kim Jong-un accompany articles about the dictatorship's nuclear weapons program. Reminders of how Seoul is a mere thirty-one miles from a "crazy" nuclear-armed state and that North and South are still technically at war are common. It is also generally assumed that, despite this rancor, the ultimate reunification of North and South must be the dream of all Koreans.

However, things are much more nuanced than that. South Korean governments have pursued a number of approaches to the North Korean question, ranging from outright hostility to the "sunshine policy" of presidents Kim Dae-jung and Roh Moo-hyun. The people themselves are also divided. The War Generation, those born before or soon after the Korean War (1950–1953), tends to be driven by fear and hatred of North Korea, and so seeks a tough response by the government to any aggression from the North. The so-called "386 generation" of 1960s baby boomers mostly favors rapprochement with "poor brother" Pyongyang. Those born in the 1970s and 1980s—the first generation to grow up without any sense of danger or capitalist-versus-communist ideological struggle—are instinctively peace-seeking, but they are also more apathetic than either the War Generation or the 386. This in itself poses a problem for the possibility of reunification in the future.

Pre-Democratization

During the days of military government, North Korea was presented as a wolf, a red monster that made it necessary for all Southerners to be on their guard at all times. South Koreans who were school-children in the 1960s recall having this message drummed into them by their teachers. Guidebooks produced at the time often contain among the list of handy expressions for visitors terms such as "communist agitators" and "anti-communist National Security Law." One vestige this era of high alert and government paranoia remains today: signs on public buses and trains offer rewards for anyone who reports "far-left activity."

The National Security Law, which has existed since 1948, continues to be used to restrict "anti-state acts" such as creating, distributing, or possessing "materials that promote anti-government ideas." Created to halt the spread of communist sentiment, it was also an effective tool for President Syngman Rhee to clamp down on political opposition. Fears about North Korea enabled Rhee to imprison some 30,000 people in the first year of the law's existence, the law's provisions making it easy for virtually any opponent to be thrown in jail or executed for being a "red." At one point, Rhee had the whole National Assembly arrested on charges of participating in a communist conspiracy, and threatened to have them all shot if they refused to vote for a dubious amendment to the electoral process that was intended to bolster Rhee's dictatorial powers.

Rhee, and later President Park Chung-hee, found the Northern threat politically useful, but at the same time the actions of the Pyongyang regime gave credence to their stark warnings. On January 21, 1968, thirty-one elite North Korean commandos, having trained for their task for two years, launched a cross-border raid with the intention of attacking the presidential mansion Cheong Wa Dae and assassinating President Park. They came within a hundred yards of their target before meeting with South Korean forces: twenty-nine of the invaders were killed, one was captured, and one escaped. Tunnels under the border, intended to facilitate a mass infantry invasion, were also discovered on separate occasions.

Given this very clear evidence of threat, and the fact that the

Korean War remained within living memory for most people, the general attitude throughout the period can be summed up by a government memo written during the Rhee administration that states: "We in [South] Korea believe there is no middle ground, no possibility of co-existence." North Korea was seen as a mortal enemy only. It is therefore entirely understandable that older South Koreans, who came of age during this period, tend to believe there is no possibility of rapprochement with the North, and that the U.S. Army bases that dot the country are a necessary bulwark against a communist takeover.

The mentality of the War Generation dies hard. A sixty-one-year-old government minister, when asked why most South Koreans cheered for North Korea in the 2010 World Cup, told a group of foreign journalists that this support was due to "communist thinking." And in 2011, a sixty-two-year-old woman with the surname Park repeatedly featured in the news for attempting to physically attack left-leaning politicians, including Seoul mayor Park Won-soon. She would show up at public events, including the funeral of democratization activist Kim Geun-tae, shout "Bbalgaengi!" (Commie!), and strike out at those who in her mind wanted to sell the country out to Kim Jong-il.

There are hardly any real *bbalgaengi*. Some pro-Pyongyang groups engage in cat-and-mouse games with South Korean authorities, setting up websites and moving their domains after finding them blocked under the National Security Law. The blunt instrument of censorship arguably need not be used against these groups, for their message is not taken seriously by most people.

Unfortunately though, there are a small handful of national assembly members who at one time or another have been too friendly with North Korea. Lee Seok-gi and Kim Jae-yeon, who both have previous convictions for "pro-North activities" and allegedly swore allegiance to North Korea's "juche" philosophy in the past, entered parliament in April 2012 on the proportional ticket of the United Progressive Party, a coalition of various old left-wing parties. They won selection via rigged internal party elections. Another, Im Soo-kyung—who won fame in her youth by travelling to Pyongyang and embracing Kim Il-sung, and in May 2012 reportedly called a North Korean defector a "traitor"—was somehow selected by the Democratic United Party as a candidate too, and gained a seat in the assembly. These developments have proven gravely embarrassing for both the UPP and DUP. None of the three will win selection again.

The Democratic Era

The 1980s saw the rise of the mass pro-democracy movement. President Park Chung-hee had his opponents in the 1970s, but it was not until the coming of Chun Doo-hwan that millions began taking to the streets to demonstrate for free speech and fair elections. The young people of that generation were tired of dictatorship and naturally distrusted everything the government said. Since Park and Chun's general policy direction had been pro-United States, staunchly anti-North Korea, and pro-capitalist (though, as we know, Korean capitalism then was not capitalism by its dictionary definition), those who opposed dictatorship started questioning all of these ideas.

The young protestors came from what later became known as the 386 generation. When the phrase was coined in the 1990s, they were in their 30s; they had attended university in the 1980s, and they were born in the 1960s—hence 386. They were a large baby-boom cohort, with the electoral and economic power their numbers entail: 8.8 million Koreans were born in the 1960s, compared to the 6.6 million born in the 1950s. Typical 386ers were suspicious of U.S. involvement in the Korean peninsula, particularly following President Chun's state visit to the White House. They felt that the United States was partly responsible for dividing their country and that it was up to North and South Koreans alone to pursue reunification. To the older generation, who thought purely in terms of capitalist versus communist, and South versus North, the 386 looked like an ultra-leftist nightmare.

The 386 were to be frustrated at the result of the first democratic presidential election in December 1987. The egotism of two longtime pro-democracy campaigners, Kim Dae-jung and Kim Young-sam, resulted in both standing for the presidency rather than one yielding to the other. They split the vote and handed victory to Chun Doo-hwan's intended successor, Roh Tae-woo. President Roh pursued "nordpolitik," in which North Korea was still the enemy, but the policy focus was more on winning over the North's friends rather than on engaging in a direct staring contest across the border. Thus, in 1988 the Soviet Union team returned from the Seoul Olympics not only with medals but also with televisions, buses, and cars, all gifts from Daewoo, a company that later would trade directly with the Soviet Union, as would LG and SK Corporation. Roh also established formal diplomatic relations with China, in January 1992.

Kim Dae-jung finally won the presidency in December 1997. The policy he introduced represented the greatest change in direction towards North Korea that the South had ever experienced. Under his "sunshine policy" (*haetbyeot jeongchaek*), he reached out to Pyongyang in an attempt to reform its behavior through better relations. Many older voters saw this as dangerous appeasement. For the 386 generation, though, Kim's approach seemed to offer the possibility of a new era of peace.

The sunshine policy derived its name from "The North Wind and the Sun," one of Aesop's Fables, in which the sun and the wind each vie to remove a man's coat. The wind blows and blows, but the man clutches more tightly to the coat, refusing to allow it to be blown off him. The sun simply shines, and the man removes the coat voluntarily because of the warmth. The aim of the strategy was the blunting of the Northern threat through rapprochement. North and South Korea of course have millennia of shared cultural history, and there was a sense that between fellow Koreans, an atmosphere of mutual trust and cooperation could be created.

Aid in the form of food, basic materials, and cash flowed generously, and joint development projects came into being, such as the Kaesong industrial complex into which Hyundai—whose founder Jeong Ju-young maintained a lifelong interest in reunification—poured millions. Attitudes were also reshaped by the fact that North Korea had fallen far behind the South and was a state desperately in need of assistance. Until the mid-1970s, North Korea had a larger economy than South Korea; but while the South continued to experience miraculous growth, the North's economy stagnated under Kim Il-sung before declining precipitously in the 1990s under Kim Jong-il. In the mid-1990s, over a million North Koreans died in a devastating famine. When President Kim visited Kim Jong-il in Pyongyang for their historic summit in 2000, he brought a gift with him: US$500 million, mostly provided by Hyundai. He later explained his munificence by saying that "a rich brother should not visit a poor brother empty-handed."

The Lee Myung-bak Presidency

Kim Dae-jung's successor, Roh Moo-hyun, continued with sunshine, despite evidence that North Korea was developing nuclear weapons rather than "removing its coat." A test on October 9, 2006, provided confirmation of the North's nuclear program. In the public mind, the sunshine policy had demonstrably failed to achieve its objectives. Lee Myung-bak, a no-nonsense conservative, came to power following the December 2007 presidential election and implemented a radical reversal of policy. Sunshine was out, and aid conditional on the abandonment of nuclear weapons was in. President Lee strongly supported U.S. sanctions against North Korea, blocking the Pyongyang regime's ability to conduct trade. He also made frequent public comments to the effect that "reunification is near," implying that the North would soon collapse and be absorbed by the South.

The North's response was to continue developing nuclear weapons and compensate for U.S.-led sanctions by conducting more business with its only remaining friend, China. China now accounts for more than 80 percent of North Korea's trade. China has taken advantage of this situation by winning access to North Korean ports and the right to mine North Korean mineral deposits. This raises obvious concerns about the amount of influence China has over the North, particularly given the fact that China once held Korea in fealty and treated it as a little brother throughout the Joseon dynasty. Many fear China's influence makes reunification less likely: to China, North Korea is a business opportunity as well as an anti-American buffer state, which Beijing would be unlikely to want to lose to reunification.

Kim Jong-il also reacted against President Lee in a way that took everyone by surprise. Having refrained from direct violence against South Korea since the 1987 bombing of a Korean Air plane in which 115 people died, he apparently ordered two deadly attacks in 2010. The first, the torpedoing of the South Korean navy corvette Cheon-an on March 26, saw the loss of 46 seamen's lives. The North hid its tracks and was silent about its aggression, and without Pyongyang's admission of guilt, South Korean society was divided. The old and the right wing instinctively felt North Korea was responsible, while the young and the left were skeptical. Some believed the sinking to be part of a conspiracy to shore up support for President Lee's tough policy. A survey by the Joongang Ilbo newspaper in 2011 found that 33 percent of nineteen- to twenty-nine-year-olds doubted North Korean responsibility. One left-leaning group, People's Solidarity for Participatory Democracy (PSPD), sent a letter to the UN Security Council expressing doubt about the South Korean government's claims of North Korean guilt. Ruling Grand National Party members responded by calling PSPD "traitors." This episode was a prime example of what is known as *nam-nam galdeung*: the South-South conflict derived from political division, as opposed to the more famous North-South conflict.

The blame for the second incident was never in doubt. On November 23, 2010, North Korean forces shelled the island of Yeonpyeong, located in a disputed stretch of sea administered by the South. Two military personnel died, but, more crucially, two innocent South Korean civilians were also killed. For young South Koreans, this was new territory: those in their twenties and thirties had known only peace, and the idea that North Korea could attack them was shocking. One young woman from Seoul who had been pro-sunshine said at the time: "I couldn't believe that they could just attack us. The government should have responded more strongly than they did." In the wake of the Yeonpyeong attack, this was a commonly held view: over 68 percent of the electorate favored a military response, according to the East Asia Institute, and 39 percent wanted air strikes. In January 2011, 31.7 percent of the public regarded North-South relations as "the most salient issue" in politics.

Just nine months later, however, that figure had plummeted to 8.8 percent. And the passing of Kim Jong-il in December 2011 was met with apathy. One thirty-something office worker recalled the moment: "I heard someone say 'Kim Jong-il is dead,' so I got up and looked at my computer screen and saw it was true. But after ten minutes of talking with my co-workers, we just got back to work." In contrast, the death of Kim Il-sung in 1994 was so fraught it caused food hoarding among South Koreans.

While the present government strives to remind people of the Korean War and the lives lost at Yeonpyeong by putting up poster displays in downtown Seoul, most voters are more concerned with the economy and jobs than North Korea. It is only when Pyongyang actually attacks that this apathy towards North Korea is temporarily broken. For Kwon Youngse, a former member of the ruling Saenuri Party (former Grand National Party) in the National Assembly and head of the national Intelligence Committee, this is a matter of grave concern. According to Mr. Kwon, South Koreans usually "act as though nothing can happen," but they "should worry more" about North Korea.

Peaceful Permanent Separation?

Though twenty- and thirty-somethings may not worry much about North Korea, they do favor rapprochement rather than confrontation. The 386 Generation prefers "sunshine"' too, while the War Generation supports a hard-line stance. Two generations against one means that 55.2 percent of the electorate favor a long-term policy of conciliation and cooperation towards the North, according to the Asan Institute. Given that this survey was taken shortly after the Yeonpyeong attack occurred, the figure now is likely to be higher.

President Lee Myung-bak's Saenuri party began a process of internal reform in late 2011. Since President Lee was perceived by the electorate to be too rightwing, Party Chairman Park Geun-hye (Park Chung-hee's daughter) has led a move to the center. Part of this effort includes a less confrontational approach to North Korea. Kwon Youngse—who is a supporter of Miss Park—contends that "we should help them (North Korea) to become a normal state." Unlike President Lee, who often hinted at the inevitable collapse of the North Korean regime, former Rep. Kwon rates the likelihood of such a breakdown as "very low," even in the wake of Kim Jong-il's death and the handover to the young, untested Kim Jong-un. Thus, instead of trying to push North Korea to breaking point by means of confrontational policies, Saenuri's future policy direction will likely contain some "sunshine." And should Saenuri lose and a center-left candidate wins the presidency, we can expect a full return to the sunshine policy, regardless of the North's nuclear weapons program.

There will be less talk of collapse and reunification then. "We should not talk about it," says Kwon Youngse, in the belief that doing so may provoke the North Korean leadership—which is itself in a transitional phase—to lash out. However, it is also increasingly the case that many South Koreans do not even want reunification. Fewer and fewer people now alive can remember life before partition and have old friends or relatives to reunite with. Furthermore, the economic divergence of North and South Korea means that the South would incur huge costs from reunification. Even the lowest estimates suggest an outlay of more than a trillion U.S. dollars to bring the infrastructure and quality of life in North Korea up to anything approaching South Korean standards.

This skepticism about reunification is especially prevalent in those under the age of forty, who have grown up with wealth and stability. "I don't want reunification. It is an expensive headache," says one thirty-two-year-old office worker from Seoul. This is an attitude that Kwon Youngse calls "individualistic," and not in a complimentary way. There are many who agree with the office worker, though: in 2008, Professor Eun Ki-soo of Seoul National University found that, while 70 percent would support North Korea in a sports match, only 12.3 percent of South Koreans thought unification "necessary," down from 58 percent in 1995. A full 45 percent said it was "unnecessary." Older Koreans are more likely to be pro-reunification: according to the Asan Institute, 20 percent of over-sixties want reunification "as quickly as possible," whereas only 8 percent of those in their twenties do. As the years go by and those who remember a united Korea pass away, the desire for reunification will diminish even more.

A survey by the Peace Research Institute showed that 30 percent of South Koreans now agree with the statement "In the past they [North Koreans] were our ethnic brethren, but now I am beginning to feel that they are foreigners." Another 9 percent went so far as to say, or agree with the statement: "North Koreans are as foreign as Chinese." It is often assumed that the greatest obstacles to reunification are the presence of two very different political systems and ideologies on either side of the border, and the influence of China over the North. However, the ultimate stumbling block to reunification may prove to be a simple lack of desire for it.

Chapter 14

Politics and the Media

In the years following the free and fair presidential election of December 1987, South Korea has developed into one of the most vibrant democracies in Asia. Few could have expected such progress. However, a number of problems remain. This country suffers from an excessively divisive political landscape brought on by regionalism, generational differences, and an entrenched left-right division. Corruption and the old "jobs for the boys" mentality also show no signs of disappearing.

The media remain a weak link in the democratic process as exercised in South Korea. As with politics itself, there is no middle ground for Korean newspapers, TV, and Internet news sources, and all suffer from bias and manipulation. At the same time, the younger generation's dissatisfaction with mainstream media has led to the development of underground and independent media, spread via social networking services like Twitter. These new outlets are starting to bring change to the mainstream.

The Framework
South Korea is a republic, with a president as head of state. Korean presidents have broad powers: they appoint ministers and preside over the armed forces as commander-in-chief. Constitutionally, they may serve only one five-year term, a condition implemented during the transition to democracy in 1987, in order to prevent a return to dictatorship. The single-term presidency has become an important cornerstone in Korean politics, but it also slows down the legislative process in the latter stages of the term, as the president loses

the ability to command his party. The transition from "imperial to lame duck" (as Professor Jang Hoon of Joongang University describes it) has affected all South Korean presidents in the democratic era, including most recently Lee Myung-bak. President Lee was an unashamedly pro-*chaebol*, anti-welfare state politician nicknamed "bulldozer" in the first half of his presidency, but he had to grudgingly modify these positions towards the end of his term.

The legislature is the National Assembly, which is a parliament comprised of 300 members and is located on the island of Yeouido, by the Han River. Two hundred forty-six of the seats are selected by direct voting in constituencies, while the remaining fifty-four are allocated via proportional representation. This extra allocation benefits smaller parties: in the 2008 National Assembly election, the Democratic Labor Party received 3.4 percent of the vote and won only two seats directly, but they won a further four via proportional representation.

There are two main parties in the assembly. One is the conservative Saenuri (New World) Party*, which is essentially the descendent of General Park Chung-hee's Democratic Republican Party. Its members have historically seen themselves as the guardians of Park's economic miracle, promoting policies that favor economic growth most of all. The other is the Democratic United Party (DUP), a liberal, centrist party that grew out of the democratization movement under the leadership of figures like Kim Dae-jung. There are several smaller parties, such as the Liberty Forward Party (LFP), a conservative party created by the losing Saenuri candidate in the 1997 and 2002 presidential elections, Lee Hoi-chang. On the left is the United Progressive Party (UPP), a broad alliance of former Democratic Labor Party members and other leftists.

The judiciary is constitutionally independent, with the Supreme Court as its highest authority. This court has supremacy on all legal matters, including the validity of presidential and parliamentary

---

* Until 2012, the Saenuri Party and Democratic United Party were known as Hannara-dang (Grand National Party) and Minju-dang (Democratic Party) respectively. South Korean political parties change names with surprising frequency.

elections. There is also however a Constitutional Court, which is specifically tasked with the role of being the "interpreter of last resort" on constitutional questions. Since its introduction in 1988, the Constitutional Court has struck down more than four hundred laws it deemed unconstitutional and has made decisions of historic importance. In 2004 for instance, the Constitutional Court overturned the impeachment of President Roh Moo-hyun, whose future as leader had been cast into doubt by a vote from the National Assembly to remove him from office. Roh had expressed his support for his own Woori Party, and, technically, a Korean president is supposed to observe impartiality in public statements.

This institutional framework makes for a reliable and democratic system. It is mostly reminiscent of the one used in the United States, and the American flavor is hardly a coincidence, given the influence the U.S. has had over this country since the end of World War Two. A republic was proclaimed in Korea in 1948 and the present version of the constitution has been in effect only since 1987, but the system has proved stable since the democratic era began. It has helped South Korea become the twenty-second most advanced democracy in the world—and number two (narrowly behind Japan) in Asia—according to the Economist Intelligence Unit's "Democracy Index" survey in 2011. This ranking is only three places below the United States, and higher than that of many European countries, including France.

Presidents and Parachutes

An institutional framework is only as good as the people operating within it, however. South Korea could rank even higher than twenty-second, were it not for the stubbornly persistent culture of corruption that ensnares too many of its politicians. According to Transparency International's Corruption Perceptions Index, South Korea is only the forty- third cleanest country in the world. This places South Korea far below neighboring Japan on corruption, and only slightly higher than Rwanda.

South Korea's inability to clean up its act stems mostly from the existence of close-knit elite networks and the jeong that prevails within them. It is frequently a source of surprise to this author how, in a nation of fifty million inhabitants, influential people from disparate fields such as journalism, law, politics, business, and academia all seem to know each other a little too well. Koreans have a strong orientation towards building up their human networks, and they will use school, army, university, or hometown connections to do so. The *jeong* that binds the members of a group can then lead to favoritist rule-bending and dishonest behavior for the benefit of insiders, and when some members have political power, corruption can result.

The best recent example of this is the network around Busan-based businessman Park Yeon-cha. Park, chairman of Taekwang Industries, was a family friend of President Roh Moo-hyun, who also came from the same region of South Gyeongsang province. He allegedly gave a million U.S. dollars to President Roh's wife, as well as money to other close Roh aides, such as Gangwon Province ex-Governor Lee Kwang-jae. Park's network extended far beyond President Roh, and eventually, when the graft was uncovered, twenty-one politicians from both main parties were indicted.

According to an editorial in the Kyunghyang Shinmun newspaper, Park Yeon-cha's corrupt network extended to "relatives by blood and marriage and close associates of former presidents, former and current politicians, close associates of the current president, high-ranking civil servants, heads of local authorities, and businessmen." The investigation exposed the "cozy relations between politics and business" that create a "structure of corruption" in Korean society, the article stated.

When corruption convictions are secured, penalties tend to be light—fines and suspended sentences are the usual outcome. And furthermore, on the rare occasion when genuine punishment is given, special presidential pardons are available to save the offender, particularly in the case of *chaebol* leaders. The chairmen of three of the top five *chaebols*—Hyundai Motor, Samsung Group, and SK Corporation—have all received presidential pardons in the 2000s.

South Korea's entrenched power networks also lead to a culture of patronage. Jobs are handed out from the top down as rewards for loyalty or friendship or to quiet potential opponents. When a new president comes to power, banks that are majority state-owned, branches of the civil service, and state media are liable to acquire new senior staff in short order. Nakhasan, or parachute employment, is also rife. Presidential staff are particularly noted for their ability to land lucrative contracts in industry despite having no experience of corporate management.

"Korean politicians, the president, and the ruling party have actively engaged in making and maintaining the networks of parachute appointment," assert Joongang University political science professors Rhyu Sang-young and Lee Seung-joo. One senior finance executive in Yeouido stated in 2010 that a friend at another bank was ordered by someone "high up in the government" to accept a nakhasan employee or face unspecified bad consequences. The government official warned the executive against saying no with the expression, "Neo geureomyeon jaemieopseo" ("if you do that, it will be boring"), a euphemistic threat in Korean.

Another banker talks of having to customarily accept older nakhasan appointees as auditors every two years, providing them with annual salaries in the mid-six figures in U.S. dollar terms. He states that the rationale for government officials in their late fifties is that, since government salaries are so low, a couple of years in a lucrative nakhasan job is seen as a kind of "retirement gift" for years of hard work and loyal service. The best way to avoid such obviously unacceptable practices would be to pay much higher civil service salaries, in the way that Singapore has done. In a sense, the government is saving money by forcing companies to pay for civil servants' retirement nest eggs.

Divided Society

Korean politics is also beset by deep divisions based on regional, age-based, and left-right ideological lines. These divisions encourage extreme shifts in policy whenever the other side gains the upper hand, and they inspire politicians to play to the gallery for votes rather than engage in mature debate. One supporter of Saenuri party Chairman Park Geun-hye claims that because of this problem, "Korea pays a very high cost for democracy."

The two protagonists of the regional rivalry are the provinces of Jeolla and Gyeongsang, which occupy the southwest and southeast of South Korea, respectively. Their rivalry has deep historical roots: the kingdom of Shilla came roughly from a part of the country that would now be called Gyeongsang. It conquered the Baekje kingdom, which corresponds roughly to the location of Jeolla, in 660 CE, before going on to unite the whole of Korea in 668 CE.

Several Baekje revival movements followed, including the breakaway kingdom of Hubaekje ("Later Baekje"), which lasted from 900 to 936. When Wang Geon—founder of the Koryo dynasty and conqueror of Hubaekje—took power, he declared the Hubaekje area a "perverse and rebellious land" and ordered that people from that region not be chosen to serve in the government. His edict finds an echo in the practice of the Gyeongsang-led military governments of South Korea from 1961 to1987, when Jeolla natives were overlooked and their region was left behind in funding for infrastructure and industrial development.

Jeolla has long been considered the rebel province, a place of fiery opposition and more recently of left-wing politics. Given the way Jeolla has been treated over the centuries, it is quite understandable that its people would have such tendencies. In 1980, Gwangju, the largest city in Jeolla, rebelled against newly installed dictator Chun Doo-hwan, a Gyeongsang native who had usurped command of the military and later the country in the wake of Park Chung-hee's assassination. Chun Doo-hwan sent in the army, killing hundreds of protestors.

In the 2007 presidential election, Saenuri candidate Lee Myung-bak beat Chung Dong-young of the Democratic Party (the old name for the UDP) by a margin that can only be considered an embarrassment for the latter. Lee defeated Chung in every province except Jeolla—where he garnered just 9 percent of the vote. By contrast, in North Gyeongsang, the most conservative part of the country, he received 72 percent of the vote. Daegu, the largest city in North Gyeongsang, gave Chung a miserly 6 percent. Quite simply, it does not matter what policies and candidates Saenuri and UDP offer in Jeolla and Gyeongsang: the result is virtually a given.

Thankfully, Seoul-centric urbanization means the problem of regionalism is not as bad as it once was. Millions of people moved to Seoul from Jeolla and Gyeongsang in the mid and late twentieth century. While the parents may have retrained some regional identity, their children are "Seoulites" and are less interested in the old regional divide. Seoul is a swing region: in the 2002 presidential election it backed liberal Roh Moo-hyun, and in 2007 it chose conservative Lee Myung-bak.

It appears as though a new divide is opening up among Seoul voters, however, and this divide is based on age. Young South Koreans suffer from unemployment and underemployment. The economy creates roughly 100,000 "good" jobs, i.e. those in *chaebols* or the government, per year, but universities churn out 500,000 graduates in that time. This discrepancy has resulted in the growth of a large cohort of disaffected, poor young people, who are well educated but have little sense of hope or trust in the political and economic system of their country.

Adults in their thirties also have money worries. Though they have jobs, the cost of raising their young children is too high, as is the price of basic household necessities like food: food price inflation reached 7.9 percent in 2011, the second highest in the OECD. The rapid rise in apartment prices in Seoul has hurt them too. While their parents have benefited handsomely from increasing property values, thirty-somethings cannot afford to buy. According to the Korea Development Bank Research Institute, the price-to-income ratio for housing in Seoul was 12.64 in 2008. This implies that the average person would have to save all of their income for 12.64 years in order to buy the average Seoul apartment. By contrast, the ratio for New York City was just 7.22. Mortgages do exist, but the inflated apartment prices mean that repayments are burdensome and seemingly never-ending.

Collectively, the unemployed twenty-somethings and struggling thirty-somethings make up what the Donga Ilbo newspaper has called "the Angry 20–40." The Angry 20–40 vote handed a defeat to the Saenuri in the October 2011 mayoral race, with around 75 percent of them choosing independent Park Won-soon, whose platform was based on expanding the welfare system and providing affordable housing. By contrast, 70 percent of the over-60s voted for the Saenuri candidate, Na Kyung-won. Such poll results are not quite as bifurcated as those created by Jeolla and Gyeongsang voters, but they are not far behind.

The election of Park Won-soon as Seoul mayor shook the traditional two-party system. Although a liberal, he was not allied to the UDP (though he did join them after the fact, in February 2012). Many voters, including liberals, have misgivings about the UDP. This explains why, despite the low approval rating of just 25 percent for Saenuri president Lee Myung-bak as of January 2012, the UDP narrowly lost the April 2012 parliamentary elections to Saenuri. Corruption scandals have frequently engulfed the UDP as well as Saenuri—the Park Yeon-cha case, for example—and UDP leaders like Sohn Hak-kyu have engaged in embarrassing policy "flip-flopping," for instance by supporting the Korea-US Free Trade Agreement, only to change their minds later. For those reasons, many Angry 20-40 voters are disillusioned with both parties. "They're as bad as each other," says one twenty-nine-year-old Seoul-based voter.

Disaffection with the two establishment parties opens the door for alternative forces. In 2011, the most popular person in Korean politics was not even a politician. Self-made anti-virus software tycoon Ahn Chul-soo was mentioned as a potential Seoul mayoral candidate by a political pundit in an interview, and he immediately became the front-runner—despite not having declared his candidacy. The liberally inclined Mr. Ahn later backed Park Won-soon, helping Park leapfrog Na Kyung-won and win the race. There is still a chance that he could run for president in December 2012, and possibly win: in a hypothetical two-horse race, he would edge out Saenuri's Park Geun-hye by around two percentage points, according to a January 2012 opinion poll. Mr. Ahn is one of the most respected people in Korea because of his personal success and philanthropic work. That he has no background in politics makes him more popular. Because he has no connection with discredited politicians, young people trust him more.

Ideology

Good old-fashioned ideology also plays a major part in South Korea's divided political culture. This is true of any democracy, but here the existence of North Korea has always pushed people to further extremes. During the presidencies of Syngman Rhee, Park Chung-hee, and Chun Doo-hwan, South Korea was largely defined by its rivalry with the North. It was an anti-communist and anti-North Korea (and by extension, anti–Soviet Union) state. The opposite of communism was considered to be pro-American capitalism, and therefore this was what South Koreans were told to embrace.

As noted in chapter 13, there was no middle ground throughout the period of military dictatorship. Syngman Rhee or Park Chung-hee defined what existed in South Korea as free-market capitalism and democracy (though it was really neither), and anything else was painted as treachery. Cho Bong-am, Syngman Rhee's greatest rival in the 1950s, had achieved popularity with a platform that was similar to European-style social democracy, stating, "We need neither a bourgeois dictatorship nor a proletarian dictatorship." President Rhee disagreed and had him executed for treason in 1959.

The lasting influence of this period means that many South Koreans aged around sixty or above still often have an all-or-nothing mentality. To such people, the sunshine policy was pro-communist rather than a strategy for dealing with a difficult situation. Measures to reduce the powers of *chaebol* chairmen, such as Kim Dae-jung's introduction of laws to protect the rights of minority shareholders of *chaebol* firms, also sometimes attracted the criticism of "leftism." This is ironic, as minority shareholder rights are a cornerstone of genuine capitalism.

What in South Korea is considered left-wing can also seem quite unusual to people from other countries, because it contains a strong dose of ethnic nationalism—something normally associated with the far right. Besides being pro-America and anti-North Korea, the Rhee and Park regimes angered many with their apparently ambivalent attitudes toward their former colonial oppressor. Sygman Rhee's security forces had an abundance of former collaborators in their ranks. Controversially, Park Chung-hee normalized relations with Tokyo in 1965 in return for US$800 million in soft loans and grants. As a student in his early twenties, even future president Lee Myung-bak protested against the normalizing of relations, serving three months in prison for his trouble.

Against this pro-U.S., Japan-friendly backdrop, South Korean left-wingers developed politics based on Korean ethnic nationalism. The left co-opted words like *minjok* (race), which was used in the masthead of left-leaning newspapers like the Minjok Ilbo. Even today, the main left-wing newspaper is named *Hankyoreh*, which means "one race" or "one people." In contrast, the right promoted *gukga*—"nation" in a political sense—which meant South Korea alone, rather than all the people of Korean blood in both halves of the peninsula.

In other democracies, left and right are divided on relatively ordinary issues, such as taxation and welfare spending. But in South Korea, the political divide is rooted in history, racial identity, and the division of Korea itself. This makes mutual understanding and reconciliation much more difficult.

The Media

South Korean media also contribute to the atmosphere of division. There are five major national newspapers: Chosun Ilbo, Joongang Ilbo, Donga Ilbo, Hankyoreh, and Kyunghyang Shinmun. The first three are the most popular, with over two million daily copies sold each. They are also all editorially right-wing. Left-wing critics lump the three together as one, taking the first syllable of their names to make the pejorative composite word Chojoongdong though in reality the Joongang is more moderate than the Chosun or the Donga. The Hankyoreh and Kyunghyang Shinmun are left-wing and less popular. This does not mean that the left are not adequately served by the media: they tend to favor a range of popular online media such as Ohmynews.com, a "citizen reporter" website with around 75,000 contributors and more than 600,000 unique users per day.

All these media outlets tend to lack balance and moderation. They present the same basic news but with different biases. During the time of the Park Yeon-cha corruption case, the left-wing media drew attention to the manner in which former president Roh Moo-hyun and his family had been singled out for rigorous investigation by the authorities, despite many other figures having been implicated. The right-wing media meanwhile focused on the negative details emerging about Roh. It would be beneficial for South Korea if a moderate, centrist major newspaper were to emerge—but then, given the entrenched political division in Korean society, it would be unlikely that many people would read it.

Manipulation of the news by the powerful is also a problem. Though South Korea is a democracy, its media are only "partly free," according to American think tank Freedom House. Freedom House points out that the problem is getting worse, reporting increases in both "official censorship" and "government attempts to influence news and information content."

Besides direct censorship, the government can influence the media through high-level *nakhasan* appointments, with those who complain facing trouble. In 2012, reporters at the three main news television stations in Korea went on strike over this, and in 2009, Amnesty International raised objections to the arrest of Roh Jong-myeon, a television journalist detained for "interfering with business" after protesting against the appointment of a former presidential aide as the boss of YTN, a television news network. Similarly, the power of the *chaebol* within the Korean economy means that harsh criticism of the likes of Samsung or Hyundai is rare in the mainstream media. If 20 percent of one's advertising revenue comes from one company, one is very unlikely to criticize that company.

Constraints on the news media have translated into a general lack of trust among the populace: according to a BBC survey, 71 percent of South Koreans think the government interferes too much in the media, and 55 percent say they do not trust the media. The so-called Angry 20-40 in particular are consequently turning to independent media. Young people read blogs and then disseminate what they read to others via Twitter, adding their opinions. According to the Korea Advertisers Association, Koreans were writing 100,000 Tweets about politics every day by November 2011, up ten-fold from one year before. Among Korean Twitter users, 87.6 percent fall within the ages of 20 and 40.

In 2011, the satirical Naneun Kkomsuda (rough translation: "I'm a sneaky trickster") became the most popular podcast in the world, with an estimated ten million listeners per episode. Its makers began the show in April 2011 with no budget or audience, but after just a few months they had built a politically powerful phenomenon. The podcast was started by founder Kim Ou-joon in response to what he saw as the corruption and greed of the Lee Myung-bak administration and the unwillingness of the mainstream media to expose it. The fact that the podcast had to exist as an "underground" phenomenon was "evidence itself that overground speech is suppressed," claims Mr. Kim. In a major break with mainstream media practice, Naneun Ggomsuda was explicitly critical of President Lee (and other individuals), running the risk of attracting defamation lawsuits. While Mr. Kim's show has attracted much criticism from conservatives, the existence of such independent media venues in the Internet age offers hope for free expression and democracy.

Chapter 15

Onward, Industrial Soldiers

A little over a century ago, Koreans were considered indolent. Legendary traveler and writer Isabella Bird Bishop visited Korea in 1897 and wrote, "Seoul is a boring, dirty, and dead city. The people are lazy and slothful." *Call of the Wild* author Jack London, who spent four months in the country, also wrote in 1904 that Koreans were "weak and lazy." The Japanese colonizers appear to have taken the same view: Okita Kinjo, in an unpleasant book named *Korea, Behind the Mask* (1905), called Koreans "the world's laziest people," adding that the country's only "products" were "shit, tobacco, lice, *kisaeng* [roughly, a Korean geisha equivalent], tigers, pigs, and flies."

Today's South Korean workers have a very different image. As the hardest working people in the OECD, they are the very model of industriousness. In 2008, the average Korean clocked a total of 2,357 hours at the office. From the 1960s onwards, they have worked under tough, somewhat militaristic conditions. Rank and organizational hierarchy are of great importance, and workers are expected to be loyal to their employers, despite a lack of genuine "jobs for life." So, how did this turnaround in image come about? Why did an extreme attitude to work develop? And how are recent economic, legal, and social changes undermining it?

Park Chung-hee, Again
General Park Chung-hee's influence can still be discerned in many disparate areas in today's South Korea, from the country's preoccupation with economic statistics to its love of unchallenging, saccharine pop ballads (see chapter 22). The way in which Koreans work

lso bears his imprint. Following his coup in 1961, General Park egan to develop an export-oriented growth model centered on *haebol*. Since South Korea was very poor and lacked capital and echnology, he realized the country would have to make up the difference through low-wage, intensive labor as the main basis of production. He needed millions of disciplined, hard-working young eople to generate rapid economic growth, in order to fulfill his twin bjectives of overtaking North Korea and lifting the nation out of overty.

General Park was fortunate in two respects. The first had to do vith education. Syngman Rhee's drive to achieve universal schooling neant that the young adults at General Park's disposal were probably etter educated than those in any other poor country. Between 1945 nd 1970, adult literacy rose from 22 to 87.6 percent. Furthermore, Korea's Confucian legacy and the traditional importance of the nemorization-intensive civil service exams had led to a school system that focused on discipline and rote learning rather than imagination. This produced a generation of young workers who were ready o take orders and not ask too many questions. In today's high-wage conomy, where creativity is increasingly required, these traits are ess desirable. However, at a time when factories needed disciplined vorkers who could follow instructions, they were very useful.

The schools also inculcated ethnic nationalism in their pupils. outh Korea was a very young state and had escaped from the Japanese colonial nightmare only to be cast into a brutal war with the North. In order to restore national pride and foster a sense of unity, he people were taught that they were the products of an unbroken five-thousand-year line descending all the way from Dangun, he legendary founder of Korea. General Park was able to harness his ethnic nationalism and put to use the sense of pride and unity fostered in convincing Korean workers to make the country great hrough industrial development. Children continued to be indoctrinated with ethnic nationalism into the 1980s. One informant now n his mid-thirties recalls, "In school, we were taught that we were pecial because we had 'pure blood.' It's ridiculous to think of it now, ut I believed it at the time."

General Park was also fortunate in having a workforce that ha undergone the experience of conscription. Because of the Nort Korean threat, all healthy South Korean males were obliged to serv for over two years in the military. (This obligation still exists, thoug it has been shortened slightly, to one year and nine months.) Mos men going to the factories at the time would have had military expe rience. As a soldier himself, General Park must have realized the po tential for harnessing the discipline and nationalism inherent in th military for use in industry. It is no coincidence that his state calle upon the people to be "saneop jeonsadeul"—industrial soldiers.

Park's government presented industrialization as a kind of "sacre quest to revive the nation," in the words of one former industrial so dier. One was not simply working for Samsung, Hyundai, or Luck Goldstar (LG): one was working to build the nation and restore th pride of the Korean race. That sacred quest required sacrifice: b 1971, the average Korean worker put in 51.6 hours per week. Thi is the recorded figure, but it is likely to have underestimated the re number of hours worked. Saturdays were also workdays. Until a leg change in 2004 abolished compulsory Saturday work at companie with over 1,000 employees, Koreans had one-day weekends.

The idea of the sacred quest was important for bringing wome into the labor force too. According to traditional Korean neo-Confu cianism, a woman's place was in the home, with the family. Gener Park, however, wanted young women to move away from their fam lies and come to big cities like Seoul, to work in factories. Accordin to anthropologist Kim Seung-kyung, this radical change was mad possible by presenting factory work as a patriotic duty, necessar only during the period of rapid industrialization. Women were t sacrifice their natural roles temporarily, out of loyalty to the natio and the Korean people.

In a book entitled *Sweatshop Warriors*, Miriam Ching Yoon Loui states that the Park government even built up South Korea's sex in dustry as a means of earning foreign exchange receipts from Japa nese businessmen and American soldiers on leave from the Vietnar War—all "for the sake of the nation." An article in the New Yor Times by Choe Sang-hun quotes one former prostitute as saying

The government was one big pimp for the U.S. military.... They urged us to sell as much as possible to the GIs, praising us as 'dollar-earning patriots.'"

The Korean Workplace

Although General Park detested Confucianism, blaming it for South Korea's earlier lack of enterprising spirit—the *yangban* aristocracy, for one, had disdained work as being beneath their station —his *chaebol* system benefitted heavily from Korea's Confucian legacy. Neo-Confucianism's influence throughout the Joseon era had ingrained in Koreans a paternalistic, top-down mentality that the South Koreans of the 1960s still possessed. A cultural habit of deference to authority enabled Park to effectively command the *chaebol* heads, who were in turn able to command their employees.

Like a Confucian father, the *chaebol* head ruled sternly but with a sense of responsibility. The hours for workers were of course long, and weekends and evenings at the factory or office were commonplace. Compulsory company outings and drinking sessions were instituted, to build up the sense among workers that they were part of a family, rather than a mere company. Daewoo Group even referred to itself as "Daewoo Gajok" (Daewoo Family). Workers would receive birthday gifts, and bosses would step in to arrange dates for staff in need of marriage partners. Such practices still occurs in many Korean firms. In 2011 it was reported in the Korean press that ten single men and women from Hana Bank and ten single men and women from Kookmin Bank were given a group blind-date by management of the two firms.

Large Korean firms have always tended to be very hierarchical. Again, owing to the influence of Confucianism, it is very rare for someone to challenge a superior or raise doubts about a particular decision. Furthermore, there is never any doubt about who is superior to whom: nearly all firms use the same range of job titles. There are up to six levels of non-executive employee: *sawon* (entry level), *daeri*, *gwa-jang*, *cha-jang*, *team-jang*, and *bu-jang* (the highest, a head of department); then, there are as many as eight executive levels: *isa* (lowest level director), *sangmu*, *jeonmu*, *bu-sajang*, *sajang*, *bu-hoehang, hoejang,* and finally *daepyo isa* (literally, "representative director," which is essentially a CEO). Among the non-executive titles, three positions, *gwa-jang, cha-jang,* and *team-jang* ("team" from the English word) correspond to different levels of manager. Among the executive positions, the *hoejang* (chairman) is usually most powerful in practice, for this title is mostly used for the company founder and/or controlling shareholder. In accordance with Confucian tradition, promotion is mostly based on age and time served, and so a brilliant thirty-three-year-old is likely to be outranked by an average thirty-seven-year-old. Top directors are typically in their late fifties or sixties.

Working for a Korean firm, particularly a *chaebol,* was never a matter of merely exchanging one's time and labor for money. Firms like Hyundai wanted to hire young men who would sacrifice themselves for the overall corporate cause and stay with the firm throughout their careers. Recruitment policies reflected this: rather than simply taking up a desk after passing interviews, new hires were subjected to tough initiation tests, as though they were joining an American university fraternity or secret society. One man who joined Hyundai in the 1970s and later became a senior executive tells of being "left up on a mountain, without a map. It was dark and cold, and we had to get to a target destination by sunrise." Hyundai chairman Jeong Ju-young was also said to be fond of challenging his employees to wrestling matches.

Chaebol had their own company songs, which new recruits were encouraged to sing in unison at training camps to which they were sent after being hired. LG's song, according to a paper by Song Young-hak and Christopher Meek on "The Impact of Culture and the Management Values and Beliefs of Korean Firms," contains the following lines:

> We are industrial soldiers leading the times,
> With our new and continuous creativity and study,
> And where we accomplish our holy mission,
> There is happiness for our race and mankind.

Here we can clearly see General Park's notion of "industrial soldiers" and the "holy mission" of export-led growth and industrialization being promulgated by one of his government's most trusted *chaebol*. The use of the word "race" is also telling, as it underscores the usefulness of ethnic nationalism in convincing people of the value of the industrialization project.

"We Are Not Machines"

Despite the power of ethnic nationalism and the occasional kindness of a paternalistic chairman, it should never be assumed that Korean workers in the 1960s and 1970s were happy with their lot. Not everyone accepted the "holy mission." In 1970, a twenty-two-year old textile worker named Jeon Tae-il committed suicide by burning himself to death, after shouting, "We are not machines!" His own work conditions were particularly terrible: he had worked at Pyeonghwa market in the north of Seoul, where tuberculosis was rampant due to a lack of ventilation, and workers were forcibly given injections of amphetamines in order to keep them working around the clock. He had previously complained to the authorities about such practices but had been told to stop being unpatriotic.

Jeon Tae-il is a hero to the Korean working class. His sacrifice raised consciousness of the plight of the workers and helped inspire the eventual growth of proper trade unions in the years following democratization. During Park Chung Hee's rule, only one union, the Federation of Korean Trade Unions, was allowed. The FKTU did not truly fulfill the functions of a union, since its executive committee was selected by the government. Park saw the FKTU's role as that of transmitting government policy down to the workers, rather than enabling the workers to resist poor treatment under the government-business compact.

Though the legions of factory workers were indeed building the nation during the 1960s and 1970s, they were not compensated well for it. One of the reasons South Korea became such a strong exporter was that wages were held down throughout the entire Park era, which served to increase the price competitiveness of Korean products. Between 1963 and 1971, GDP per capita increased from US$100 to

$289. Wages though rose only 58 percent during that time. The lion's share of the benefit of growth accrued to the *chaebol*.

Similarly, while workers were encouraged to devote themselves to their companies and think of their companies as being like family, there was no real "jobs for life" culture in exchange, as there were in Japan. Workers were expected to be loyal to their employers rather than move from place to place as is the norm in Western countries. Their loyalty was not fully reciprocated by the company, though, as most workers were forced into retirement around the age of fifty. Unless a worker was promoted to an executive role, it was expected that he would take retirement without making a fuss. Partly this was because older workers earn higher salaries than younger ones, but age hierarchy was also an issue. In Korea, one is expected to show respect to one's elders. It is very uncomfortable for all concerned when a forty-five-year-old boss has to deal with a fifty-five-year-old subordinate. There was even an expression that crystallized the company point of view: "oryukdo" is a contraction of the Korean words that mean, "If you're here in your fifties or sixties, you're a thief." Forced early retirement still exists, and as a result there are many middle-aged and old men scraping a living driving taxis, operating small convenience stores, or working as security guards.

The IMF Era

Despite the introduction of democracy in 1987 and the flowering of trade union activity that this political change allowed, South Korean work culture remained essentially unchanged into the 1990s. Hours were still long—from 1991 to 1996, Koreans worked almost 48 hours per week on average, only 3 hours less than in the early 1970s—and again, this figure is very likely to underestimate the real number of hours put in. Corporate culture, particularly at *chaebol*, could be said to have become even more paternalistic. Under pressure from the newly emboldened unions, the largest firms began offering generous benefits rather than higher salaries, such as life insurance and help with children's tuition expenses.

The family illusion was about to be shattered, though. Over the years, the *chaebol* had loaded up on debt in order to fund expansion nto as many industries as possible. Reliance on debt had been a fundamental part of the *chaebol* system since the 1960s and had been fully encouraged by successive governments. Throughout the mid-1990s, borrowing in foreign currencies—particularly the U.S. dollar—also increased dramatically, from $89.5 billion in 1994 to $174.9 billion in 1997. Furthermore, the government effectively encouraged short-term borrowing of foreign currencies by demanding detailed disclosure of how long-term borrowings would be used. Korean companies were therefore taking on short-term debt in foreign currencies to finance long-term projects.

Throughout 1997, successive *chaebol* began to totter under the weight of their obligations. The debt-to-equity ratio of the average *chaebol* was 519 percent, far out of line with any reasonable yardstick. In January 1997, iron and steel maker Hanbo—then the fourteenth-largest *chaebol*—collapsed, owing US$6 billion. By November, seven of the thirty largest *chaebol* were insolvent, including Kia Motors. Smaller firms that relied on orders from *chaebol* fell into trouble, and the unemployment rate started rising. Meanwhile, foreign investors began pulling out of Korea, provoking heavy selling of the won. The value of the currency plummeted from 800 per U.S. dollar to 1700. This meant that the cost of repaying short-term foreign debt in Korean won more than doubled, further exacerbating the problem.

The result of all this was the bankruptcy of flagship names such as Kia, which ended up in the hands of Hyundai Motor, and third-largest *chaebol* Daewoo, which had attempted to ride out the crisis by expanding even further. Unemployment rose from just 2.2 percent to 7.9 percent between 1996 and 1998. By the standards of Europe or the United States, 7.9 percent may still sound like a reasonable figure, but South Koreans had become accustomed to near-full employment before 1997.

A survey by the FKTU at the time showed that among the unemployed, 81 percent blamed politicians for the crisis, and 67 percent felt the *chaebol* were also responsible. A mere 16 percent blamed the International Monetary Fund. The IMF "bailed out" Korea with a US$58.3 billion aid package, but in return it imposed its customary "shock therapy" conditions: short term interest rates, for example, were raised dramatically, surpassing 30 percent by December 1997 This caused further bankruptcies through 1998. The period of 199; to 1998 has become known as the IMF era by Koreans, but despite a belief among many foreign businesspeople that Koreans blame the IMF for causing the crisis, the majority does take the view that the root cause of the problem was the government-*chaebol* compact which had bred an addiction to debt and reckless expansion.

Though South Koreans worked long hours and faced enforce early retirement, there has been at least a tacit understanding tha by joining a Korean firm, one would have a long, stable career. Tha changed in the wake of 1997. The implicit contract of job security was gone. Even Hyundai, which, more than any other *chaebol*, incul cated its workers to believe in the company-as-family mindset, wa not immune to layoffs. Between January and September 2008, 1(percent of workers at the five largest *chaebol* were made redundant.

The crisis of 1997–1998 had wide-ranging implications for Ko rean society and the economy. As well as undermining the bond o trust between company and worker, it increased inequality. In 1999 a survey by Hyundai Research Institute showed that 44.6 percent o Koreans felt "middle class," but a further 19.7 percent said that the had fallen out of the middle class due to the crisis. Between 199; and 1998, the bottom 20 percent of earners lost 17.2 percent of thei income, while the top 20 percent only lost 0.8 percent of theirs. Fur thermore, Seoul's homeless population of 2,500 shot up to 6,000 domestic crime (i.e. spousal abuse) rose by 46 percent, and divorce rose by 34.5 percent, all in that one year. A source of historic shame to Koreans, the overseas adoption of Korean babies registered its first increase since 1987.

The Decline of Loyalty, and Other Changes

Even in the post-IMF era, firms still attempt to instill loyalty in thei employees. At some firms, new recruits fresh out of university are sent on four-week-long training programs, in which they are woken up early, made to participate in physical exercises, indoctrinated with the company's values, and sing the company song. LG's program is re portedly run by former military personnel. The recruitment process itself is designed to make would-be employees value the company: Samsung, for instance, runs its own "Samsung SAT" exam; this contributes to the belief that Samsung employees are smarter than the average Korean.

Such efforts are not as effective as they used to be. One Hyundai Capital employee says, "Some of our staff are loyal, but not me. In fact I'm grateful to those loyal guys, because it means less competition for me if I apply for other jobs." He is not alone: a recruitment agency, Job Korea, found that 70 percent of Korean workers would now switch employers if given a better offer; only 12 percent of men and 4.6 percent of women stated they were "truly loyal" to their firm. This would have been unimaginable in 1980 or 1990.

Another survey by TNS in 2003 showed that Korean employees were in fact the second most disloyal out of a cohort of thirty-five different industrialized countries. At the time, this was taken as a surprise, as Korean workers were still perceived to be company loyalists. According to the survey, women and older male employees were especially disloyal. This is because Korean firms still discriminate against both these groups. In 2010, the top *chaebol* hired three men for every woman through their entry-level recruitment programs, and the gender pay gap in Korea is 35 percent, the highest in the OECD. Older employees are still put out to pasture too soon.

Another factor in declining loyalty is the use of temporary contracts by employers. This trend began in the aftermath of the 1997–1998 crisis but picked up pace throughout the 2000s. In 2001, 16.6 percent of Korean workers were on temporary contracts, but by 2006, this figure had increased to 28.8 percent. As of 2012, around one in three Korean workers is a temporary employee, intern, or part-timer. Such workers have fewer legal rights, and so companies have found this type of hiring to be a useful way of gaining the upper hand over labor. Yet, as a consequence of this practice, workers worried about job security may outwardly proclaim loyalty to their employers but inwardly will harbor resentment and readily switch jobs when a better alternative becomes available. Only 48 percent of Koreans would recommend their employer as a place to work, compared to 75 percent of employees worldwide, according to TNS.

It is commonly believed by foreign businesspeople that South Korea has inflexible labor markets and that it is thus difficult to "hire and fire" as one wishes, but this is an incorrect perception, especially in the era of the temporary contract. The OECD ranked South Korea thirteenth out of its thirty member states in terms of employment flexibility in 2008. The belief that Korea's labor market is rigid comes mainly from the strength of unions at particular companies, such as Hyundai Motor, and the umbrella union covering Korea's bank workers. In 2011, the Hyundai Motor Union even tried to win a concession from management that the children of current workers be given extra consideration in the recruitment process. This kind of zero-sum demand—one that will hinder other applicants—is emblematic of the two-tier labor system that has come into being since 1997. Those with long-term work contracts at highly profitable companies like Hyundai Motor are extremely well protected; meanwhile, the rest of the workforce faces poor job security.

The Korean office is changing in other ways. Thanks not to a cultural change but to a legal one, the length of the average workweek is falling. In 2004, the Roh Moo-hyun administration introduced a 40-hour maximum, 5-day workweek, with a maximum of 12 hours paid overtime. This is mandatory for companies with 1,000 or more employees. In reality, it is not strictly adhered to: Koreans still put in a 44-hour basic workweek (plus many hours of uncounted, unpaid overtime), but at least the average is falling. Company drinking parties are also becoming less common than they used to be. "We used to go out twice a week and get really drunk, but these days, we go out once, and maybe just have a few beers," says one bank worker.

The increasing numbers of foreign firms with Seoul offices is changing to the way some Koreans work. In particular, foreign firms are taking advantage of the *chaebol's* apparent lack of interest in hiring women by taking their pick of most well-qualified women they can find. U.S. investment bank Goldman Sachs' Seoul office contains more women than men. Executives there say it has always been easier for them to hire a talented woman than a talented man, as there is less competition from *chaebol* and major Korean banks.

Yoon Jeong-eun, a thirty-four-year-old woman, has built a career in PR entirely at foreign firms. She is now the lead PR director of the Seoul office of a multinational consumer products firm. Given her age and gender, she would never have achieved this had she remained entirely within local companies. She has subordinates ten years older than herself. One forty-four-year old male PR manager, she notes, is bitter about having a young, female boss but has to accept the situation. Miss Yoon has been promoted rapidly due to her ability, and because of flatter organizational hierarchies (which means fewer levels and job titles to pass through), she has reached the top at a young age.

At major Korean firms, age-based promotion through a long list of job titles still largely prevails. However, with the dawn of the Internet economy, a new breed of Korean firm is rising. For instance, online game maker Nexon, which is valued at US$6 billion, had (as of 2012) no director above the age of forty-four, and a thirty-four-year-old chief financial officer. From roughly 2010 onwards, South Korea has been going through a venture capital-led Internet and technology boom pioneered by entrepreneurs in their twenties and thirties. In some sectors of the economy at least, the traditional importance attached to age and hierarchy is beginning to break down.

tend to believe in the wisdom of the Latin expression, "in vino veritas."

In building a strong relationship, mutual sacrifice is important. For this reason, one must expect to "take a hit" once in a while, says Peter Underwood, who has been running his Seoul-based consultancy firm, IRC, for over twenty years. Not every transaction will be profitable. Mr. Underwood tells the story of an American car parts entrepreneur who came to Korea with an approach of "I won't do anything unless I can make a profit on it." This would seem a perfectly sound philosophy in the United States or the United Kingdom. According to Mr. Underwood, though, the attitude the man should have had was, "It goes for a hundred, and you want me to sell for ninety? Well, I'll do it this time, but next time I want a hundred and ten." If both partners engage in give-and-take, a long-term relationship of mutual benefit can be established. While one may lose money on a deal today, one may get a better price next week, protecting oneself from undercutting competitors.

The relationship the *chaebol* had with President Park Chung-hee illustrates the effectiveness of this give-and-take practice. The chaebol built Park's roads, bridges, hospitals, and other infrastructure, sometimes at prices they knew would lose them money. They did so because they also knew that Park would reward them in the long run. Even before Park's time, Jeong Ju-young of Hyundai accepted a net loss of 70 million won on a project to build the Goryeong Bridge, when he could have simply walked away from it. The total contract size was 54 million won; for every single won coming in from the government, 2.3 won was going out on the various costs associated with the project. Though he realized the loss was coming, he insisted on completing the bridge and risk bankrupting his company, because he knew the best long-run approach was to secure his relationships by keeping his word. The result was, as he says in his autobiography, that Hyundai was "thought of very highly by the Ministry of Home Affairs. After that, we didn't have difficulties in getting construction contracts from the government."

Signaling Care and Respect: Etiquette, Hospitality, and Gift Giving

The importance of face in Korean culture, as well as general human courtesy, dictates that one must show care and respect to one's prospective business partner. It is not advisable to say "no" directly to a particular proposal. Generally speaking, it is rude to utter a blunt refusal, though perhaps not quite to the extent that it is in Japan. A statement like, "that would be difficult," would probably suffice and cause less social friction. Adhering to basic etiquette like this, as well as being aware of the importance of hospitality and gift exchange, is recommended for anyone seeking to do business in Korea.

There are several important rules of business etiquette that are second nature to Koreans, and indeed to foreign businesspeople living in Korea, that may not be obvious to outsiders. Business cards are extremely important and should be treated with proper respect. When one exchanges business cards, one should present one's card with two hands and then receive the other person's card with two hands. One should then examine the card one has just received and nod approvingly. Taking a card one-handed and simply placing it in one's pocket with just a cursory glance would be considered rude.

The card will have print on both sides—one side will have Korean, and the other English. Many Koreans use English nicknames for international business purposes, in the belief that Korean names are impossible for anyone other than Koreans to remember. So it may be the case that the English side of your counterpart's card says something like "John Jeong-won Kim, Head of Department" (note the reversal of the usual surname-first given name-second order). In Korea, one would never address a person one just met by their given name. However, the English nicknames are considered more acceptable to use. So, depending on the context, it may be acceptable to say "Hi, John" but not "Hi, Jeong-won."

That said, a foreign businessperson who learns how to correctly address someone in Korean will make a good impression. This is done by combining the surname with the job title and then adding the honorific suffix "nim." As we saw in the previous chapter, the head of a department of a Korean firm is known as *bujang*. So, in this instance, "John Jeong-won Kim, Head of Department" would be "Kim bujang-nim." Foreign nicknames can be useful for the neophyte, but ultimately they are just nicknames. There will always be a certain distance between two people when one does not know the other's real name.

When the alcohol flows, the rule of two hands still applies. One should not pour one's own drink; instead, one should hold out one's glass with two hands and allow the other person to pour it (with two hands). Then, one should return the favor, pouring the other person's drink for them in the same way. If Kim bujang-nim asks, "One-shot?" this means, "Shall we drink the whole glass in one go?" One may politely decline, but taking the "leap of faith" and one-shotting one's *poktanju* will get things off to a good start.

If two groups, rather than two individuals, are meeting, Confucian-derived hierarchical relations will come into play. There will be an overall atmosphere of deference towards the leader of each group, with the focus of the conversation naturally falling on the most senior person from each side. When drinking, these two people will clink glasses first and probably offer a few words about the hope for a bright future relationship. If one is playing a supporting role, one should not speak before the two leaders have spoken or drink before the two leaders have drunk. Traditionally—but less so these days—junior members of the group are supposed to turn their heads away as they drink, and also make sure the rim of their glass is lower than the rim of a senior member's glass when they are clinked together.

Business drinking sessions in Korea also relate to the tradition of showing great hospitality to guests. Peter Underwood jokes, "When guests come, Americans hide their best whiskey, but Koreans keep theirs waiting for you." If one visits Korea on a business trip, one will be taken first to an excellent restaurant and then probably to an up-market bar and given expensive whiskey—even if that whiskey later ends up being mixed with beer and one-shotted. If one is male, one may also be taken to a "room salon."

Room salons are hostess bars. Patrons go down a flight of stairs and into a room with a large table, a karaoke machine, platters laden with fruit, and bottles of expensive whiskey. (South Korea is the world's sixth-largest importer of Scotch.) Drinks are served by young women in their twenties, who in high-end places make more money than some of the men around the table. Though the room salon is not specifically about prostitution, prostitution of such women does occur; many a deal was done with the aid of such a service for a prospective business partner. Large *chaebols* devote substantial budgets for room salons, drinking, and other forms of *jeopdae* (corporate entertainment) and employ staff to oversee them. This culture will die out eventually as the role of women in business is increasing. For now, though, it continues to hold great importance.

According to Choi Mi-jung (not her real name), a room salon hostess, "there are four types of customer: those who want to touch the girls, those who want to talk to them, those who want to sing, and those who just want to drink with their friends." The room salons provide pretty girls who can also hold a conversation (and are adept at feigning interest in everything the guests say), a karaoke machine, and vast amounts of whiskey. "This place has everything men want. That's why they bring business partners here," she says. The room salon is a form of hospitality designed to make men feel like kings.

Hospitality may well extend to being picked up at the airport in a limousine and being given trips around Korea's tourist sights, depending upon the resources of the Korean partner. The important thing for foreign businesspeople to remember is that the business relationship is about give and take—so when a Korean partner comes to visit one's own country, one should go to similar lengths for them. It is all a matter of showing mutual respect and care for each other.

The same is true of gift giving. Many Korean firms send out gifts to suppliers, clients, investors, and so on, on the two major national holidays of Chuseok (Autumnal Harvest Festival), and Seollal (Lunar New Year). These presents usually consist of gift-boxed food items rather than anything especially expensive. The important thing, again, is they signal that the company values the recipient. It is unlikely that many non-Korean businesspeople would send gifts on Korean national holidays, so being the rare Westerner who did would stand one in very good stead. Chuseok and Seollal are movable feasts, so make sure to look up the correct dates.

When meeting a prospective partner face to face, a more individualized gift would be most appropriate. The best type of present would probably connect the two of you: for example, if one is from New York and meeting a baseball fan, an item of New York Yankees memorabilia may go down well. One does not need to go completely overboard on the cost but rather signal one's consideration of the other person's interests and emphasize the things that are shared between you, in spite of your cultural differences.

Reputation

The importance of showing good face cannot be overstated, as Korean businesspeople care deeply about their reputations. It is surprisingly common for bosses of Korean firms to commit suicide in the wake of image-destroying scandals: in 2011 and 2012, after a series of mutual savings banks were found to have committed bribery and illegal lending, the heads of three separate banks killed themselves. Korean firms also respond aggressively to reputation-harming criticism. In a 2009 column, author Michael Breen made satirical reference to Samsung's past corruption scandals. Samsung responded by suing him for a million U.S. dollars—despite the fact that he had said nothing untrue (in Korea, defamation can be found even when the criticism is correct). In the text of the lawsuit, specific reference was made to the "mocking tone" of Mr. Breen's words. Eventually, Samsung dropped the case, most likely due to the negative publicity it was earning them.

Kim Woo-choong, founder of Daewoo, famously said, "It is too bad if you lose money, but money is one of those things that it is okay to lose, since you can always make more . . . but you should never lose your reputation. You should treasure it as dearly as life." He knew this better than anyone. In the wake of Daewoo's bankruptcy in 1999, Mr. Kim was convicted of accounting fraud, sent to jail, and ordered to pay back the equivalent US$22 billion.

Knowing that reputation is of such importance, one should think very hard before criticizing a Korean partner firm or a member of the partner firm in front of their colleagues. One should have a private conversation first and even then resort to open criticism only as the nuclear option when other avenues have been exhausted. Harsh

ies. In Korea, a marriage is not merely between two people but also between two families. One's partner should be a good match for one's family and one's social milieu as well. One could probably relate this idea of marriage to Confucianism, in the way it places value on the family and social harmony. A person introduced by a friend, or by an acquaintance of one's mother, naturally stands a better chance of fitting the bill.

The custom of *jungmae*, or matchmaking, has existed for many years. When the time came for their son or daughter to get married, a couple could seek out a professional. The *jungmae-in* were usually older women who had a large network of contacts within a particular social circle. The matchmaker would maintain books with pictures and information on a range of single people, and when a new client came, she would search through the book to find a suitable partner to recommend. Meetings would be arranged, and if the two young people liked each other and their respective families were satisfied, a wedding would be booked in haste. Only then would the matchmaker receive her fee. In the case of rich families, this fee could run into the many thousands of dollars.

The marriage-oriented dates arranged by matchmakers are known as *seon*. *Seon* can also be arranged by non-professionals. An *ajumma* (middle-aged lady) in Korea will typically have a substantial network of acquaintances. A friend in need of a son-in-law may approach her with a request for *seon*. The *ajumma* will ask around her network if any suitable young man is available. Though this is amateur matchmaking, she will still likely earn a fee. One friend of the author received 3 million won (almost US$3,000) in this way. However, the couple divorced one year later, and she was pressured into returning the money.

Given the high stakes involved, *seon* is a stressful experience. Parents push *seon* on unmarried children in their early thirties out of fear that it will soon be too late for them to marry at all. The expression "time bomb" has sometimes been used to refer to unmarried thirty-somethings, particularly women. If a woman is unsure whether she likes her prospective partner, her parents may put pressure on her to marry the suitor anyway. Some couples agree to wed a mere month or two after their first meeting.

Jungmae matchmaking is still common, although due to the likes of Duo, it has become a larger, more organized industry. And since the 1960s and 1970s, with the growth of independent city living away from parents, young people have sought more casual alternatives to *jungmae.* The most popular such alternative is the *sogaeting.* *Sogaeting* is a hybrid Korean-English word derived from *sogae* "introduction" and the final syllable of the word meeting. In a typical *sogaeting,* a man and a woman who know each other will each bring another friend to a café. The four will make polite small talk, and at some opportune moment the matchmakers leave, hoping that the two strangers will hit it off.

The newly introduced pair will proceed to a restaurant, while the other two await text messages, which invariably read, "Thank you so much!" or "What were you thinking?" In the case of the former, the two introducers will feel the pride of a job well done: some enjoy matchmaking so much that they are constantly on the lookout for opportunities to set people up, and maintain counts of how many couples they are responsible for creating. There are also serial *sogaeting* recipients, who seem to enjoy spending every other Saturday wearing their finest, eating pasta, and making awkward conversation with friends of friends.

Another type of introduction comes via specially arranged group singles' meetings, known by the English word meeting. For example, if a young man meets a young woman from a different social circle, he may suggest that they both invite their respective single friends to a group meeting. If she accepts, then they will each bring perhaps three or four friends to an agreed location, usually a bar. Meetings are usually favored by university students and people in their early twenties, and are not at all serious. Often, the whole evening will be passed playing drinking games, in which forfeits, such as having to kiss one of the other participants, are handed out with great regularity. Participants may then stagger to a *noraebang* (singing room), where they can try to impress those they had their eye on with alcoholically impaired vocal stylings.

The most casual type of arranged meeting occurs in a traditional Korean nightclub. Korean clubs are very different from the Western variety. They contain row upon row of tables and a relatively small dance floor, because patrons in fact do not go there to dance. Typically, around four or five men will sit down at a table and be served expensive whiskey and fruit. They are assigned a waiter, who will go around the other tables to find a group of women, whom they bring over to the men's table. This process is known by the English word booking. The waiter does this in return for a tip. The larger the tip, the prettier the women he will bring. If a man and woman get along well, they will exchange phone numbers. In this day and age, one-night stands from such meetings are very common.

For women, booking also means a cheap night out. Waiters maintain lists of attractive women's phone numbers and will call them up and offer free, or very cheap, tables and drinks for them and their friends. This is more than compensated for by the price men will pay. Men will happily lay out 150,000 won (almost US$150) each in table fees and tips. Despite the cost, some men go very often. In fact, there is an expression, night-jukdoli, for a man addicted to booking and nightclubs. The female equivalent is a night-juksooni.

When one considers the practice of booking, it is hard to agree with the now outdated conception of South Korea as a "conservative" country. Booking has an old-fashioned Korean element to it—the introduction from the waiter—but the way in which it is now used suggests that young South Koreans today are sexually rather liberal. Not everyone likes booking, though: these days, most go to Western-style nightclubs, and there too, people meet randomly and engage in behavior that is anything but conservative.

Marriage Agencies

These days, more and more singles urgently seeking to wed join one of the country's large matchmaking agencies. The agencies are more efficient than *seon* arranged by friends of their parents and offer larger networks that a professional *jungmae-in* with only a local network. The market leader, Duo, was founded in 1995 and has 24,000 members, who each pay between 1 million and 4 million won (roughly US $1,000–4,000) in membership fees, depending on the level of service they require.

Kim Hye-jeong explains that, prior to the advent of such firms, matchmaking was not systematic, with many professional matchmakers "just using handwritten records" and relying on their instincts to set people up. Duo's method is to turn matchmaking into a kind of science by asking each new member 150 questions about their character, family, educational and work background (documentary evidence of these must be provided), and the exact characteristics of the person they are seeking before matching the member up with prospective partners by computer. Those who expect too much are asked to "lower their eyes," as the Korean expression goes—for instance, when a woman only wants to meet doctors, as is sometimes the case according to Ms. Kim. Members are given between seven and ten "suitable" introductions from the Duo database, which is often enough. The company claims to have introduced 22,500 couples who eventually married. In 2010, they were responsible for a full one percent of all Korean marriages.

Ms. Kim fondly recounts the tale of two people who had been scheduled to meet via Duo and appeared to have stood each other up, the reason being that each had been involved in separate accidents at the exact same time. By chance, they were even taken to the same hospital. The two strangers had their scheduled date later and are now married. Be it destiny or not, the system seems to give people what they want in the end.

Later and Later

These days, destiny has to wait a while. As recently as the 1980s and early 1990s, women typically expected to marry soon after graduating from university. Now the average age at which females marry has risen to twenty-nine, while for men, it is almost thirty-two. The rise in women's marriage age has led some men to think that women do not really want to get married anymore and are becoming believers in *dokshinjuui*—deliberate, independent singledom. There is an expression, "gold miss," to describe a thirty-something woman with a career, a social life, money—and no husband.

Many may envy the lifestyle of the gold miss, but few Korean women genuinely want to remain single forever. It is more a case of today's women having more choice and seeking out opportunities to build careers (and also travel and enjoy life a little) before tying the knot. In a sense, this suits men's aims too: according to Ms. Kim, today's Korean male is seeking not merely a beautiful woman but one who can also bring a stable income to the table.

The fact that recent graduates face a tough job market—with higher unemployment and many workers stuck in temporary contracts—is an extra cause for delayed marriage. Many people simply cannot afford to get married, even if they want to. The cost of marrying and setting up house together has risen dramatically in recent years: on average, couples and their parents must shell out 208 million won (around US$185,000), according to a survey commissioned by the Chosun Ilbo newspaper. In 1999, it cost just 76.3 million won. The rise can be attributed mainly to the increase in real estate prices.

Furthermore, since raising one child costs an average of over 10 million won per year (almost half of GDP per capita), it is becoming necessary for both marriage partners to work. Whereas today's sixty-year-old Korean man probably sought to marry a woman who had no greater ambition than be a good *jubu* (housewife) and stay at home to raise the children, his thirty-year-old son is likely to want someone with a strong educational background and a decent career.

Male pickiness in choosing a mate is more than reciprocated. In the past, women were simply looking for *gyeongjaengryeok*— "competitive ability," a euphemism for the ability to make money, states Ms. Kim. "Before, if a man was successful but short, a woman would accept him. But now, she wants a man who is tall and handsome, as well as successful." Increasingly, both sexes want to have it all, which reflects the highly competitive nature of Korean society. For some, a PhD-level education or model-like looks are expected, rather than ideal or exceptional.

Finding one's *isanghyung*—ideal type—is not the end of the process, of course. Marriage in South Korea is not merely about two people tying their futures together. It is about the union of two families, and one in which the parents continue to play a decisive role. It is common to hear tales of people forcibly separated from their "true love" due to the parents' opposition, usually on the grounds of social status as related to the education, career, or financial background of the intended in-law and his or her family. While young people are starting to conceive of marriage as a matter for the couple alone to decide, they still generally defer to their parents, who subscribe to the opposite view. According to Duo's internal research department, seven out of ten would not defy their parents when it comes to marriage.

The Wedding

If both sets of parents are satisfied, a date is set, and a home for the happy couple is sought. Traditionally, the husband's parents provided a house for the couple and the wife's parents filled it with furniture and other necessities. These days, much depends on the relative wealth of all concerned. Due to today's highly inflated apartment prices, the parents may avail themselves of *jeonse*, a uniquely Korean system of property rental in which a large deposit is paid to allow the couple to live rent-free, but ownership is not transferred. *Jeonse* seems to be slowly declining as a practice, though, as mortgages are more commonplace than they once were. There is also a customary exchange of expensive gifts and money between the two families. The most problematic is likely to be *yedan*, gifts sent from the bride to the groom's family, on which around 10 percent of the total cost of the bride and groom's new home should be spent. For one friend of the author, this amounted to 40 million Korean won (around US$36,000).

A charming tradition that may take place prior to the wedding is selling *hahm*. *Hahm* is a box containing gifts, which are brought by the friends of the groom to the bride's family home. The young men stand outside, making as much noise as possible and shouting, "Hahm saseyo ("Please buy *hahm*"). It is the job of the leader of the group, the *hahmjinabi*, to "sell" the box to the family, who will ignore him at first but will eventually let him in and lavish all manner of food and drink on the group. The *hahmjinabi* is readily identifiable because he masks his face with a very unusual item: a dried squid. Unfortunately, as most people now live in apartments with

neighbors very close by, the selling of *hahm* is considered by many to be a noisy disturbance, and so the custom is less common than it used to be.

On the wedding day, if the couple are both Christian, they may well marry in a church. For non-Christians, there are two typical options: a hotel banquet hall or a purpose-built "wedding hall." The former is considered to be more up-market. The ceremony is generally quite short, and guests may come and go as they please and talk among themselves as the vows are being made as well as during the lecture given by the *jurye*. The *jurye*—typically the most respected old gentleman the two families can muster up—will deliver his thoughts on longevity of marriage, respect for parents, and so on. However, most people seem not to listen.

The couple is dressed in Western-style wedding attire for the main vows but then disappear for a few moments and re-emerge in hanbok, traditional Korean dress, to greet their guests. Proceeding to a special room called the *pyebaek-shil* (wedding gift room), they will bow to both sets of parents. In the past, only the husband's parents received this honor, but Korea's growing spirit of equality and changing family roles has resulted in this important symbolic change. The groom may also carry his bride around the room on piggyback, symbolizing his obligation to her.

For gifts, guests simply put money in an envelope. Considering the high cost of the ceremony—particularly in the case of a hotel wedding—this is entirely understandable. One friend told the author, "It is important that I get married before my father retires." The reason for this is financial: his father, a bank executive, has been attending the weddings of co-workers (and co-workers' children) for many years, filling envelopes with money each time. If he retires before his son marries, most people from the bank will not come to the wedding, and he will not receive his "investment" back.

The more people who turn up, the more money will be collected. The size of the turnout can also be a matter of pride, and some sets of parents, particularly high-status ones, may feel the need to invite as many guests as possible in order to bolster their image as important people. This can lead to much grumbling among the newlyweds

themselves, who complain about the large number of attendees whom they barely know.

What about Romance?

Korean dating and marriage as described so far may seem to have more in common with free market economics than love, but it would be incorrect to characterize this country as unromantic. The early stages of a relationship tend to be full of anniversaries (a hundred days since first meeting, a hundred days since first becoming a couple, and so on), which invariably result in trips to the theater, weekends away, and a steady stream of bouquets of flowers and chocolate boxes. In the early days, romantic gestures are very common: there is a special English-derived phrase, event man, to describe the kind of boyfriend who serenades his love from outside her window or shows up to her office with a hundred roses.

The calendar also contains an abundance of special romantic days, mostly created by firms seeking to sell products. Besides Valentine's Day, there is Diary Day, when one is supposed to buy a diary for one's lover to record all the special moments in the year ahead; Rose Day, when roses are exchanged; and White Day, when men give candy to women. Amusingly, November 8 is Bra Day, when men are encouraged to buy said item for their significant other. On Green Day, couples are supposed to dress in green clothes and go for a walk in the woods. Singles may console themselves on that day by drinking the alcoholic spirit named *soju*, which comes in green bottles.

Among products promoted in the name of romance are "couple rings," which are a step down from engagement rings but still signal to the world that a person is attached. A rather bizarre fashion trend is known as "couple style," in which the besotted pair dress in the same way: if the woman wears a red sweater and blue jeans, the man will also wear a red sweater and blue jeans. Nobody admits to liking couple style, but plenty of couples adopt it.

If It All Goes Wrong

For many years, divorce was considered unconscionable, and social pressure strongly discouraged it. A couple at war, or no longer in

love, was expected to stay together for the sake of family unity and honor. In the 1970s, though, the number of divorces began a steady rise, and between 1980 and the early 2000s the rate quintupled to 3.5 per 1,000 people per year. Towards the end of this period, the rate of increase was startling: there were 116,300 annulments in 1998, and 166,600 in 2003 (against 303,000 new marriages that year). Meanwhile, the rate of marriage was reaching historic lows: throughout the 1980s, there were around nine marriages per 1,000 people per year, but by the early 2000s this figure had fallen to just over six.

The rapid increase in the divorce rate between 1998 and 2003 may in part be attributed to a backlog of people who had long wanted to divorce taking advantage of the change in social mores, as well as the fall-out of the economic crisis of the late 1990s. Indeed, the rate has since returned to 1998 levels. However, attitudes about divorce have changed for good. The number of bachelors marrying divorced women, for instance, almost tripled between 1980 and 2009, and 23.5 percent of marriages in 2009 involved one or more divorced partners, up from 10.7 percent in 1990. A growing trend of celebrity divorces has contributed to the climate of acceptance. Single parenting, while still generally frowned upon, is also a trend: there are over a million Koreans raising children alone.

According to a survey by Professor Shin Yeon-hee of Sungkyul University, 73.4 percent of men and 67.2 percent of women support the idea of cohabitation before marriage, mostly on the grounds that it allows the couple the chance to get to know each other, reducing the risk of divorce in the future. This is still not something that most parents of adult children would readily accept, but it may well be a normal state of affairs one generation from now.

Chapter 18

English Mania

Though Korean culture is shot through with a hearty dose of national pride—and by extension, pride in the native tongue—one of the first things a visitor to South Korea will notice is this country's obsession with the study of English. The language is taught all the way through a child's school years, sometimes starting with specialized English kindergartens and continuing with private after-school institutes known as *hakwons*, which, if run well, can make their owners rich. Parents will stop at almost nothing to ensure their children can speak English, and even in adulthood, many people continue to work on improving their fluency. English ability is a ticket to better employment opportunities as well as a badge of pride.

The rationale for such heavy emphasis on learning English is that if South Korea is to compete effectively, company workers and entrepreneurs need to speak the international language of business—a way of thinking found in most advanced economies. Yet Korea's excessively competitive approach to education has freighted the study of English with serious social problems that may well outweigh the benefits of having an English-speaking population.

The Extent of the Obsession

As reported in the New York Times as well as many domestic newspapers, there are doctors in South Korea who offer special tongue surgery that some people believe will lead to better English pronunciation. The operation is called lingual frenectomy and involves cutting through the part of the tongue connected to the bottom of the mouth to free the tongue up more. Though millions of Western-born

ethnic Koreans speak English perfectly well without the need for such a bizarre procedure, some parents are apparently so driven that they insist on having it performed on their children.

This example is of course extreme, but that the surgery exists at all is telling. For most people, the way to master English is through endless hours, days, months, and years of study. Throughout the land, parents believe that their children cannot succeed in life without English fluency, and thus, even before being able speak their own language properly, many kindergarten-age kids will be sent to English nurseries, where they will be taught in the foreign tongue all morning, every morning.

When children start attending school, the final bell of the day does not mean the end of lessons. Most children will then go to *hakwons*, or private academies. These teach all manner of subjects, from art to mathematics and music, but the most costly and popular are for English. *Hakwons* import native-speakers as teachers all the way from the United States, Britain, Canada, Australia, Ireland, New Zealand, and South Africa, and provide them with free accommodation and a reasonable salary. Due to the historic influence of the United States, American accents are in most demand. On the other hand, many people view British accents as high status, though more difficult to understand. Often, the teachers are not required to have any specific teaching qualifications or experience. The demand is so great that "anyone with a pulse and a white face will do," in the words of Mark James (not his real name), a *hakwon* teacher in Gyeonggi Province.

The goal of all this study, both in school and in *hakwons*, is to score well on tests such as the TOEFL (Test of English as a Foreign Language). A high score is probably more important than genuine fluency. As with the *suneung*, and the Joseon civil service exam administered in earlier centuries, success on the TOEFL can improve a South Korean's life—much more than can fluency. This is because top companies, besieged with applicants, use a candidate's English score as an extra criterion for selection, even when the job in question does not require English ability. A study by Incruit, a recruitment firm, found that a full 50 percent of Korean companies use such English test scores to whittle down the list of applicants.

Since Korean culture places a premium on success, poor performance is unacceptable. Parents will spare no amount of effort or expense to ensure that their child's future university or job applications will never be relegated to the bottom of the pile because of a low score in English. But when everyone is desperately seeking to achieve the highest percentile, the result for the majority has to be disappointment. Even those who do well have been convinced by a society that only accepts one hundred percent that they need to do better. The expression "I'm sorry my English is so poor" is one of the most commonly used English phrases in South Korea—and is usually not accurate.

The pressure to score well continues far into adulthood. One friend of the author reports, "My dad is in his sixties and is an executive at a large Korean paint company. He has never needed to use English at work, but if he wants another promotion, he has to show them a good TOEFL score. It makes absolutely no sense at all."

The Cost

According to Park Il-jin (not his real name), a *hakwon* owner, "In Seoul, the average family's after-tax income will be about 3 million won per month (around US$3,000), assuming the mother stays at home. A good English kindergarten will cost 1 million per month. That means they are spending a third of their money on private English education for their kid. And that really isn't unusual."

After the child enters regular school, and starts to attend *hakwon* in the evening, the cost to parents is a few hundred thousand won per month. On top of that, there are fees for tests, textbooks, and quite possibly, one-on-one private lessons with native English instructors. Such tutoring (known as *gwa-wae*) costs around 50,000 won or more per hour. The government tries to discourage parents from using *gwa-wae*—it is actually illegal for foreign teachers to offer them—but in the quest for perfect English, rules take a back seat.

Families who can afford to may send their children to schools abroad, typically in the United States or Canada, in order to get them ahead of the pack. Families sometimes "break up" over English. The phenomenon of the *gireogi appa* ("goose father") is an example of this. The goose father is a man who remains in Korea to work while his wife and child go and live abroad, for the purpose of improving the child's English. By some estimates, the number of such men extends to the low six figures. Of course, some of them may well enjoy the return to quasi-singledom.

Not surprisingly, the amount of money spent on English education is vast. The combined profit of *hakwons* in 2009 was 7.67 trillion won (around US$7.3 billion), which was greater than the operating profit of Samsung Electronics (by far Korea's largest firm) that same year. Probably around half that comes from English *hakwons*. And this figure excludes the additional amounts made by the vendors of private lessons, textbooks, tests, electronic English dictionaries, and overseas study programs.

Some parents and experts claim that such investment in education is far-sighted and good for South Korea. But, granted that English ability may be valuable for some, is it really worth a third of any family's income? According to Professor Chang Ha-joon, the cost of education is "the biggest reason [Korean people] don't have more kids." English tuition is the largest single part of this cost. The cost of education, and in particular English education, is thus a major factor in Korea's exceptionally low birth rate of around 1.2 children per woman, which threatens the economic future and vitality of this country.

The Costs Outweigh the Benefits

In so competitive a society, many other problems are associated with excessive study, in particular that of English. *Hakwons* in busy parts of Seoul remain open very late—although *hakwon* operation between the hours of 10 p.m. and 5 a.m. is illegal. High school students often wake up at dawn to study before leaving for school, and then go directly to a *hakwon* after school. With homework from both school and *hakwons* factored in, it will be a lucky high school boy or girl who is able to sleep for more than six hours per night. The saddest part is that everyone knows this is a bad thing, but when other parents force their kids to study when they should be sleeping, it is hard for people not to feel pressure to do the same—especially since failure to keep up may result in their child being rejected from the top universities that will make his or her career and lead to success in life.

In public schools, English classes focus too much on grammar rules rather than the ability to communicate. The way English is taught in *hakwons* is better but not without problems. Parents constantly demand "level ups" into higher classes to show that their child has made progress, and get them into a more difficult level. *Hakwon* owners, fearful of defections, are often happy to massage results in order to oblige. Consequently, parents feel better, children feel relieved (since failing to progress would bring incessant parental nagging), and owners keep their revenue—but true improvement will not have necessarily occurred.

In most subjects, Korean students score among the best in the world. In 2010, the OECD's Program for International Student Assessment (PISA) ranked Korean children the best in mathematics and reading among all member countries. However, this achievement comes so inefficiently that "kids get the result . . . by working for twice as long and having twice as much money spent," in the words of Professor Chang. As a counterexample, he cites Finland whose youngsters also regularly top PISA rankings but are still able to play, socialize, and generally enjoy their childhoods. If the quality of education could be improved and children were able to "study smart, not hard," and get enough sleep, this country could be much more productive, not to mention happier.

Thus, a cost comes with devoting excessive amounts of time and money to the study of English. Korean and English are, as anyone who has the slightest knowledge of both will admit, about as different as two languages can be. An hour spent by a Korean on the study of Chinese or Japanese will yield greater progress than an hour spent on English, other things being equal. Now that China has overtaken the United States to become South Korea's number one trading partner, reducing some of the focus from English in favor of Mandarin may make sense.

The push for English fluency is also a factor in social inequality. After the Korean War, this country basically started over. There existed no real entrenched elite like the old *yangban*, and in the 1960s and

1970s, President Park Chung-hee tried to ensure that the benefits of growth were spread around. In recent years, though, a neo-*yangban* class has started to form. This group can be defined as a social elite whose status is based not on lineage but on a self-reinforcing cycle of better education and greater wealth. From roughly the 1980s onwards, those who had studied hard, attended "SKY"—Seoul National, Korea, and Yonsei Universities—and got the best jobs began to pull away from the rest. Having more money, they were able to help their own children pull ahead too, through costly private education. This has been especially the case with English education. Top scores on English proficiency tests are one of the most important factors in university and job applications, and so those with enough money will hire native English speaking tutors or send their children to schools in the United States or Canada to perfect their English.

The heartland of this new elite is the Gangnam area of Seoul. Children from Gangnam and, increasingly, an area of western Seoul called Mokdong have great advantages over others. The government developed these areas by building good schools there, which encouraged parents to move into the newly built apartments nearby. Over time, competition for places was resolved by free-market economics. Apartment prices rose so much that the ability to attend those good schools depended upon how much money one's parents had. The best private tutors and *hakwons* then followed the money to Gangnam and Mokdong. The result is that by 2005, a high school graduate from Gangnam was almost ten times more likely to be accepted by Seoul National University than one from the north Seoul district of Mapo—an area not even considered especially disadvantaged.

Gangnam is a symbol for the excesses of modern South Korea. It is the center not only of English mania but also of competitiveness, not to mention conspicuous consumption. Young women in parts of Gangnam such as Cheongdam-dong or Apgujong-dong carry US$2,000 handbags as a matter of course. Young people expect to go to a SKY university, or increasingly, an American Ivy League school, and if they fail, they and their parents are likely to be sorely disappointed. Tellingly, Gangnam also contains 70 percent of Seoul's plastic surgery clinics but only 5.5 percent of its population.

English Teachers as a Necessary Evil

The largest minority group in South Korea is the Chinese. However, probably the most noticeable foreigners are native English teachers from countries like the United States and Canada, so much so that any Westerner in Korea will at some time be asked, "Where are you teaching?" rather than "What brings you here?" English teachers are in such demand that 15,000 visas for English teachers were issued in 2006, and this probably represents a small fraction of the actual number who come. Many overseas Koreans (who have special visas), foreign husbands or wives of Koreans, and pure illegals on tourist visas also teach English here.

Foreign English teachers have a relationship with Korean society that is strangely reminiscent of the *musok-in*, or shaman. When asked about foreign English teachers, the average Korean will express a negative opinion—and yet at the same time, they are well paid and always in demand, just like the *musok-in*. But much depends, sadly, on the ethnic background of the teacher. For unsophisticated people, a white face equals English, and blue-eyed, blond-haired young white women are in particularly high demand for lessons. This author's first job in Seoul was at a *hakwon*, the owner of which had an unofficial policy of hiring only white people. The owner explained at the time, "I know it's stupid, but that's what the parents want."

Of course, the foreign teachers influence how Korean people think about their native countries through their performance in the classroom and behavior outside of it. Many who remember a good teacher will have fond feelings when a sports team from their ex-teacher's home city appears on television. However, there have been numerous scandals too. The number of young male English teachers is large, and as a group they do all the things that young men like to do when they go abroad. This behavior, combined with sensationalism in the media and old-school ethnic nationalism, has produced a widespread belief that people from Western countries are libertines.

One website, called English Spectrum, was at the center of a controversy regarding messages on its forum, which featured content written by male English teachers who claimed (among other things) that Korean women were easy to sleep with. Defensive nationalism reared its head, and an online group called Anti-English Spectrum was formed. AES operated a website and forum dedicated to exposing "bad foreign teachers." Some of its members have been known to stalk English teachers and harass them in public.

The mainstream media contributes to this atmosphere. For example, when teaching quality is found to be poor, the media will set off on an anti–foreign teacher crusade rather than blame the *hakwons*. Newspaper articles frequently associate foreign English teachers with criminal behavior such as drug dealing, despite the fact that as a group, they display no greater level of criminality than the rest of society. One English-teaching acquaintance of the author was even tricked into appearing in what he thought was a TV drama but which actually turned out to be a fake documentary. While following a supposed script, he was filmed encouraging underage-looking girls to drink beer, and thus unwittingly contributed to the demonization of his profession.

Konglish

An abundance of loanwords and English-like words have entered the Korean language because of South Korea's English obsession. Konglish echoes the kind of semi-English vocabulary that developed in Japan (where people say "pasocon" for "personal computer"), and many examples of it are cute or amusing. For example, In South Korea, a "mama-boi" (mama's boy or mummy's boy) who spots another child cheating on a test may tell him to stop "cunning." Cunning here is used as a verb. "Window shopping" is known as "eye shopping;" "touchy-feely" people are described as having a lot of "skinship"; and a woman with a large bosom may be considered "glamour style".

It would surely disappoint the British fashion company Burberry to know that public flashers in South Korea have become known as "Burberry men," on account of the company's famed long coats, which are considered to be particularly appropriate for such activity. Some companies benefit from Konglish by employing it in their advertising campaigns. Memorable examples from recent ad campaigns are "well-being," used to denote any supposedly healthy product, and "S-line," to describe the shape of an attractive woman's body.

There are literally thousands of foreign, mostly English, loanwords circulating in South Korea. If the two Koreas ever do unify, North Koreans will no doubt be mystified by how their mutual language has changed and is now spoken in the South. North Koreans have steadfastly maintained their original vocabulary. For instance, *son-gicheok* means "hand indication" and can be used to make a sound on a door before one enters the room. South Koreans simply call this a "knock."

PART FOUR

In the Hours Not Spent Working

Chapter 19

Living Space: From *Hanok* to Apartment Houses and Back Again

Visitors to South Korea often remark on the unattractiveness of the big cookie-cutter apartment buildings that blanket the capital and other major cities, and seem to bear little relation to their surroundings. These buildings arose from two factors: first, this is a small, mountainous country with a large population in its capital, and high-rise dwellings make the most efficient use of available land; and second, postwar economic development and urbanization occurred at such a rapid pace that city planning and aesthetics were matters of little concern to the authorities of the time.

Yet Korea does have a strong legacy of traditional residential architecture, in the form of the *hanok*, the classic Korean home. At the turn of the millennium, the *hanok* was considered a thing of the past that had no place in Korea's future—it was perhaps even "chonseureopda" ("country style"), or outmoded. Increasingly, though, South Koreans are seeking connections with their traditional culture. They are demanding greater sustainability and beauty in addition to functionality in the objects that fill their daily lives, and as they do some are discovering that all of these can be found in modernized versions of the houses they turned their backs on years ago.

The *Hanok* and *Pungsu-jiri*
What is a *hanok*? In the words of architect and modern *hanok*

specialist Hwang Doo-jin, it is a style of house that is the "result of a very long-term process in which Korean nature and Korean culture worked together" to develop a habitation suitable for people to live in. Built from natural materials such as wood, clay, and stone, its dimensions will vary depending upon its location. *Hanoks* in the north of the peninsula, where the climate is colder, tend to be constructed in a closed square shape, while those in the south are typically based on a more open rectangular shape. Ideally, in either case, the *hanok* would be positioned facing a river, and with a mountain to the back, in accordance with a geomantic principle known as *baesanimsu*.

The importance of correct house location was first promulgated in Korea by a monk named Doseon (827–898) as part of his geomantic philosophy called *pungsu-jiri*. *Jiri* simply means "geography," but *pungsu* will probably resonate most with Westerners—it translates as "feng shui," the Chinese art of positioning physical objects in a way that promotes the correct flow of *qi* (*gi* in Korean). Doseon's system is influenced by Chinese feng shui but focuses on macro-scale features: he was more concerned with the location of houses, communities, and even the *gi* of the whole nation in relation to geographical features like mountains and rivers. Chinese feng shui is concerned with the location of houses but also with the placement of the objects within them. *Pungsu-jiri* was so influential, it inspired a rebellion against the Koryo dynasty: in the late 1120s and early 1130s, a monk named Myocheong attempted to overthrow the government and establish a new state with Pyongyang as its capital, at least in part because he believed Pyongyang a more auspicious location than Kaesong, the city in which the Koryo court was based.

In a *hanok*, slatted windows and doors are covered with *hanji*, a type of mulberry paper treated in a way that renders it waterproof, yet breathable. *Hanji* panes give the *hanok* a sense of natural light and aeration. The *hanok's* roof, the *cheoma*, has a curved edge, the length of which will vary according to the need to allow in light and heat. Wealthy *yangban hanok* owners had roofs covered with clay tiles known as *giwa*, while poorer people had to make do with thatch. *Yangban* also liked to situate their houses on high ground. They were able to look down, literally, on the tenant farmers who served them, and on their smaller, more humbly constructed homes.

The typical *hanok* of the past reflected Confucian social mores. There were separate rooms for the men and women of the house. These were known as the *sarangchae* and *anchae*, respectively, the former being a place in which the gentleman scholar could receive guests, while the ladies kept to themselves in the latter. Even so, there are regional variations on this theme. The province of Gyeongsang-do, which is known to this day for its conservatism, adhered to strict division, while in the more liberal Jeolla-do Province one can find *hanoks* with *sarangchae* provided for women to entertain their own friends.

Encroaching Modernism

The twentieth century saw vast changes in Korean residential architecture. As early as the Japanese colonial period, apartment buildings were being constructed in areas of Seoul like Sindang-dong and Jangchung-dong. These buildings were intended mainly for Japanese workers, who had been sent over to participate in transforming Korea into a Japanese industrial powerhouse that would aid the island state in its plans to extend its dominance to Manchuria and beyond. These structures were typically two or three stories in height, and contained between fifty and seventy units. Later, buildings available for general lease to Koreans as well as Japanese were erected, such as the Yurim Toyota Apartments at Chungjeongro (1932).

The year 1942 saw the first Korean-built apartments, in the northern Seoul district of Hyehwa. However, not until the Park Chung-hee era of rapid economic development that begun in the early 1960s did apartment living really take off, with the completion of the Mapo Apartments in 1964, in the Dohwa-dong area of Mapo, Seoul. This was the very first large residential complex of the sort that millions now live in.

As the population of Seoul swelled—half the country's population now lives in or around the capital—the *hanok* became less and less viable. New residents of Seoul needed cheap housing, and that meant building high, stacking their homes on top of each other.

The spirit of the times was growth at any cost, which meant that no emphasis was placed on aesthetics. Apartment blocks were built as quickly and cheaply as possible, with no design flourishes. Planning was not much of a concern, either: buildings were erected in any available space, regardless of the effect they might have on the surrounding area. People "simply needed a space to live in," according to Mr. Hwang.

"I don't one-hundred-percent denounce apartment living, because we had our reasons to do it," he adds. Like many of the changes in Korean society of the past half-century that created unwelcome side effects, apartment living was a practical step on the road to economic take-off. One could compare it to the building of endless rows of two-up two-down terrace houses found in mill towns all over Northern England, which, though most seem ugly today, served a particular purpose at that time.

Apartments are also supremely convenient. Many say *hanoks* are difficult to keep warm compared to apartments. And while maintaining a *hanok* takes a great deal of effort, if one lives in an apartment, window cleaning, security, external repairs, and so on are no longer one's own responsibility. South Koreans pay a *gualli-bi*—a management fee—to the apartment complex's maintenance firm every month, and in return all of these things are taken care of. For those working 51.6 hours per week (plus uncredited overtime), as the average person did in 1970, this is entirely understandable.

Many believe that this apartment culture has resulted in increased alienation. People no longer live in true communities, and the enclosed isolation of this living space causes a disconnect from nature and one's neighbors. On the other hand, one might argue equally that apartment alienation is a reflection of the atomized, lonely reality of the large industrial city, where citizens working all day long in an office or a factory lack the energy and inclination to develop any neighborhood spirit in the little free time they have.

The End of the *Hanok*?

Hanoks used to exist in large numbers throughout all towns and cities, but industrialization and population growth meant that vast swathes of *hanoks* were knocked down to be replaced by apartment buildings and factories from the 1960s onwards. By some estimates, the number of *hanoks* nationwide declined from over a million to just ten thousand by the year 2000. People began to see these traditional houses as relics, quaint throwbacks to old Korea, and in a country where anything old was considered undesirable, the *hanoks* had to go. By the 1980s, architecture students like the young Mr. Hwang continued to learn about *hanoks*, but never expected to work with them. *Hanoks* were regarded as anachronistic and inconvenient, especially in comparison to apartments.

The apartment has thus become the default residence in South Korea. Even in the countryside, one sees giant, gray concrete blocks, neatly divided into units, offering convenience for their residents but utter incongruity and even ugliness for their surroundings. Giant construction companies that specialize in such brutally generic structures are among the largest firms in South Korea, and have managed to use their influence to propagate the view that the apartment is the only viable solution for living space.

However, there is a growing glimmer of hope. Since around the turn of the millennium, some members of society have started, albeit slowly, to shift their priority from hyper-growth functionality to quality of life. This is evidenced in a number of areas: greater interest in art and public beautification, an increased environmental awareness, the growth of cultural industries, and stronger demand for leisure time, to name a few. Furthermore, people are now starting to rediscover the past.

As we saw in chapter 12, Koreans have felt a sense of shame over their history, and this makes them prefer to look forward rather than backward. However, the elite classes (both financial and cultural) are now beginning to find value in the historic. This emerging interest has touched a number of areas: old Korean music, traditional *hanbok* clothing, and furniture, to name a few. In the case of *hanok*, the trend for nostalgia has led to the construction of new *hanoks* and the preservation of old ones. Whereas the elite once sought to trade in their *hanoks* for apartments, now they are leading a trend in the opposite direction.

Hanoks have a great many advantages with regard to twenty-first century concerns such as energy consumption and sustainability. Since *hanoks* are constructed from basic materials like wood and stone, they have less environmental impact than cement (producing a ton of cement causes the release of almost a ton of carbon dioxide, several kilograms of nitrous oxide, and particulate emissions). Due to simple features like the elongated, overhanging roof, they naturally draw in heat in the winter, when the sun is low, and provide shade in the summer, when the sun is high. This eco-friendliness is winning the *hanok* new admirers.

Purists and Progressives

Of course, concerns about cost, practicality, limited land for building, and economic realities mean that Koreans will never completely turn against apartment living. However, demand is growing for the construction of "modernized" *hanoks*. Because of the cost of land, this option is available only to the wealthy at present, but there are plans for generic *hanoks* and *hanok* complexes, which would naturally reduce prices somewhat. Mr. Hwang has even proposed *hanoks* with basements and multiple stories to meet the challenge of high population density. They would be constructed from traditional materials, but in a more mass-produced way. Both concepts are new, representing a kind of hybrid of traditional Korean and modern urban living, and both have skeptics. For example, traditionalists do not like the sound of a multistory *hanok*, and others question its energy efficiency.

The modernized *hanok* generally features the kind of conveniences found in apartments or Western homes, such as bathroom suites and air conditioning. Some even make use of concrete as a building material. While such innovations are drawing back those who dismissed *hanoks* in the past, they are also causing a divide between so-called progressives and purists, particularly in the historic Seoul neighborhood of Bukchon.

Bukchon, located near the fashionably leafy district of Samcheong-dong and in the vicinity of the presidential mansion, has had a history of changing fortunes. Originally a *yangban* residential district, it has spent much of the modern era as an overlooked, depressed neighborhood for the poor, with property values below those found in other districts. However, in 1999, the government instituted a policy of preservation in which those who invested in the redevelopment of *hanoks* received generous subsidies. This has drawn in a new breed of *hanok* owner. Furthermore, the government's policy coincided with the development of the modern *hanok*, and, as a consequence, Bukchon has undergone rapid gentrification. Many old homes were simply knocked down rather than renovated and were replaced with large, modernized (and subsidized) super-*hanoks*. Bukchon is now a nouveau riche area that attracts legions of foreign tourists armed with DSLR cameras.

The Bukchon purists argue that since that district is virtually the only place left in Seoul with beautiful, traditional-style *hanoks*, it ought to be maintained in a traditional way, rather than exposed to hybridization. Several of the strongest proponents of this view are in fact Westerners, long-term residents of Korea who bought their *hanoks* for bargain-basement prices back in the days when Koreans did not want them. The debate has split local opinion, with some voicing support and finding it sad that it apparently falls to foreigners to protect Korean heritage. Others consider the purist campaign romanticist meddling over houses too "inconvenient" for modern living.

The Future of Seoul?

As Korean society begins to accept the need for reduced consumption of energy and resources, a contradiction is becoming apparent. "There is no sense in creating an eco-friendly society if people have to commute for two hours every day," generating considerable emissions of greenhouse gases, according to Mr. Hwang. It is clear that the Seoul megalopolis, a sprawling octopus of a city, occupies too much space. The tendency of the capital since industrialization has been to suck in people from other areas and then expand outwards, overtaking surrounding cities and subsuming them in the greater Seoul conurbation.

Yet, while there are blocks of giant apartment buildings, it is worth noting that the average number of stories in smaller Seoul buildings is just 2.5, much lower than in Paris or New York, for instance. Commercial buildings, such as those used for shops, are typically low-rise. If the average number of stories could be doubled, through mixed-use buildings of around five or six stories that feature shops on the ground floor, offices in the middle, and residential units on top—as is the case in Paris—a great deal of space could be saved. This would reduce the need for giant apartment blocks and allow for more urban *hanoks*, parks, and so on. The future of Seoul could arguably be smaller, yet taller, and greener.

As some are now realizing, developing other areas of the country in order to create a more geographically balanced nation would make a great deal of sense. Without a concerted effort to limit the growth of Seoul, South Korea risks becoming a Singapore-style city-state with tens of thousands of square miles of countryside attached, give or take Busan and a handful of other cities. Educational, business, and administrative capacity is concentrated inordinately on Seoul. One could say that Seoul has double the clout in South Korea that London has in England. This imbalance is wasteful and creates excessive competition for space, excessive property prices, and excessive commutes and traffic jams, which reduce productivity. And with armed-to-the-hilt North Korea about a marathon run's distance from Seoul, there is also a slight chance that it could be catastrophic. Though achieving any meaningful rebalancing would be a massive political challenge, it would certainly be worth a try.

Chapter 20

Four Seasons at the Dinner Table

Whenever he goes abroad, complains one member of the National Assembly, all people ever want to discuss besides North Korea is dog meat. Korean food is undoubtedly as misunderstood and underappreciated as its country of origin. Yet Korean cuisine is rich and varied beyond what one might expect from the peninsula's small geographical area, and its most celebrated dishes easily become addictive to those who accustom themselves to the strong and sometimes fiery flavors.

The reputation for spiciness is perhaps overstated, however. Dishes like *dakdoritang* (a kind of chicken soup with vegetables) and *kimchi jjigae* (kimchi stew) are indeed on the hot side, but traditionally, Korean cooks use only one particular spice for heat: red pepper. More important to the Korean culinary experience is the practice of fermentation. No Korean kitchen will be without *gochujang, doenjang* and *ganjang*—three fermented condiments that are to be found in a vast range of meat, seafood, and vegetable dishes. Similarly, Korea's most famous representative food—kimchi—is a fermented vegetable. This method of preserving food has been part of Korean cuisine for millennia, and foods based on fermentation are as ubiquitous as rice, the staple food of Korea that comes with most meals.

Foundations
The principle of balance is also fundamental, and, accordingly, the Korean meal is never about one single dish or one single flavor. The

proper culinary experience derives from multiple dishes that offer harmony in respect to each other. Thus, a meal will include various separate platters and bowls containing vegetables, meats, and soups, for instance, each offering variety and contrast in temperature, spiciness, saltiness, and so on. At a particularly lavish meal, the number of *banchan*—side dishes—may go into double figures.

According to Han Young-yong, a restaurateur, food columnist, and author from Jeolla (the province considered to be the home of the best cooks), there should also be "four seasons at the dinner table." Korea's climate is variable: cold and crisp in the winter, hot and humid in the summer, and warm and clear in between. The average temperature in Seoul during January reaches well below zero degrees centigrade. The types of vegetables that can be grown naturally vary by season, so then how is a balance to be achieved? The answer is, through fermentation. Vegetables like spinach, eggplant, and bean sprouts have long been enjoyed in this way. Mr. Han points out that fermented food is even suggested in Korea's creation myth. Ungnyeo, a bear who became a woman after remaining in a cave for a hundred days, subsisted for the entire period on cloves of garlic and mugwort given to her by Hwanung, who later became the father of her child, Dangun—the legendary founder of Korea. In order to last for such a long period of time, the garlic must have been fermented, implying that the concept of preservation by fermenting would have existed at the time of the story's creation, and probably predated it. Perhaps the taste for seasonal balance stems from this tradition born of necessity.

Kimchi

The most famous of such fermented foods in Korean cuisine is undoubtedly *kimchi*. This pickled vegetable dish is probably the most recognizably Korean thing in existence. Indeed, *kimchi* has become a byword for Korea in itself, to the point where cliché-loving outsiders refer to the country as *Kimchi*-land. And many Koreans themselves will tell you that a meal not accompanied by *kimchi* simply feels wrong. If one were to stop ten people on the streets of Seoul and ask, "What can Korean people not live without?" probably at least seven would instantly respond, "Kimchi." When going on business trips, executives commonly take boxes of *kimchi* and noodles with them, in order to avoid the relatively disappointing fare on offer at the restaurant in their five-star hotel.

The most common *kimchi* is spicy cabbage, which is instantly recognizable through its pungent aroma and red coloring, imparted by red pepper. Yet this is only one of the roughly two hundred varieties of pickled vegetables that are labeled *kimchi*. *Nabak kimchi*, for instance, a mixture of radish and cabbage allowed to ferment in red pepper, garlic, and onions, comes in water and is thus very refreshing. Another type is *oi sobaeki kimchi*, cucumbers stuffed with seasonings, and left to ferment for one or two days. As with many fermented foods, with *kimchi* it is a case of "try it once and hate it, try it ten times and love it forever." At first, Korean parents may have to force their children to eat kimchi, but once the taste for it develops, a lifelong passion is born. Thus, even in pizza restaurants, it seems natural to Koreans to offer pickled Western vegetables as an accompanying side dish.

When non-Koreans express distaste for *kimchi*, often it is because of the spiciness of some of the most popular varieties. Classic cabbage *kimchi* is smothered in *gochujang*, a red-pepper based condiment, before it is left to age in large stone pots. Many varieties of kimchi are similarly peppered. However, other kinds are much lighter in flavor. *Yeolmu mul kimchi* (water radish kimchi), for instance, is very mild, and considered most suitable for the hot summer months.

Jang

Of the three fermented condiments on which Korean cuisine relies, *gochujang*—a mixture of red pepper, fermented soybean paste, and salt—is the one most responsible for giving Korean food its spicy reputation. However, seen through the lens of this country's long history, it is a relatively recent invention. Its base, red pepper, was brought over by Japanese invaders in the period known as the Imjin Waeran, the attempted conquest that took place between 1592 and 1598. According to Mr. Han, it was the peasant class that popularized its use: the brutally cold Korean winters could be very hard on the poor, who found the heating effect provided by this foreign import so attractive that, soon after its introduction, red pepper was being cultivated by everyone and used in every meal. Tobacco was also introduced to Korea during the Japanese invasion. By the time Westerners began settling in Korea in the late nineteenth century, Korean food was spicy and majority of the population smoked pipes.

The fermented soybean paste used in making *gochujang* is important in itself. Known as *doenjang*, this condiment is the base for a number of popular dishes, such as a brothy soup called *doenjang jjigae*. *Doenjang jjigae*, which is somewhat similar to Japanese miso (Korean chefs claim that the latter was originally inspired by the former) can be eaten with rice as a meal in itself or found as an accompaniment to more complex meals, such as the so-called Korean barbecue so beloved by patrons of Koreatown restaurants in the United States. For many, including this author, Korean-style barbecued pork or beef simply does not taste the same without a bowl of *doenjang jjigae*—and of course, a side dish of *kimchi*.

Last is *ganjang*, essentially a kind of soy sauce and also made from fermented soybeans, which is used as a base for dishes like *jjimdak*, a braised chicken stew with noodles and vegetables. *Ganjang* is a product of the same process that produces *doenjang*. Soybeans are boiled and ground and then compressed into blocks known as *meju*. *Meju* are allowed to dry for a week and then fermented in brine in a pot. This produces a liquid and a solid residue; the former is *ganjang*, and the latter *doenjang*.

Besides these three major condiments and red pepper, a variety of other condiments, herbs, and seasonings are found in Korean kitchens. Sesame oil can be used as an ingredient in cooking but also as a dip for barbecued meats. Garlic is very common in the preparation of various types of kimchi as well as more complex dishes like stews. Ginseng is occasionally used in foods considered beneficial to health, such as samgyetang, a chicken soup. Ginger is also sometimes used in marinades and in the making of refreshing after-meal drinks, such as *sujeonggwa*, which also features cinnamon. Sugar is found in some *gochujang*-based dishes (such as *dakdoritang*), tempering the spicy flavor, and salt is used in the cooking process to bring out the flavor in most recipes but not placed in a shaker on the table.

Meats

Among non-Koreans, barbecued meats such as *galbi* (pork or beef ribs) and *samgyeopsal*, are the most popular Korean dishes. A charcoal grill at the center of the table is used to cook the meat, which can then be wrapped in lettuce leaves along with *ssamjang*, a sauce based on a mixture of *gochujang* and *doenjang*. An optional bowl of rice—the staple that goes with just about anything—can provide for a more filling experience if desired.

One of the best parts of this kind of meal is the collective experience that it provides. Except perhaps for the rice and sauces, everything is placed in the middle of the table. The meat, the *doenjang jjigae*, and lettuce leaves, for instance, are all communal, as are the assorted bowls and plates of *kimchi*. Many non-Koreans find the fact that everyone can dip their spoon into the same bowl of soup distasteful. However, those who can overcome this feeling may be rewarded with a sense of greater closeness, from participation in Korea's culture of sharing.

Surprisingly, Korean barbecue dishes such as *bulgogi* bear strong foreign influence. During the Shilla and Koryo dynasties (668 onwards), Buddhism held sway, and the prevalence of Buddhist ethics resulted in a reduction in the consumption of meat. It was not until the Mongol invasions (1231–1270) that grilled meats came back into fashion, due to the marauding northerners' more red-blooded culinary tastes. *Mandu*, a kind of meat or vegetable-stuffed dumpling, is also a Mongolian import. Throughout Central Asia and beyond, cousins of this dish with similar names—*manti*, for instance, which can be found as far west as Turkey and Armenia—testify to the astonishingly widespread influence of the khans.

Mandu, barbecued meat, and red pepper are far from alone as examples of political developments changing Korean food culture. The practices of individual rulers sometimes also had a powerful effect. King Yeongjo, the son of King Sukjeong and his concubine—a former water maid—had extremely spartan tastes. To honor his mother's humble background, he would eat only three *banchan* (side dishes) with his meal, and rarely consumed meat. His asceticism set off a period of austerity in the national diet, for if the king himself could limit himself to three *banchan*, there was no reason for anyone else to consume more. Thankfully, King Yeongjo's influence over Korean cuisine has since diminished.

Seafood

Surrounded by water, Korea is a paradise for seafood enthusiasts. Though the squeamish will probably not want to try *san-nakji* (live octopus), there is a wide variety of fish dishes, such as *hwai* (which is comparable with sashimi), clams and shrimp from the extensive mudflats found especially on the west coast, eel, and grilled mackerel, which can be enjoyed by anyone. Grilled mackerel is a particular favorite among patrons of *pojang macha* (street tent bars) in the Yeouido financial district, who like to wash it down with *soju* after a long day's work. A visit to a fish market in seaside cities such as Busan or Sokcho ensures the freshest and finest seafood. There, one may choose a live fish from a vendor's stall and watch as an *ajumma* (middle-aged woman) grabs it and expertly lines it up on the chopping block, severs its bewildered head, guts and slices its body, wraps it up and then puts it in a bag—a feat completed even before the unfortunate creature's gills have stopped ventilating.

Lee Jin-ho is a young, European-style chef who, despite being just in his twenties, has his own segment on a breakfast TV show as well as magazine columns on cuisine. Lee speaks fondly of the surprising diversity of seafood available in Korea. On a visit to a coastal town named Uljin, he recounts, he bought a fish that was identified only as *japeo*—which simply means "caught fish"—because no one knew what it was. Yet, "it was so great," he enthuses. "It tasted as good as monkfish."

Most visitors would probably fail to muster the same enthusiasm for *hongeo*, a fermented fish from Jeolla Province that tastes strongly of ammonia. Just one piece is enough to completely overwhelm one's nostrils, mouth, sinuses, and tear ducts. Of all the different kinds of food on offer in this country, *hongeo* has to be the most extreme: "if you enjoy it," you may well be told, "we should just give you a Korean passport."

Also Try These

Chicken dishes are plentiful, too. One personal favorite of the author is *dakgalbi*, a spicy chicken dish served in a hot pan with vegetables such as onions, cabbage, and sweet potatoes and a sauce based on *gochujang*. This is just one of several chicken casserole–type recipes. The one considered most hearty is *samgyetang*, in which a whole chicken is stuffed with rice and cooked with ginseng in a broth. Served piping hot, *samgyetang* is considered best on *boknal* days (the height of summer). Koreans tend to like sweating their heat out, hence their fondness for this tradition as well as their love of hot springs and saunas. One can observe Koreans eating piping-hot *samgyetang* in the sweltering heat and exclaiming, "Ah, shiwon-hae!" ("Refreshing!"), much to the puzzlement of foreigners who have not been in Korea very long.

There are also fusion dishes, such as *budae jjigae*. *Budae* means "armed forces," and the dish comes from the sad days when the only people with enough good food to eat seemed to be the American soldiers stationed around the country. It is a *gochujang*-based stew but can contain such incongruous GI leftovers as spam and macaroni, and, though South Koreans are now thankfully light years beyond needing to eat such an odd mixture, they have acquired a taste for it. In fact, Spam—an object of ridicule in the West due to its cheapness and association with Monty Python sketches—is so well regarded in South Korea that people give special gift-wrapped boxes of it to friends on national holidays.

Some of the best Korean dining experiences can be found at the cheapest end of the market. An entire nationwide street-food culture is based on little vans and kiosks that sell snacks like *ddeokbokki*, a simple dish of rice cake and *odeng* (a kind of fish cake) served in a *gochujang*-based sauce. *Ddeokbokki*, along with *dak-kkochi* (grilled chicken sticks) and sweeter treats like *hotteok*—a kind of pancake filled with sugary syrup—draws long lines of evening commuters looking for a quick bite to eat on their way home. Another common Korean snack is *kimbap*, which consists of rice and vegetables rolled up in seaweed. As a quick, filling bite for those in a hurry, this hand-rolled meal might be compared to the sandwich.

Bibimbap and the Problem of Recognition

According to Mr. Han, the food that sums up the Korean culinary experience most of all is *bibimbap*, a dish concocted of various vegetables of different colors, rice, meat (in some varieties), and *gochujang* for flavoring. The ingredients are laid out in neat piles within a single bowl, and the diner mixes them together himself with his spoon (the word *bibim* means "mixing"). It makes a good representative dish for Korean cuisine as it features a balance of spice, vegetables, and rice, and as such, it is the food most commonly chosen as in-flight food by airlines flying in and out of Korea.

Bibimbap tastes great, but within that bowl of mixed vegetables and rice may lie the reason for Korean cuisine's relative lack of worldwide fame in comparison to other Asian cuisines, such as Japanese, or Thai. Once the ingredients are mixed together in the bowl, bibimbap looks ordinary and unimpressive in its presentation. As Lee Jin-ho observes by way of example, compared to Japanese food, Korean food is not presented elegantly. "We don't know how to make food into a product," he argues. The result is that Korean food remains a niche in world cuisine, despite numerous government initiatives and even *bibimbap* advertisements being placed on a number of occasions in papers like the New York Times.

Lee Jin-ho continues: "'Food as art for the eye' is not a concept in Korea." While holding that Korean *doenjang jjigae* is the inspiration for Japanese miso soup, he feels frustrated that superior Japanese presentation skills have resulted in the latter becoming world famous, while the former remains unknown to the vast majority of non-Koreans. "Korea doesn't have a culture of serving yet. People just say, 'Hello, what would you like?' We don't appreciate that 50 percent of getting a Michelin star is about service and presentation. Even in the Zagat guide to **Seoul** (his emphasis), none of their top ten restaurants are for Korean food," he laments.

Lately, a few Korean chefs have begun addressing this problem. Edward Kwon (Kwon Young-min) is probably the most famous of these. He has enjoyed a career working in hotel restaurants in Seoul, Dubai, and San Francisco. He also presents a TV cooking show called *Yes, Chef!* based on the *Hell's Kitchen* series starring Gordon

Ramsay and has achieved a high profile in the United States, having cooked for former president George W. Bush. Kwon has made it his mission to further "the globalization of Korean food," describing his food as using Korean ingredients for "a flavor profile created with global techniques." His restaurants elevate the notion of service and presentation and will probably do more to promote Korean food worldwide than any number of government initiatives.

The Obligatory Section about Dog Meat

Yes, dog is part of traditional Korean cuisine. The fact is, though, that Korea is far from alone, with other Asian countries including China, Vietnam, and the Philippines being notable consumers of this controversial meat. All of these nations have a long history of cooking with dog meat and regard breeds raised for their flesh as entirely different to those raised as pets.

Typically, in Korea, dog is seen as something that old men eat once in a while. Rarely will you find a young man, or a woman of any age, who consumes it. People will tell you they had it a few times when they were children, with their parents telling them what this soft meat (which tastes a little like greasy beef) really was only after they finished their bowl.

The manner in which dogs are killed, however, can be very cruel. The old-school method, still used in the countryside, is to beat them to death, in order to flood the meat with adrenaline, which is believed to make it taste better. For this reason—as well as basic affection for man's best friend—many people will not touch the meat. It is unfortunate that one of Korea's least popular dishes sometimes seems to command the most attention, based entirely on the controversy it generates. Those who are wary of Korean cuisine due to the dog meat image should go to their nearest Korean restaurant and try some barbecued meat with *doenjang jjigae,* or a hearty bowl of *bibimbap.*

Chapter 21

Cinema: Boom, Bust, and Brilliance

The South Korean film industry is this country's greatest modern cultural achievement. On a domestic level, it is one of the few national cinemas that can challenge Hollywood, both creatively and financially. Western fans may be familiar with the likes of *Oldboy* (2003), a film famed for its violence and shock ending as much as its visual brilliance. However, the "extreme Asia" image that movie inadvertently helped to create belies a diversity of works in many genres that continue to impress audiences.

The Korean film industry underwent a transformation in the late 1990s, and its subsequent success came somewhat out of the blue. According to Kim Kkobbi, star of the 2009 low-budget breakthrough hit *Breathless*, the breadth of its output makes the question "What is Korean film?" impossible to answer, other than to punt with "It is film made in Korea." However, Korean cinema does have distinctive characteristics: a certain directness, a willingness to show violence and tragedy in a realistic manner, and a deep strain of melancholy based on *han*, for instance. These qualities contribute to the unexpected popularity of Korean cinema throughout Asia and beyond.

Censorship and Quotas

In the days of President Park Chung-hee, filmmaking was tightly restricted, particularly during the time of the Yushin Constitution in the 1970s. A policy of censorship blocked anything that might be considered politically or socially "edgy" in favor of run-of -the-mill action flicks and melodramas. Censorship applied to both domestic and international films. The author of a book on Argentine cinema was jailed at the time, on the grounds that since no Argentine films had ever been allowed in Korea, he must have been watching them illegally.

Censorship was only half of the problem, though. A quota system aimed at promoting the Korean film industry ended up backfiring and promoting its decline. Distributors wishing to import one foreign film were required to produce three domestic films in order to "offset" it. Accordingly, they did the rational thing and simply made the cheapest pictures they could in the quickest possible time. Typically, the foreign film was a big-budget American blockbuster, the kind of work that only served to reinforce the perception that there was no way that Korea could ever catch up.

This is not to say that there were not occasional masterpieces during the period. Critics single out eccentric filmmaker Kim Ki-young as arguably the greatest Korean director of the time. His film *Hanyeo* (*The Housemaid*, 1960) depicts a cold temptress seducing her married employer and doing it so well that audiences were known to yell, "Kill the bitch!" at the movie screen. Even during the darkest days of the 1970s, the likes of Kim and Ha Kil-jong, who studied at the UCLA Film School with Francis Ford Coppola, were able to produce respected films like *Iodo* (1977) and *March of Fools* (1975), respectively.

Democratization, and Opportunity from Crisis

The legacy of dictatorship could in some ways be regarded as a blessing in disguise for the generation of directors who came of age during the 1980s, the most notable being the likes of Park Chan-wook, and Bong Joon-ho. Darcy Paquet, an American film critic living in Seoul (and creator of Koreanfilm.org, an excellent English language resource for fans of Korean cinema), speaks of this group as like children without fathers, in the sense that they entered an industry that had been left in a near-dormant state and so were freed of overpowering influences. This allowed this new generation of directors to be guided almost completely by their own artistic sense. A certain amount of pent-up creativity was finally able to see the light of day in the 1990s, which helps explain the sudden explosion of great cinema that began later in the decade.

Many directors were also involved with and inspired by the 1980s democratization movement. Bong Joon-ho, the man behind *Memories of Murder* (2003) and the most popular Korean film of all time, *The Host* (2006), was arrested for political activities, according to Darcy Paquet. His films are full of mistrust for authority and frequently highlight subjects like police incompetence and brutality. It is no exaggeration to state that one of the great themes in modern Korean cinema is the authoritarian era, with President Park Chung-hee a common point of reference. Arguably the most entertaining Park-related film is also the most controversial: Im Sang-soo's *The President's Last Bang* (2005) deals with his assassination and portrayed him in a unflattering light, resulting in legal action from the Park family, and criticism from the conservative press. It is a tense and taut film, shot through with black humor.

The Asian financial crisis of 1997–1998 changed the nation's work culture and economic structure, and also had a major effect on Korean cinema. Prior to the collapse, *chaebol*, like Samsung and Daewoo, were the principal investors in Korean film. Their approach was hands on, to the extent that casting decisions would frequently be made by *chaebol* managers rather than film professionals, which naturally led to poor film-making more often than not. However, by 1997 the *chaebol* were losing interest in the industry. The crisis then made clear the need for them to get back to their core activities. Samsung and Daewoo began to pull out of film production, although ironically, the former's penultimate picture (the spy thriller *Shiri*) proved to be a huge hit in 1999, quickly repaying its $8.5 million budget and outselling *Titanic* in the domestic market.

In their place came a new breed of backers, venture capitalists who sought to invest passively, allowing talented directors the chance to work with minimal interference. This group benefited from virtually perfect timing, in that the economic crisis resolved itself swiftly. It was followed almost immediately by the Internet-led venture boom, which saw vast amounts of cheap money flooding the economy, supported by a government eager to promote smaller-scale entrepreneurialism.

South Koreans had always been great film fans, even in the days when it was restricted and censored. In the late 1960s, the average Korean went to the cinema six times per year. With the new era of freedom from both political interference and meddling investors, the venture capitalists realized that there were huge opportunities to make money from this undeveloped market. In South Korea in the late 1990s, Internet companies were not the only hot investments.

Some entrepreneurs capitalized on the combined Internet and Korean cinema mania by creating websites that allowed the general public to invest in new productions. One of the greatest Korean comedies, Kim Ji-woon's *The Foul King* (2000), which starred popular actor Song Kang-ho in his breakthrough leading role, raised 100 million won in this way. The 464 people who invested in it each ended up making a return of 97 percent. One site, Simmani.com, allowed investment rights to trade freely, like stocks. Thus, the value of one's participation in a film could rise or fall every day, depending upon factors like the changing star power of the leading actors.

The Golden Years

Early success bred greater enthusiasm from audiences and investors, creating a virtuous circle of creativity and commercial payoff. It was in this environment that *Oldboy*, a brilliant and extraordinarily dark production, which deals with themes like torture and incest and features the shocking on-screen demise of an octopus (or rather four, given that multiple takes were required to complete the scene), could become the fifth-highest grossing film of 2003 in Korea—and then go on to take another $15 million worldwide. Its star, Choi Min-sik, and director Park Chan-wook became hot properties on the international festival circuit, with the latter claiming the 2004 Grand Prix at Cannes and garnering rapturous praise from Quentin Tarantino.

A more mainstream hit was *My Sassy Girl* (2001), which starred model-turned-actress Jun Ji-hyun as a capricious yet charming character who makes life hell for her love interest, an engineering student played by Cha Tae-hyun. This film has proved such an enduring success that Chinese survey respondents chose it as one of "the ten things that come to mind when you think of Korea." *My Sassy Girl* even caught the eye of Hollywood and Bollywood producers, who ended up filming remakes, which were of course nowhere near as good as the original.

Other popular and brilliantly executed pictures of this golden era were Korean War epic *Taegukgi* (2004); *JSA* (2000), a more mainstream offering by a pre-*Oldboy* Park Chan-wook; gangster tale *Friend* (2001); the smash hit *The King and the Clown* (2005), homoerotically charged and set in the Joseon era; and— perhaps the most outstanding of all—*Memories of Murder* (2003), a dramatization of the true events surrounding a small town living in fear of a serial killer.

One of the best aspects of the period was the diversity of work being produced. The year 2002, for instance, saw the release of two outrageously raunchy sex comedies in the shape of *Sex is Zero* and *Wet Dreams* (both top-ten hits in the year-end charts); *Chihwaseon*, the beautifully-made tale of a tormented artist (another showcase for Choi Min-sik's talents); *Too Young To Die*, a surprisingly graphic romance between two retired people; *Public Enemy*, a straight-up action thriller; and the masterly Lee Chang-dong's *Oasis*, an emotive depiction of the relationship between a man of limited mental capacity and a woman afflicted by cerebral palsy (the latter played by the gifted Moon So-ri), which also reflects on society's attitudes towards the disabled.

This golden period saw the entry of a new word in the vocabularies of people across East Asia. The term *Hallyu*, or "Korean Wave," came into use to characterize the growing interest around the region in Korean films, music, and television shows. *Hallyu* is now a very general term and describes any cultural product from Korea that gains popularity elsewhere. In the cinema, the first major *Hallyu* success was probably *My Sassy Girl*. Its star Jun Ji-hyun is still very popular in China and even made it as far as Hollywood under the name Gianna Jun. Actor Bae Yong-joon was the greatest beneficiary of *Hallyu*: his star power in Japan is so strong—particularly among middle-aged women—that fans in one town erected a statue of him. He has earned a reported fortune of US$100 million, generated mainly on the back of his Japanese fan base.

The Bursting of the Bubble, and Creative Recovery

Unfortunately, the glory days of the early 2000s could not last. By 2005, the increasing popularity of Korean films around Asia, particularly in Japan, had led to inflated actor salaries and a focus on simply securing the most famous stars, rather than making good films. For instance, Jun Ji-hyun was hired for a number of weak star vehicles such as *Daisy* (2006). This phenomenon resulted in an overall decline in quality and an eventual backlash from the countries that had begun to look to Korea as a cultural innovator. Export earnings from films peaked at US$75 million in 2005, but collapsed to $24.5 million in 2006. By 2010, they were no greater than $14 million.

The popularity of Korean films in the domestic market began to tail off as well, with foreign films holding a market share of 53.4 percent as of 2010, compared to just 36.2 percent in 2006. This took the industry roughly back to where it was in 2001, when the boom was just getting started. According to Darcy Paquet, "the middle [was] falling out of the industry." Big hits like *Scandal Makers* (2008) and *Haeundae* (2009) still come along, but the average film struggles to recoup its investment.

The industry is learning from its mistakes, however, and is now going through a period of retrenchment. Big-name *Hallyu* movies are on the way out, and low budgets are seen as one way forward. In 2010, a film called *Daytime Drinking* won several awards despite being made by a first-time director who completed the whole project with just 10 million won (around US $10,000) borrowed from his grandmother. Another unexpected success was *Old Partner* (2009), a documentary film about a farmer and his cow, which 3 million people went to the movie theater to see.

The creative talents who built the original success story are still active. Park Chan-wook released in 2011 the first ever "cinema-standard" movie made using the Apple iPhone as the primary means of recording. Lee Chang-dong's most recent film, *Poetry* (2010), won he Best Screenplay prize at Cannes. Its lead actress, Yoon Jeong-hee, ook the 2011 Los Angeles Film Critics Award for Best Actress. Just one year previously, Kim Hye-ja won the same award for her role n *Mother* (2009), another highly-regarded work by Bong Joon-ho. Perhaps more important, a new generation of indie filmmakers is rising, the product of a surge in enrollment numbers in Korean film schools. Artistically, they sometimes reach the heights of the golden era, though their work is not yet generating significant revenue. For nstance, Yang Ik-jun's *Breathless*, in which Kim Kkobbi stars, won hirteen awards at international festivals.

Within Asia, Korean cinema continues to be held in high esteem egardless of the *Hallyu* bust. At the 2011 Asian Film Awards in Hong Kong, the prizes for best director, best actor, best supporting actress, and best screenplay all went to Korean talent. Korean actors are also ecognized further afield, especially on the European film festival circuit. Individual talents such as Jeon Do-yeon are well recognized in Europe; Miss Jeon took the Best Actress prize at Cannes in 2007 for ner tragic role in *Secret Sunshine* (2007), another Lee Chang-dong offering.

Why Korean Film?

The reason *Breathless* struck a chord with audiences, female lead Kim Kkobbi feels, is that it "touched people's essential feelings." The film features characters living through some of the worst imaginable family situations, yet at the same it provided something the audience could relate to "even if they didn't have such an experience" themselves. Yang Ik-jun, who wrote and directed the film and starred as the male lead, offers that the story was "five hundred million percent" inspired by his own life and experiences, adding that acting for him is a way of "han-puli"—releasing his *han*.

This truth applies to many contemporary Korean films. There is a directness about Korean cinema, a sense of realness, and emotionalism, which comes from directors and actors willing to truly convey feeling rather than cloak themselves in excessive sophistication. *Han* and *heung*, the sorrow and joy of life found in strong measure in this country, are very much part of the cinematic landscape too. This is true regardless of genre; even gangster epics like *Friend* (2001) register heavily in this regard. Emotionalism "is an aspect of Korean culture," says Darcy Paquet, and directors "don't shy away from emotional impact."

Sometimes the criticism is made that Korean film is too melodramatic, and certainly in less artistic hands this can be the case. Classic tear-jerking themes such as bereavement and lost love are often mined for maximum payoff. Melodrama helps explain the mass popularity throughout Asia of stars like Bae Yong-joon, and there is a particular tendency to portray male leads as highly emotional (while still masculine) when dealing with painful situations, a concept that has led women across East Asia to view Korean men as representing the height of attractiveness.

Among Western audiences, a subset of film fans like Korean cinema for rather different reasons. Directors like Park Chan-wook and Kim Ki-duk, though very different in style, have gained a reputation for so-called "extreme" film through their use of morally ambiguous characters, darker themes like murderous revenge, and very direct presentation of violence. For those jaded by the Hollywood fare of good guys and bad guys and victims who die cleanly and immediately with one gunshot, Extreme Korea provides a new kind of thrill. Director Yang Ik-jun goes so far as to say that Western fans "aren't really interested in Korea—they're interested in Park Chan-wook and Kim Ki-duk."

However, given the international praise heaped on his own film, his skepticism may be overstated. *Breathless* proved a hit with European fans, not for its use of violence (though it does have its share) but for its emotional core. The movie provides a "curiously good-hearted" story of "hard-boiled moral redemption," according to the British Film Institute, which made it their Film of the Month in March 2010.

Special Feature: Interview with Choi Min-sik

As the star of *Oldboy*, Choi Min-sik is the most recognizable face of Korean cinema in Europe and America. His portrayal of Oh Dae-su, a man imprisoned for fifteen years—apparently without reason—is a triumph of both physical and mental prowess. However, he has also portrayed a wide range of characters in a long list of some of Korea's best films, including *Failan* (2001) and *Chihwaseon* (2002). Here, he gives an exclusive interview about his work and motivations.

What did you think when you first saw the script and plot for Old-boy? *Did you imagine it could become such a phenomenon?*

I actually felt a certain freedom, due to its unique subject matter and format. In fact, I was more concerned there could be more un-favorable reactions from the audience than favorable ones... But to be honest, audience reaction isn't something I take into too much consideration when I'm involved in film creation, so it wasn't such a big burden. Because I was like a wolf—thirsty for characters, so to speak—at the time (and I still am), I was so glad that *Oldboy* came around. As for the wide disparity in reviews and reactions, I had ex-pected it somewhat.

Between the fight scenes and the legendary octopus scene, it looks like it must have been a very physically demanding film to make. What was the toughest part of making Oldboy?

Of course, there was a certain physical fatigue involved. But, as the film progressed to its conclusion, the satisfaction and pleasure I got from it were all the more palpable. For instance, let's assume I'm building a house in the style that I want. There will be trials and errors, and, of course, fatigue from physical labor. But as I can feel the house getting close to completion as time goes by, that physi-cal fatigue soon turns into happiness. The physical hardship I felt in this film was nothing more than the sweat of happiness. I did agonize over one thing, however, and that was the character of Oh Dae-su himself. The portrait and character of a man who had been impris-oned for fifteen years while not even knowing why... I could only rely one hundred percent on my imagination. The situation couldn't be analyzed according to any basis in reality. But in the end, since such a situation wasn't possible in real life, it allowed me freedom to delve in creating the part.

Why do you think Oldboy *has become such a success among Western film fans? And are you glad that the planned U.S. remake seems to have been canceled?*

I feel *Oldboy* had a very philosophical and classical subject matter, which also meshed well with its commercial film style, allowing it to communicate effectively with audiences in the West as well as in the East. Some may say they are sometimes uncomfortable with director Park Chan-wook's cinematic style, but I find it very refreshing. I also value highly the fact that he always tries to extricate himself from falling into routine—or from going through the motions. Although I'm not too thrilled about remakes in general, I was also curious [about the proposed remake]. It would have been interesting to see the difference in interpretation and expression. So in one way, I'm somewhat disappointed it didn't happen.

Which of your films is your personal favorite?

Because I've always thought deeply about it before deciding to take on any film I became a part of, I have a great deal of affection for all of them, regardless of whether they were commercially successful or not. However, smoothness of communication with the director is important when working on a film: *Oldboy* and *Failan* can be considered ideal, in terms of that communication.

And who have you most enjoyed working with (any particular actors, directors)?

Ryoo Seung-beom of *Crying Fist* (2005)—shall I say, an uncut gem? I believe some of the most important qualities in an actor are an earnest and sincere approach to work and innocence in character, as well as uninhibited ways of thinking, that are yet to be tamed. I can say that he is someone who has all these qualities. I'm looking forward to seeing what he'll be like in the future, compared to how he is now. As for directors, it's none other than Park Chan-wook. He's an artist. I learn a lot when I work with him.

Your acting has a great deal of range, from the tormented artist in Chihwaseon *to a low-life gangster in* Failan. *What do you look for in a role, and is there any type of character you'd like to tackle that you haven't had the chance to try yet?*

First and foremost, when I consider whether to take on a given film, I see if its cinematic world convinces me, regardless of its genre—such as if I am instantly mesmerized by the script. Then I consider which directors create such attractive worlds. It wouldn't matter if the script was the best ever, if the director's mindset was not clear-cut. Other considerations include the "presence" of the characters, in both main and supporting roles, along with how much the film would contribute to the world of films in general... [As for which characters I would like to try,] All characters that exist, be they fictional or real.

Can you tell me about the project you are working on now?

Director Yoon Jong-bin's *War on Crime* [working title] will start shooting in April [2011]. It's a powerful human drama with many lessons, involving an ordinary family man working as a customs officer who uncovers a smuggling operation. [*War on Crime* was released in January 2012.]

Who do you think are the best actors and directors working in Korea?

All directors and actors in Korea who go about their work with sincerity and earnestness, I believe, are the best.

Why do you think this country is particularly strong at the art of cinema?

Koreans have an artistic character that comes from our history. Even in the midst of war and political chaos, Koreans have been a people who supported and encouraged each other through their culture, enjoying entertainment, humor, and satire in their daily lives. These elements resist political and ideological constraints. They burst out in the desire to communicate... It's also because these same sensibilities are found in the creators who work in the visual media industry— along with the "pure" arts like literature, fine art, and music.

Chapter 22

More than K-Pop

K-pop—the sound produced by manufactured boy and girl "idol" groups working for South Korea's three major record labels, SM, YG, and JYP Entertainment—has enjoyed a boom in recent years. K-pop songs are popular both in Korea and throughout East Asia, in countries like Japan, Thailand, and China, and they are beginning to attract small followings farther afield.

In Korea, K-pop groups battle for chart supremacy with singers of romantic ballads. While the word ballad in English can mean any soft, emotional song, it has more specific connotations in Korea. Ballad singers are trained to produce a distinct warble, which, when combined with piano and over-wrought orchestral arrangements, produces saccharine, clichéd songs. It is common to hear even Koreans say, "All ballads sound the same."

Mainstream Korean pop music lacks variety, but it was not always this way. In the late 1960s and 1970s, pioneers like Shin Joonghyun—Korea's first real rock star—made music that was creative as well as commercial. There have also been genuine maverick outliers, like rock-meets-dance-meets-rap star Seo Tai-ji, who dominated the Korean music scene in the 1990s. Today, the best music is in the clubs around the student district of Hongdae. Hongdae bands are rarely found on TV or radio, but are gaining increasing popularity through live shows and the Internet.

Park Chung-hee, Yet Again

No individual comes even remotely close to matching President Park Chung-hee's influence over modern South Korean society. This holds true not only for the economy and the fierce work ethic of the South Korean people, which he kick-started following his 1961 coup. His influence also extends to pop music. During the 1970s, as President Park's regime grew more authoritarian, it banned any song deemed to "disturb social morals." Musicians were required to include a *geonjeon gayo* (wholesome song) on every album. This generally meant something with lyrical content that praised the Park administration or exhorted the people to work hard to help build Park's new nation. Before any record could be released, it had to have the approval of government censors. The result was the development of a popular music culture devoid of imagination, which featured jolly, empty pop songs or lachrymose love ballads, since very little else was deemed acceptable.

Those who defied the censors met with severe restrictions. Korea's "rock daebu" (godfather of rock), Shin Joong-hyun, was asked to write a song praising the administration in 1972. He declined, saying, "I don't know how to do that. Ask someone else." Following that demurral, he became a target for police harassment, and many of his records were banned, including his single "Mi-in" ("Beautiful Girl"), his most popular hit. *Mi-in* was deemed "noisy and degenerate" by authorities, according to Mr. Shin, a problem made worse by the way young people liked to twist its lyrics: the English translation of the song's first line would be "I look at her once, I look at her twice, I want to keep on looking," but kids at the time liked to sing "I screw her once, I screw her twice, I want to keep on screwing."

In 1975, he was arrested for marijuana use (some hippie fans of his had given the marijuana to him) and jailed. He was also tortured at an infamous detention facility near Namsan in central Seoul and forcibly committed to a mental institution for several months as part of his punishment. Journalists came to take pictures of him and paraded him through the papers as a crazed drug addict. Following the completion of his sentence, he was prohibited from releasing music or performing publicly, a ban that continued until Park was assassinated.

Shin Joong-hyun
Despite his almost five-year-long enforced hiatus, Mr. Shin is

regarded as the fountainhead of rock music in Korea. Having lost his parents to the Korean war of 1950–1953, he "strayed around" for a few years, working as a servant in people's houses and learning guitar in his spare time. Eventually, he decided to take his guitar along to one of the U.S. Army's open auditions, announcing himself as "Jackie Shin." The Eighth U.S. Army took entertainment for its personnel very seriously. Officers flew in from the United States to hear each crop of would-be base musicians and divided them into four groups according to ability. Mr. Shin, who had been listening to Armed Forces Korea Network (AFKN) radio for years, was already well versed in country, rock n' roll, blues, and jazz standards and thus was given the top grade. He proved popular with the servicemen of the late 1950s: "The Americans would shout, 'We want Jackie! We want Jackie!'" he recalls. Following that, he created Korea's first proper rock band, Add 4, with fellow base performers.

In those days, young Koreans would go to live music cafes such as C'est Si Bon in Mugyo-dong, downtown Seoul, or gather with friends in special music rooms, where they would go to hear a DJ play records rather than dance to a live band. According to Mr. Shin, sophisticated urbanites favored Western pop sung by the likes of Frank Sinatra and Elvis Presley, while everyone else listened to a form known as *trot*, a "residue of Japanese colonialism" in that it was a style of music derived from the Japanese enka tradition. In contrast, the U.S. Army stage and AFKN Radio were cutting-edge and served as conduits through which the music of Korea's future entered the country. Other well-known Korean singers such as Patti Kim, who only retired in 2012 after 54 years in the business, got their first breaks on a U.S. base, all the while absorbing the influence of American music.

Throughout the late 1950s and 1960s, Mr. Shin continued to perform on base, while recording for Korean audiences as well. In those days, there were just two recording studios in Seoul, one of which "was in someone's house," he recalls. There were no multi-track recorders back then, so "we all just gathered around one microphone in the middle of the room." In 1968, he wrote and recorded an album with a female duo named the Pearl Sisters. They too performed on the American base and were due to go off with Mr. Shin to entertain the troops serving in Vietnam. However, when one of their songs, "Nima," became a hit, record companies offered to buy them out of their contract with the US Army. They stayed behind in Seoul and had further success with the single "Coffee Han-jan" ("A Cup of Coffee").

Because of this, Shin Joong-hyun gained a reputation as someone who could produce hits for others, and a stable of young hopefuls gathered around him. Many went on to become major stars in Korean pop music. Kim Chu-ja, for instance, was a university student who hung around Mr. Shin's office day in, day out, until he finally gave her an audition. His style of guitar music—increasingly influenced by psychedelic bands like Jefferson Airplane, but with a certain Korean melodic sensibility—suited her smoky, expressive voice perfectly, and together they made an album titled *Neutgi-jeone* (Before It's Too Late). Today, original vinyl copies of this record are highly sought-after by collectors. Those who are interested though can purchase the album on CD, as well as the *Shin Joong-hyun Anthology*, which gathers the best of his solo work, as well as songs he made with Kim Chu-ja, the Pearl Sisters, Add 4, and Kim Jung-mi, with whom he made a wonderful folk-meets-psychedelic album titled *Now* in 1973.

Though Shin Joong-hyun's career was curtailed in 1975 following his incarceration for marijuana use (he claims he used it only one time because it "just made my head hurt and stopped me from concentrating on my music"), his consistent influence and brilliance displayed during the 1960s and early 1970s make him the most legendary popular Korean musician. In a survey in 2010, 7 percent of Koreans picked him as the modern cultural figure who best represents their country. He was the top-ranked musician in that poll.

Meanwhile *trot*, the music Shin Joong-hyun helped to marginalize in the 1960s and 1970s, is still with us. This style, also sometimes known as *bbongjjak* (an onomatopoeic word derived from its oom-pah rhythm), is popular among old people and can be heard at country festivals and dances held in public parks. Though not respected by music lovers, *trot* has been undergoing something of a renaissance, with current stars like Jang Yoon-jung choosing to take on the genre.

Trot singers make music that is unashamedly fun and over-the-top in its lyrical sensibilities, appealing in particular to people looking for a touch of escapism and something to dance to.

From Folk to Ballad

The 1970s saw the rise of the protest folk song in the Bob Dylan mode. The best-loved creator of protest songs is probably Kim Min-gi, who wrote "Achim Iseul" ("Morning Dew"), a big hit sung by Yang Hee-eun (another one-time Shin Joong-hyun protégé). The song became an anthem for the democratization movement, and Kim, like Shin Joong-hyun, attracted the wrath of the government. He recorded an album in 1971 that contained "Achim Iseul," and soon after the record was banned and all known copies were recalled and burned. That song in particular was subjected to the severest of restrictions, with cover versions by other artists deemed illegal as well. Nevertheless, dedicated activists, particularly in the universities, always found ways of obtaining underground copies of this and other banned records and distributing them to like-minded friends.

Officially banned from appearing on stage or recording, Kim continued to work, writing plays and musicals that would eventually see the light of day following democratization in 1987. One of his musicals, *Line One*, had a run of thirteen years in Seoul, such was its popularity. Kim also worked as a producer, helping the likes of Kim Kwang-seok to record his first album. Kim Kwang-seok, whose plaintive voice spoke to people's real emotions, sadly died by his own hand at the age of thirty-one. Having sold five million records, an extraordinary number for a Korean artist, he remains a presence, and his status will never be in doubt.

During the late 1970s and 1980s, probably the biggest star was a singer named Cho Yong-pil, who played pop, rock, and old-fashioned *trot* style music. Like Shin Joong-hyun, he also got his start playing for the US Army, before becoming a mainstream Korean success. At the height of his fame, he played a show in front of one million people in the city of Busan. The 1980s was also a time in which the electric guitar returned to the fore in rock groups such as Deul-gukhwa and Sanullim. So-called big hair rock, influenced by kitschy

Western acts like Poison and Whitesnake, made inroads too, as did proper metal bands like Sinawe.

However, the 1980s also saw the rise of the saccharine love ballad. The ballad format in some ways grew out of the acoustic folk song but had a very different kind of spirit and lyrical content. Taking on pop gloss and elements of R&B, it evolved into a distinct sound. Ballad songs today are almost always sung by vocalists trained to be technically flawless but with a cynically over-emotional warble designed to push the right buttons. In each song, the phrase "sarang-hae" ("I love you") crooned at least once is virtually compulsory, particularly at the end of the chorus. Ballads may reflect Korea's tendency towards *han* culture and emotionalism, but they lack depth, which may be attributable to the environment of censorship that prevailed during the genesis of the genre. Shin Joong-hyun complains that the Park and Chun administrations "didn't like people who think," and so encouraged a music culture with no imagination or artistic value. "This culture has prevailed and is still going on even now," he says.

Seo Tai-ji

The year 1992 saw the arrival of Seo Tai-ji, a one-man revolution in dance, rock, and hip-hop. Extraordinarily for a South Korean, he had dropped out of school because, in his view, it did nothing but destroy creativity. He wrote songs indicting the education system, such as the controversial "Gyoshil Idea" ("Classroom Idea"), which laments the standardization of "the minds of nine million children across the country." Young people loved him, of course, and he quickly earned a status far beyond that of an ordinary pop star as the so-called President of Culture.

Musically, he was something of a magpie, picking up on new trends in Western music (rap, metal, electronic dance, drum n' bass, and so on) and introducing them to Korean audiences for the first time. His real achievement was to do this in a way that was creative rather than imitative and to move from genre to genre without alienating his enormous fan base. He remains virtually the only artist in South Korea to be both experimental and a consistent chart-topper. If one hears unusual or defiantly un-poppy music in an ordinary Korean main-street shop or on TV, there is a good chance it will be by Seo Tai-ji.

As the man who first popularized rap in Korea, he opened the door for a whole generation of hip-hop artists, who began to find a large audience in the late 1990s and 2000s. The best of these include Drunken Tiger, Dynamic Duo, MC Sniper, and Epik High. Perhaps surprisingly, South Korea now has a well-developed hip-hop culture that goes beyond music and into fashion and dance. There are around ten Korean break dance groups that are considered world class and regularly compete in international competitions.

Hongdae

The late 1990s also saw the flowering of the Hongdae district indie scene. Hongdae is named after Hongik Daehakgyo (Hongik University, a school famous for its art department), but in fact, there are another three major universities close by: Sogang, Yonsei, and Ehwa Womens' University. It was therefore natural that a music scene should develop there. Unfortunately, the milieu of artists that sprang up from Hongdae has had difficulty establishing its music among ordinary Koreans. The average person still listens mostly to pop songs or over-emotive ballads, making the delineation between the mainstream and the underground very sharp in South Korea.

Consequently, it is relatively rare to see Hongdae bands on TV or mentioned in the press. This is unfortunate, because several of the best acts would probably attract a big following and become genuine stars if they came from London or New York and sang in English. With the exception of punk band Crying Nut, and perhaps three or four others, no musicians from the scene are able to survive without day jobs. This is in contrast to the British music scene, in which a great many popular bands have graduated from playing small clubs to touring the stadiums of the world.

Thankfully, the scene mentality in Hongdae being what it is—music for music's sake—this does not stop the performers. There are many great acts working in all manner of styles. Among the best are Windy City (a funk/reggae outfit led by hyper-talented singer-drummer Kim Ban-jang), Nastyona (a quirky grunge-meets-piano group), Galaxy Express (highly energetic garage rock), The Black Skirts (tuneful pop-rock), and Heureun ("Flowing") a solo singer who combines electronic beats with folk.

The pick of the crop is Third Line Butterfly, a group that sometimes combines noisy experimentalism with a grunge sensibility and at other times offers the listener a gentle ballad or a standout song like "Gipeun Bam Angae-sok" ("In a Deep Night Fog") that starts out simply but builds into a towering crescendo, driven by one of the most powerful voices you can hear in Korea or anywhere else.

The owner of that voice is Nam Sang-ah, now a veteran of the Hongdae scene. She and fellow bandleader Sung Ki-wan met in 1999: "I was a member of [indie band] Huckleberry Finn, and his group was on the same label as us. He asked me to add vocals to one of his songs, and we just clicked," she recounts. Since then, they have recorded three full-length albums and an EP, and, having been consistently excellent for over a decade, are spoken of in reverential terms by newer Hongdae acts.

Sadly, such appreciation does not extend very far beyond the bounds of the university district. "About once a year, someone recognizes me in the supermarket, when I'm wearing shorts and my hair is a mess —but that's about it," says Ms. Nam. Most people in the Korean indie scene accept this lack of recognition as is their lot, but given the outsize talent of some of them, it is still a pity.

The Corporate Era

At the other end of the spectrum lies the "K-pop" of hugely successful girl and boy groups assembled by companies like SM Entertainment and JYP Entertainment. Since the 1990s, these companies have been recruiting sometimes alarmingly young adolescents and putting them through years of training in dancing, singing, and foreign languages in preparation for a future career as teen idols. When deemed ready, the young performers are assembled into groups like 2NE1, the Wondergirls, or 2AM. They are then ready to step out onto the stage in front of hordes of screaming teenage girls.

Some of the songs produced by these labels are extraordinarily catchy. Park Jin-young—for whom JYP Entertainment is named—in particular is a master of melodies that stick in people's heads. Certainly, the increasing enthusiasm for K-pop from all over the world is testament to its charms. Pop star Rain, for example, has played at New York's Madison Square Garden and is huge all across Asia. In Time magazine's online poll of the "World's Most Influential Person," obsessed fans have clicked and reclicked votes for him so often that they put him implausibly ahead of the likes of Barack Obama and Hu Jintao.

K-pop is becoming a big business. In 2010, SM Entertainment recorded revenues of 86.4 billion won (around US$80m). Clearly, SM is not in the same league as Samsung, but revenue has been doubling every two years recently, putting the firm at the center of a growth industry. The market capitalization (total company value) of SM on the Korean stock market is almost a billion U.S. dollars. Competitor YG Entertainment is worth US$250 million. Their performers not only sing but promote all manner of products, from mobile phones to soft drinks. Journalists often get invited to events to celebrate the launch of a new cell phone or television, with special guest performances from the latest boy or girl band. Many of these "idol stars" also cross over into television or film. Lee Hyo-ri for instance, who was a member of a girl band named FinKL, went on to have a solo singing career, before appearing in TV dramas, panel shows, and working as the advertising model for a seemingly infinite list of products from soju and electronic gadgets to Korean beef. This combined music, TV, and sponsorship revenue strategy—which all takes place under the watchful gaze of Svengali-managers who have no interest in producing music of genuine emotion—is reminiscent of the Japanese J-pop industry.

Enormous investments of time and money go into creating teen idol bands, so nothing is left to chance: the life and image of each performer is very strictly controlled. Furthermore, the band members' cut of the profits is extremely small. This has led to several high-profile legal showdowns between members of groups such as Dongbangshingi (TVXQ to non-Korean fans) and their creators. The young singers and their parents are nonetheless fully aware of what lies in store when they sign up: years of hard training in dancing, singing, and foreign languages; endless media appearances and commercial recordings from early morning to late night; no private life; and, a poor deal financially at the end of it all. The would-be star's hope is for longevity and the eventual lucrative solo career, as experienced by Lee Hyo-ri among others. For the majority, this remains a distant dream.

Reportedly, revenues from recorded music have declined by 90 percent from their peak in the late 1990s, mostly as the result of illegal downloading. Where once there were thousands of small record shops across the country, now there are just a handful, usually catering to music-obsessive university students in places like Hongdae and Sinchon (Purple Record and Hyang Music are among the best-known survivors.) The likes of SM Entertainment, whose average listener is a teenage girl, are under pressure to find other sources of revenue. Besides sponsorship, the big labels are now heavily involved in concert promotion and are seeking out new audiences overseas.

Meanwhile, Koreans over the age of thirty complain that "there's nothing for me to listen to." Pop music in Korea is almost entirely aimed at teenagers, and with a few exceptions—such as the more mature, soulful pop of bands like Clazziquai or Rollercoaster—it is artistically disappointing. Older listeners are just ignored by the industry. Shin Joong-hyun says, "In England, bands can be influenced by old music. But in Korea there's no connection between the music of the old and the young. And young people seem to think music just comes from MP3 players. They never heard real live music coming out of big speakers," he laments.

Chapter 23

Work All Day, Stay Out All Night

Though it may be hard to imagine, from 1945 to 1982 South Koreans were not allowed on the streets between the hours of midnight and four a.m. This national curfew was a vestige of the chaotic post-Second World War and Korean War era, which ended up being extended through the military dictatorship period. Throughout the Park Chung-hee years, a mixture of authoritarianism, paternalism, and the determination to keep the workers as productive and compliant as possible resulted in regulation of such things as skirt length, hairstyles, and the simple act of going for a night out. Liberated from this sort of government control today, Koreans have the freedom to go to extremes in all three areas, and many do. Nightlife in particular is a vibrant and widely embraced part of daily activity. Though not known for it internationally, Seoul is a party city.

An oft-repeated stereotype about Koreans brands them "the Irish of the East"—meaning that Koreans are a people who love singing and dancing and the time-honored tradition of getting drunk. Korea's own self-image of *eumju-ga-mu* ("drinking, singing, and dancing") certainly lends credence to that perception, and when followed, this motto naturally results in many an entertaining evening. Drinking can also be a matter of necessity: compulsory company drinking sessions with the boss, known as *hwaishik*, are extremely common.

Alcohol, Revisited

According to the World Health Organization, South Koreans drink the equivalent of 14.8 liters of alcohol per year per person, putting them slightly ahead of the British, as well as their Celtic comrades, the Irish. They are the heaviest-drinking non-Europeans. More tellingly, their 14.8 liters are not consumed steadily, in the form of a couple of beers here and there or a glass of wine with a meal. As in Northern Europe, people either stay in and have an early night or go all-out until the small hours—led on by the rallying cry of "Mashigo-jujka," which means, "Let's drink and die!"

Koreans have long been known for their capacity to imbibe: at a 2010 lecture to the Royal Asiatic Society, historian Robert Neff recounted that when Western sailors began to show up in Korea in the nineteenth century, Koreans were able to drink them under the table. However, many say that it was not until industrialization in the 1960s and 1970s that the practice of drinking oneself unconscious became commonplace. *Hwaishik* drinking parties were instituted as a way of bringing people together as a team after a typically long, hard day's work, but in practice, the parties often became excessive. In 1983, 494 per 100,000 deaths in South Korea were from liver disease; by 2009, the number was 4,417 per 100,000, according to Statistics Korea data. This tenfold increase in the death rate and surging incidence of liver disease that it suggests are strongly linked to *hwaishik* culture and way it has legitimized the binge.

What exactly do Koreans drink, though? This country is blessed with abundant choice where alcohol is concerned. Beers, spirits, and wines from around the world are readily available, along with a wide variety of local brews. The most common is *soju*, which was traditionally made from rice. While some high-end *soju*, such as Andong *soju*, is still rice-based, mass-market *soju* can also be made from potatoes or other starches. *Soju* is far from being a sophisticate's drink, but it does offer the advantage of being cheap: a 375 milliliter bottle of 20 percent ABV (40-proof) *soju* from a convenience store will cost no more than 1,500 won (about US$1.40) and around 4,000 won in a restaurant.

Soju is the people's spirit. It tastes of nothing and costs only

slightly more than nothing, but it does its job exceptionally—some would say excessively—well. It is usually drunk neat, in shot glasses, but many like to mix it with beer to make *so-maek*, a lethal "poktan" (bomb) that can be drunk in "pado" (wave) formation, with each member of the group following the last in downing the whole glass. Cocktail *soju*, a mixture of the spirit with fruit juice or yoghurt drinks to give it a more pleasant taste, is the ultimate in deceptive drinking experiences. It tastes completely unalcoholic and convinces the drinker that he is not even tipsy—until he stands up and finds his legs unwilling to comply with his brain's wishes.

Soju, like *mandu* dumplings, has a Mongol connection, for these thirteenth-century invaders brought a forebear called *arak* with them. The origin of *arak* can be traced to the Levant, from which it spread eastward to Asia and northward to places like Bulgaria, where its descendant is known as *rakia*. In North Korea today, some regions still refer to *soju* as *arakju*. *Soju* is part of the long Silk Road story of proto-globalization and trade, linking seemingly unrelated cultures together.

Other drinks delivered in shots include *baekseju*, a tastier and less alcoholic spirit also brewed from rice, and made with herbs and ginseng. The name means "one hundred year life drink," implying that you will become a centenarian if you drink it. Nobody believes this of course. Some enjoy mixing *baekseju* with *soju* in a combination they call *oshipseju*, which implies a life of only fifty years. There is also the fruity *bokbunja*, made from a kind of native raspberry, and *cheongha*, which tastes slightly similar to Japanese sake.

There are in fact far too many types of Korean spirit to mention. The Cultural Heritage Administration of South Korea lists 86 traditional alcoholic drinks, many of which are regional and not produced in large amounts. The king of spirits, though, will always be *soju*, of which Koreans over the age of twenty drank an average of ninety bottles each in 2006, according to the website of KBS World (the national broadcaster). The text accompanying their report says it all: *soju* is "the energy source of Korea"; it "heats the hearts of lonely people" and "creates not only new relationships but also strengthen (sic) the old ones."

Among fermented beverages, a variety of rice wine called *makgeolli* has a milky color and is drunk in larger cups. It tastes great, but those who imbibe in quantity know that it can cause absolutely devastating hangovers. Traditionally, *makgeolli* was a farmers' drink and thus shunned by urbanites, who viewed it as unsophisticated. However, it underwent a renaissance in the late 2000s, due to its relatively low calorie count. Trendy bars now serve *makgeolli* at high prices to people who would not have been seen dead drinking it not long ago. Old-style *makgeolli* is still on sale, and can be bought for as little as $1 per bottle in supermarkets.

How to Drink in Korea

Kkang-soju—drinking *soju* by itself—is not the standard way of consuming it. For Koreans, alcohol should be accompanied by food. Such food is referred to as *anju*. Tourists who sit down at a bar and order a beer have been known to become confused and annoyed when asked to buy a plate of French fries or fruit that they do not particularly want. Koreans believe that particular foods and spirits belong together: for example, *samgyeopsal* (pork on a "Korean barbecue") and *soju*, *makgeolli* and *jeon* (a kind of pancake), or fried chicken and beer. The latter pairing is a modern institution. Venues serving only chicken and beer can be found in every busy area. A unique Korean sauce, *yangnyeom*, can be added to the chicken if desired. Young people have devised the word *chi-maek*, a combination of chicken and *maekju* (beer) to celebrate this marriage made in heaven.

Since one must generally order food at a drinking establishment, drinkers stay in one place for several hours and then perhaps move to one or two other establishments as the evening progresses. Over the course of a complete evening, which can last as long as ten hours potentially, one may visit perhaps three or four places. For instance, one may start in a *gogi-jip* ("meat house," literally) for *samgyeopsal* and *soju* and then move to a *hof* (a German loan-word for "pub"), where more *soju* or beer (or indeed both) is accompanied by snacks such as nachos or a plate of fruit.

Another sort of venue is the *pojang macha*, an outdoor tent bar that is usually covered with an orange tarpaulin and has plastic chairs

and tables inside. Such places will invariably be run by an *ajumma* or *halmeoni* (middle-aged woman and "grandmother," respectively) sporting a fine crop of permed hair. She will serve up seafood and *soju*, and in smaller places, it will be very easy to strike up a conversation with her or the other customers. For a foreign guest, this is a chance to be part of something genuine and entirely unrelated to dull tourist-oriented fare. In a *pojang macha*, one can feel the warmth and character of this country, the alcohol aside.

The authorities are forever trying to suppress tent bars and roadside snack joints, and they redouble their efforts to remove them whenever an event like the Olympics, World Cup, or G20 summit comes to town. Officials hold the misguided view that this sort of popular eatery looks backward and gives a bad impression to visiting foreigners. They believe instead that the best way to attract visitors is by providing a sanitized—and, boring, it must be said—view of the country, consisting entirely of palaces, kimchi, traditional dance, and the like. Such a policy seems doomed to failure given the close proximity of countries like China, whose Forbidden City frankly trumps anything old that Korea has to offer. By promoting rather than destroying some of the singular experiences that can be found here—such as *pojang macha*—they would probably have more success.

Singing and Dancing

When a group of drinkers feels sufficiently lubricated, a trip to a *noraebang* may well ensue. This is a private room that may cost between 10,000 and 20,000 won per hour (roughly US$10-20), in which you can sing karaoke to your heart's content. Many English-language songs are available in addition to Korean songs. One has the opportunity to murder almost any Beatles classic, for instance. Those who are not singing at any particular moment will probably be up on their feet, dancing and shaking tambourines, which are also provided. Some luxury *noraebangs* offer themed rooms. For example, one in the Hongdae area of Seoul has a band-themed room, with stage and a drum kit.

Hongdae itself is the most famous area for music and dancing in the country. As a mecca for clubbing, Hongdae grew out of bars in

nearby Sinchon, which would play rock music videos for their patrons to dance to back in the 1980s. Some moved down the road to Hongdae, since rents were cheaper there. Later, punk rock took off with the opening of Club Drug (where the first Korean punk bands, like Crying Nut, would play), and dance music came with the advent of Pachulso (Power Station), which was opened by a local university graduate. There were also bars dedicated to particular emerging genres of music, such as reggae, shoegaze, and hip hop. Few of these pioneering places made money, but owners would run them more as a labor of love. As a result, Hongdae became the area for young people looking for fun.

Clubbing and music districts can now be found in all major cities, usually near universities. Pusan has clubs in the area surrounding the Pukyeong and Kyungsung Universities, for instance. And, around lunchtime on a Sunday, it is not unusual to see people stumbling out of afterclubs—clubs that open just as others are winding down. The Gangnam area of Seoul is particularly known for such establishments.

Older people have their venues, too. For those in their sixties, the music of their youth was mostly *trot*, old-style pop music with a one-two, one-two rhythm. Dance clubs for this kind of music open even in the afternoon. One located near a former home of the author is called Seongin Cola-tec (Adult Cola-tec), which is a play on the old Cola-tec clubs for teenagers that sold soft drinks rather than alcohol. In certain areas like Tapgol Park in the Jongno Sam-ga district of Seoul, one can sometimes see old people engaged in impromptu outdoor dancing, having derived courage from *makgeolli*.

In Korea, old people tend to enjoy outdoor activities more than do the young. As in China, there are parks that fill up with old men playing board games, such as *janggi*, a relative of the Chinese game *xiangqi* (Chinese chess). Those who are not playing are invariably making bets with each other on the outcome. And when trekking up a mountain in Korea, one is also likely to come across (or even be overtaken by) groups of sprightly old men and women. They are almost certain to be carrying *soju* or *makgeolli* in their backpacks.

Itaewon

Multicultural Itaewon in Seoul is a rising party destination for locals. It was not always so, though. For years, this district was considered by Koreans as a place of infamy and otherness. According to some sources, Itaewon originally got its name from an act of mass rape perpetrated on the nuns of a local monastery by Japanese invaders, during the Imjin Waeran invasions of 1592–1598. *I* meant "different" (as in foreign), *tae* meant "fetus," and *won* "home." The nuns who were impregnated were given a place there in which to raise their children, and thus the area became known as Itaewon. Understandably, a less shocking potential source of the name Itaewon has become the officially adopted one. *I*, *tae*, and *won* can also mean "large pear tree" when put together. The Chinese characters for this rendering of Itaewon are the ones that appear on the subway map.

In the early twentieth century, occupying Japanese troops maintained a garrison nearby at Yongsan. Yongsan Garrison was taken over and expanded by the U.S. Army following the fall of imperial Japan in 1945. It became the headquarters of US-ROK Combined Forces Command, and many American soldiers and support staff came to live in the area. Around it, Itaewon developed throughout the 1960s and 1970s as a place of shopping and evening entertainment for the U.S. military personnel.

The presence of soldiers naturally meant that prostitution flourished. Though prostitution is not legal in Korea, it is tolerated to the point where it has become a large industry. Itaewon has been no exception to this rule. To this day, there remains an area within Itaewon known as "Hooker Hill," which targets foreign men as customers. The prevalence of prostitution, combined with general prejudice against American soldiers, meant that Itaewon was out of bounds for any Korean hoping to preserve a good reputation. This was particularly the case for women, who would be demonized as *yanggongju* (Yankee princess) and subjected to taunts in the street if they were seen in the company of foreign men. Films such as *Yeowangbeol* (*Queen Bee* 1985) reflect this sense of Itaewon, depicting it as a hive of depravity full of Western men waiting for their chance to corrupt any available Korean girl.

In 1997, an infamous murder took place in the toilets of the Itae-won Burger King and appeared to confirm to ordinary Koreans that Itaewon was an intimidating, immoral place best avoided. Yet in the late 2000s, a remarkable transformation began to occur. After a series of crackdowns by military police on the late-night partying of American soldiers, a new era of gentrification began. People like Hong Seok-cheon, Korea's first openly gay celebrity, commenced opening bars and restaurants in Itaewon, offering more upmarket entertainment at upmarket prices. Rents soared, and now many of the old bars that cater to GIs are closing down. These days, the majority of people enjoying nights out in Itaewon are Korean. They tend to be "yuppies," who do not mind spending US$10 for a glass of beer. The imminent closure of Yongsan Garrison and relocation of its personnel to another city is certain to enhance this trend. Those wishing to invest in real estate in Seoul could do much worse than to buy in Itaewon and its environs.

From around the mid-1990s onwards, Itaewon has also become the main gay area of Seoul. As an historic place of otherness, it was natural for the district to fulfill this role too. But Itaewon's recent gentrification, led by Hong Seok-cheon, has given its gay scene more mainstream appeal. In 2012, it is not so unusual for young Korean women to visit gay bars or even watch transvestite shows there. Not so long ago, few would have even known about the existence of such places.

Coffee and Clothes Shops

Though alcohol fuels most evenings out, South Korea is also a nation of coffee drinkers—or more accurately, coffee shop addicts. Large cities like Seoul, Busan, Gwangju, Daejeon, and Daegu have international franchises such as Starbucks, local chains like Caffe Bene (which went from zero to five hundred stores in three years), and independents on every busy street. Groups of women in particular will spend entire evenings chatting over Caramel Macchiatos, Mocha Frappucinos, and other drinks that would have seemed obscure or unpronounceable a decade ago. Starbucks opened its first Korean shop near Ewha Women's University in 1999 and by 2011 had a network of 360 outlets nationwide.

This startling growth stems not so much from a love of coffee as from the social function of the coffee shop. Korea is a gregarious country where people have a strong preference for gathering rather than being alone. When bored, Koreans love to arrange impromptu get-togethers rather than simply go home. If they do not want to have alcohol, they will probably end up in a coffee shop. Day and night, coffee shops are full of people. They are so common that in the downtown area of Jung-gu, one of Seoul's twenty-five districts, there are around four thousand of them. Some remain open twenty-four hours a day.

If you happen to be having a late-night coffee in the Dongdaemun area of Seoul, you might decide to go out and buy some clothes—at four a.m., if you so desire. This district comprises thirty thousand shops, most of which are small stalls situated in dedicated market buildings such as Migliore and Hello aPm. Such buildings do not truly come alive until late: many stalls open at eight p.m. and go on doing business until after sunrise. For that reason, the whole area is referred to in tourist guides as Dongdaemun Night Market. Stall operators live an upside-down life that most likely skimps on sleep, but in that—in a country that exemplifies the motto of "work hard, play hard"—they are probably not too different from everyone else.

PART FIVE

More of "Us," Less of "Them"

Chapter 24

Defensive Nationalism

Long treated as a stepping-stone or strategic asset by greater powers, Korea has developed an ethnic nationalism based on an "us against them" mentality. Older Koreans will sometimes recall being instructed in their schooldays in the importance of their "pure blood," which purportedly came from a single, 5,000-year-long unbroken family tree originating with the first Koreans. This notion largely developed in the early twentieth century as a reaction to Japanese colonialism, during which time the invading power sought to portray Koreans as a subset of the Japanese race. Ethnic nationalism was later promoted by South Korea's military governments as they aimed to foster a sense of unity and pride in country in order to encourage the people to support economic development—a goal itself inspired by the need to transcend Korea's tragic history.

Korea's brand of ethnic nationalism is the product of outside interference, or the fear thereof. Because of this, it is defensive rather than aggressive. As South Korea justifiably gains in confidence as a now-wealthy country with increasing cultural and political clout, that fear has started to dissipate. At the same time, Koreans are opening up more to foreigners in a number of ways. The foreign population of South Korea has risen dramatically, and the proportion of mixed-nationality marriages is now over 10 percent. The nation's famed xenophobic edge is becoming blunted.

Japan

Throughout the Joseon era, China exercised dominant political and cultural influence over Korea. For the intellectual, Confucian elite,

China was a big brother and the provider of philosophy, ethics, and literature as well as the source of the beautiful *hanja* characters with which they wrote letters, literature, and official documents. Korean monarchs paid tribute to China three to four times a year as part of a policy of *sadae*, or "submission to the stronger." It would have been an insult for a Korean king to build a palace grander than those found in Beijing.

Relations with China were unequal but largely peaceful. Relations with Japan during the same period were hostile; when the Japanese shogun came knocking, it was not to extract tribute. During the Imjin Waeran invasions by the Japanese armies of shogun Toyotomi Hideyoshi, from 1592 to 1598, hundreds of thousands of Koreans perished. The invaders' catalogue of brutality included mass rape and the collection of dead Koreans' ears and noses as war trophies. Astonishingly, some 38,000 or more such body parts fill the Mimizuka (Ear Mound) in Kyoto, a monument that stands today, just down the road from the shrine to Toyotomi Hideyoshi.

The annexation of Korea by Japan from 1910 to 1945 was also an exercise in brutality. Resisters to colonial rule were imprisoned and tortured, or executed. Koreans were forced to adopt Japanese names and speak Japanese. Many thousands of women were forced into sexual slavery. It is hardly surprising that negative sentiment towards Japan remains. There are Japanese people who understand this completely but also many others who, never having been taught about this sad episode in school, have no idea why "emotional" Koreans would hold a grudge against their country.

Prior to the colonial period, ethnic nationalism in Korea was not strong. The concept of *minjok*—the nation, based on blood and ethnicity—was popularized only in the 1920s by the likes of independence activist, anarchist, and historian Shin Chae-ho. Shin Chae-ho wrote of a "single pure bloodline" traceable all the way back to mythical founder, Dangun—a suspect concept for certain, but one that strengthened the people's sense of resolve against the foreign power. Imperial Japan claimed that Koreans were a subset of the Japanese race, and this provided one rationale for the annexation. Shin's purpose was at once to refute this claim and construct a solid

Korean identity. In its inception, Korean ethnic nationalism was in large part born of a desire for independence and resistance to foreign domination.

Post-division

Following the fall of Imperial Japan at the end of World War Two, leading independence activists and fighters, who were mostly based overseas, returned to Korea. They, along with the Soviets and Americans, had competing ideas about the direction their country would take. Among the most prominent were ex-guerrilla fighter Kim Il-sung, who wanted to establish a communist state; Kim Gu, who formed the Korean Liberation Army in Chongqing, China, and pursued national independence and unity above all ideology; and Syngman Rhee, the Harvard and Princeton-educated, pro-American who openly espoused democracy but later ruled South Korea as a dictator.

The end result of the wrangling between the USSR and the U.S., and the various Korean factions, was something that no Korean could have truly wanted: the nation was divided in two. One part ended up ruled by the Soviet-backed Kim Il-sung, for the Ministry of Foreign Affairs in Moscow believed he would make a good puppet. His regime—which evolved into a de facto monarchy—has outlasted the USSR, with his grandson Kim Jong-un remaining in power today. The other part was ruled by Syngman Rhee. Rhee had once been president of the Korean Provisional Government in Shanghai, but was removed in 1925 after being accused of embezzlement by Kim Gu. By 1945 his authority lay mainly in the trust the U.S military had in him, based on his American education, Christian beliefs, and professed democratic values.

The division, and the war that followed, showed Koreans that despite the termination of Japanese rule, their destiny was not in their own hands. The two states—North and South—were created because of the involvement and interests of Moscow and Washington, and when North and South went to war in 1950, foreign forces enabled each to survive. Following the North's invasion on June 25, 1950, the Soviet-backed communist Northern forces quickly took the whole of Korea, save for the area around the southern port city of Pusan. General Douglas MacArthur's famed September 1950 landing at Incheon, combined with a "breakout" of UN troops from Pusan, then pushed the North Koreans back all the way up to the Chinese border region, almost taking the entire peninsula. It was Chairman Mao's decision to send the Chinese People's Liberation Army into the fray just over one month later that forced the UN into retreat, ultimately resulting in a stalemate situation and eventual armistice declaration, with a demarcation line being drawn around the 38th Parallel.

It was naturally hard for Koreans to escape the perception that their country was a pawn in a game played by the more powerful—just as was the case when China, Russia, and Japan competed for influence over the peninsula during the twilight years of the Joseon dynasty. Both South and North Korea owed their very existence to the financial and military backing of the respective capitalist and communist superpowers. The division of Korea separated family from family, and friend from friend, creating personal trauma on a mass scale. It is hardly surprising then that division fed a current of fear and distrust towards foreign countries. Furthermore, the emergence of two competing Koreas meant that the governments of each felt the need to show they were the true keepers of Korean nationhood, rather than foreign puppets. The division of Korea certainly did not result in the end of ethnic nationalism.

In the period following the Korean War, the one thing that raised South Korean men's nationalistic ire most of all was probably the sight of American soldiers with "their" women, Korean women. The British view of the GI—"oversexed, overpaid, and over here"—was felt even more intensely by South Koreans. Women who hung around with GIs were labeled prostitutes and traitors for betraying the supposed "pure blood" of their ancestors, or were seen as victims of a kind of sexual colonialism and in need of rescuing. Sadly, this attitude has not really died away among older men, even though South Korea now is a wealthy and modern country.

The Power of the Bunker Mentality

"Pure-blooded nationalism...was used as an effective tool to make people obedient and easy to govern," states Kim Seok-soo, a Kyung-pook National University professor of philosophy, as quoted in the Korea Times. The Syngman Rhee regime made so-called *ilmin juui* ("one people-ism") an ingredient its propaganda at least partly to draw attention away from the number of former Japanese collaborators in the administration's ranks. Promoting a Korean ethnic nationalist image, President Rhee thought, would give his government greater legitimacy in the eyes of the people. The Park Chung-hee administration (1961–1979) also adopted pure-blood nationalism in order to encourage the people to follow President Park's economic development plans.

To transform South Korean citizens into Park's "industrial soldiers," there had to be something worth fighting for. That something was the survival and prosperity of "the great *han* race," according to Professor Shin Gi-wook, a leading expert on Korean ethnic nationalism. Thus, government-produced school textbooks taught children about the importance of their "pure blood"; teachers encouraged pupils to believe that Koreans embodied a pure, unbroken 5,000 yearlong bloodline. When they graduated and joined the workforce, they were exhorted in official poster campaigns to "beat Japan"—the country that had previously humiliated Korea—and make the nation powerful by working twelve-hour days, even on Saturdays, and under tough conditions. As seen in chapters 21 and 22, General Park also co-opted the nation's cultural industries to help spread his nationalistic, pro-development message. He even wrote a song of his own, "Saemaeul Norae" ("New Village Song"), in which he exhorts the people to "build a new fatherland as we work and fight." Of course, it was played constantly on the radio after its release in 1971.

As in many East Asian countries, a fear of Chinese business prowess was widespread, and Park's response was to protect Korean companies from it. As well as discouraging schools from teaching Chinese characters (he placed greater emphasis on native Korean *Hangeul* characters), President Park restricted the ability of Chinese residents to own land and operate businesses, resulting in the emigration of around 10,000 Chinese. General Park also strove to project an image of himself as a user of Korean products such as *makgeolli* (rice wine) rather than expensive foreign liquors. The notion that buyers of foreign products were traitorous aided the mercantilist development policy of the time, providing moral justification for the heavy tariffs that were placed on imported goods.

A more recent event reveals the defensive nature of Korean nationalism and the potential it has to inspire people to vast collective efforts. In 1997 the Asian Economic Crisis hit, and once-proud "tiger" economies like South Korea teetered on the brink of ruin. Politicians and business leaders blamed the crisis on foreign lenders and investors for pulling their money out of short-term investments (such as Korean stocks) and causing the won to crash. When the IMF extracted painful conditions in return for its bailout package, the result was a gut feeling among many Koreans that the country was under attack, not militarily this time but financially. Past history helped lead them to that conclusion.

The *chaebol*, which rightfully should have accepted plenty of the blame due to their debt-laden balance sheets, responded with a nationalistic "under attack" message. In a book on the crisis, journalist Donald Kirk writes of a Hyundai manager claiming, "The IMF and America are trying to break up the *chaebol*," the companies consistently promoted as "national champions" by Korean governments since the days of Park Chung-hee. Mr. Kirk goes on to say: "On television and in the press, Koreans complained that the IMF had been guilty of egregious imperialistic meddling. To hear Finance Minister Lim (Chang-ryul) tell it, the country had gone down to defeat in a hard-fought war." The public reacted to this perceived assault, as the BBC reported at the time, by stigmatizing any Koreans "taking holidays abroad or (buying) foreign-made luxury products."

The "hard-fought war" mentality reported by Donald Kirk may have been misguided, but it did have benefits for the Korean economy, in that it provided impetus for the country to unite and dig itself out of trouble. Just as Park Chung-hee had done in the 1960s, corporate leaders and the government both appealed to the people's sense of nationalism and collectivity. For instance, Chung Mong-koo, chairman of Hyundai Motor, staged a rally in front of company headquarters and declared, "Hyundai has to raise the flag high to contribute to the development of the Korean economy." The company *sa-ga* or anthem was sung and fists were pumped. Hyundai employees were encouraged to feel they were working to save the country and not just to build cars or contribute to the success of the company. *Chaebol* also organized a campaign exhorting citizens to send gold to the treasury. This call resulted in a reported eight tons of the precious metal being collected, mainly in the form of jewelry, in the first week. The campaign provided both a material boost to the nation's reserves and a morale boost from the impressive display of unity that allowed it to happen.

If one talks to foreigners about living in South Korea, one frequently hears criticism of Koreans' bunker mentality, their over-sensitivity about perceived threats from abroad, and their "readiness to play the victim." This is sometimes fair criticism, but Korea's defensive nationalism creates highly effective social glue that can be used whenever the family heirloom starts to crack. Given how divided South Korea is internally—politically, regionally, and increasingly between young and old, and rich and poor— the sense of purpose and unity that springs up when there is a perceived threat is quite incredible. In the wake of the 1997–1998 financial crisis, Korea's trade unions, large corporations, and the government formed a "super-committee" that produced a grand bargain over *chaebol* reform and labor policy in just twenty days. The agreement was painful for both the *chaebol* and the workers: the former had to accept the liquidation of many inefficient subsidiaries as well as tougher accounting standards; and the latter had to consent to a new era of flexible labor laws that still aggrieves them today. Both quickly agreed to the bargain for the sake of national recovery.

The humiliation felt during the "IMF period" helps explain why South Korea has a tendency to be extremely sensitive to criticism of its economic policies from abroad. During his tenure as the UK's Chancellor of the Exchequer, Alistair Darling held a series of meetings with fellow finance ministers from other countries at a summit in London. While others came to discuss regulation in the wake of the 2008 financial crisis, his opposite number from South Korea reportedly just wanted to know "Why does the Financial Times, a British paper, keep criticizing me?" Darling could only reply, "Well, you should see what they write about me!"

The 2002 World Cup

Just four years after the Asian economic crisis came a watershed moment in the nation's history: the 2002 World Cup, which South Korea hosted together with Japan. As a global event watched by billions of people, it represented South Korea's first real opportunity to show itself off to the world as an advanced nation. Though the 1988 Seoul Olympics was an event of equal international status, Olympic-era South Korea was a country with a GDP per capita of US$4,500, and a still-uncertain transition to democracy taking its course. By 2002, Korea had recovered from the 1997–1998 crisis, had advanced to a GDP per capita of over $12,000, and was enjoying stable, democratic government. The estimated one million people who visited South Korea for the World Cup saw not just impressive stadia but also an advanced country nothing like the one shown in the TV series *M*A*S*H*.

The national team dramatically exceeded expectations, reaching the semi-finals, which seemed to underscore the national success. Team captain Hong Myung-bo calls this achievement "more than ultimate" and said it showed Koreans that "we can do anything when we put our mind to it." Victories over Spain, Portugal, and Italy inspired intense national pride, spurring millions of Koreans into the streets, all wearing red, the color of the team's jerseys. The "Red Devils" supporters club brandished slogans like "We are one, we are Korea." Young Koreans, long criticized by the older generations for having no patriotism, painted their faces in the national colors and draped Korean flags over their bodies.

The combination of pride from foreigners acknowledging their country's progress and the unexpected joy that resulted from reaching the semi-finals may have been Koreans' first experience of positive, proud nationalism—as opposed to the defensive, threat-driven variety. The World Cup planted the idea that interaction with foreigners could bring a mutually beneficial exchange, and even fun.

Korean World Cup supporters, according to Florence Lowe-Lee of the Korea Economic Institute, "redefined nationalism to include a renewed sense of national confidence and pride." She contrasts this with the traditional Korean nationalism, centered on "seeking liberation from foreign occupation" of one sort or another. Similarly, in a book entitled *Football and the South Korean Imagination*, Choi Yoon-sung argues that the national pride created by the World Cup enabled Koreans psychologically to rectify or purge some of the pain of their national history.

That this was accomplished with Guus Hiddink, a foreign manager, in charge of the team is important. For his efforts, Hiddink was made an honorary citizen, the first time South Korea had ever conferred citizenship on a foreigner with no Korean blood. In a paper entitled "South Korea's 'Glocal' Hero" (2007), researchers at Pusan University claim that this award of citizenship could inspire "fundamental changes, both culturally and legally, in how race, ethnicity, and citizenship are defined. They add that Korea's sense of ethnic homogeneity "may be preparing to change." The election in 2012 of Philippine-born Jasmine Lee, the first non-ethnic Korean National Assembly member, is evidence that this change is now fully underway. Admittedly, there are many who do not like it—Ms. Lee received threats from "netizens" in the wake of her election—but such hostility looks like mere friction in the path of an irreversible trend.

The Decline of Ethnic and Defensive Nationalism

Lately, pure-blood nationalism and the general suspicion of non-Koreans have seen a marked decline. Foreigners in Seoul used to complain, "Why do people stare at me with angry eyes?" Now they are more likely to ask, "Why don't people look at me anymore?" Intermarriage is increasingly accepted too. Only 9 percent of Koreans say they would never marry a foreigner, according to a 2011 survey by the Ministry of Gender Equality and Family. Immigrant workers find it easier to get visas and residency permits, which reflects a shift in thinking by those in power. By contrast to the "pure blood" teaching of the past, today's South Korean government engages in poster campaigns encouraging people to accept multiculturalism.

The number of foreigners living in this country has soared, reaching 1.4 million, a figure that would have been unimaginable even at the turn of the millennium. Imported products are everywhere. This is the consequence not just of reduced tariffs brought on by the end of South Korean mercantilism and the new era of free-trade agreements. It also stems from a change in attitude among the public towards foreign goods, and the resulting decline of nationalistic purchasing. The owner of a Mercedes is now perceived by most people as affluent and cool rather than a flashy traitor too arrogant to drive a Hyundai, as he once was.

Traces of Korean defensiveness do remain but rise to the surface much less frequently than before. Since 2002, the only major incident said to be of this nature was the "summer of protest" of 2008. The government of President Lee Myung-bak had made a deal with the United States to allow the importation of American beef for the first time since 2003, when it had been banned due to the discovery of a cow infected with bovine spongiform encephalopathy in Washington State. Opponents, particularly on the left, contended that President Lee was selling out the health of Koreans in return for favorable relations with the U.S. Driven initially by rather hysterical media coverage that exaggerated the danger, hundreds of thousands of people began gathering for candlelight protests on the streets of downtown Seoul. They were the biggest displays of anti-government anger since democratization.

However, when considered in context, the protests were also a product of general anger towards President Lee; the apparent threat of BSE-infected, foreign beef was only a part of this. Having been elected in December 2007, President Lee had set about quickly reversing many of the key policies of the Kim Dae-jung and Roh Moo-hyun years—a period termed "the lost decade" by Lee supporters. The sunshine policy, for instance, was out, and pro-*chaebol* economic policies were in. This naturally infuriated the left, but Lee had also become unpopular with average voters, too. Despite his landslide election victory, by June 2008 his approval rating stood at just 17 percent, the result of a general belief that he had gone too far to the right, and was poor at communicating with the public. So there was already a strong undercurrent of anti-government sentiment based on domestic political concerns.

That summer, beef protestors were joined by opponents of President Lee's educational reforms, planned privatization of public corporations, and costly river restoration programs in a general display of grievance to an unpopular president rather than one of pure defensive nationalism provoked by health fears over a foreign product. Statistics appear to back this up: after its reintroduction in 2008, American beef quickly claimed a 20 percent market share in Korea, and by 2011, that figure had risen to 37 percent.

South Korea's sense of nationalism among the young is not particularly strong, as shown by a 2010 survey of 2,400 schoolchildren by South Korea's Ministry of Patriots and Veterans' Affairs. In the poll, youngsters in South Korea as well as the big three (as far as Korea is concerned) of China, Japan, and the United States, were asked about the extent of their national pride. By the ministry's index, China scored 84.2, the U.S. 70.6, South Korea 62.9, and Japan 55.3. When asked about willingness to fight for their country, Koreans came second with a score of 56.3, but only slightly ahead of America and far behind China, which registered a rather frightening 74.8.

Chapter 25

Multicultural Korea?

Though many older Koreans may not welcome it, South Korea is opening up as a society as its economy becomes more advanced and internationalized. Increased immigration is resulting in greater ethnic diversity. The foreign population rose from around 200,000 in 2001 to 1.4 million by 2011. Half of these are Chinese, but the number of countries that have provided thirty or more immigrants to Korea is almost in the triple figures. Many foreigners have married locals, and more than 10 percent of Korean weddings now involve a foreign partner. The change has come very quickly: in the year 2000, the international marriage rate was just 3.5 percent, and in the 1980s it was so low as to have looked like a statistical anomaly. The children of these mixed couples are starting to blur the once obvious lines between Korean and non-Korean.

Statistics suggest that the younger generation is beginning to embrace a new era of openness in attitudes to foreigners. This change mirrors the increasing willingness of Koreans overall to accept alien cultures in cuisine, art, imported products, and so on. After years of defining nationality by race, Korean society shows signs of allowing foreigners to put one foot in the "us" (*woori*) camp rather than excluding them as a pure "them" (*nam*). For non-Koreans, it is becoming possible to develop deep social networks in Korea rather than remain excluded, as was the case before. This is fortunate, because the presence of foreigners provides an obvious and practical solution to a serious social problem: the nation's drastically low birth rate.

Drops of Ink in the Han River

During a 2006 meeting between North and South Korean delegates, the former brought up the issue of South Korea's so-called race mixing. When a Southern representative (falsely) stated that the amount of mixing amounted to no more than a "drop of ink in the Han River," the reply from the North was blunt: "Not even one drop of ink must be allowed to fall in the Han River."

Of course, North Korea is not your average communist state. Perhaps the true inheritor of the mantle of the Hermit Kingdom, it promotes a strong brand of race-based nationalism that somewhat resembles fascism. Regardless, the Northern delegation was laboring under a delusion. Throughout the history of Korea, intermarriage and a mixing of genes has taken place with Chinese, Mongols, and many other peoples from across the region. There is even a Korean clan, the Deoksu Jang (a family with the surname Jang originating from a place named Deoksu), that was founded by an ethnic Uighur from Central Asia during the reign of King Chungnyeol (r. 1274–1298). The founder's original name was Samga, and he came to Korea in the retinue of a Mongol princess, who was sent to marry none other than Chungnyeol himself. Particularly in Koryo dynasty Korea, these were not isolated cases.

Pure blood is a fiction, but as we have seen, in Korea as in many other places, it has proved a very useful one. Koreans locked in the struggle to overcome Japanese colonialism embraced the concept of national unity based on shared blood. Following the devastation of the Korean War, the unifying ideology of ethnic nationalism was employed in the service of nation building, to great effect.

One consequence of this ideology was prejudice toward anyone who chose to look beyond the "pure blood" in-group of the Korean *minjok* (race) and marry a foreigner. Especially women who went for American soldiers were singled out for hatred and subjected to harassment and epithets such as "yanggongju" ("Yankee princess"), a term far more derogatory than its translation sounds. Families forbade their daughters from marrying non-Koreans and in some cases disowned those defiant enough to go ahead with it. Children produced by such marriages were ostracized. Both a woman who married a foreigner and her child were essentially no longer part of the national in-group.

In the 1980s, international marriage was so uncommon that the Unification Church, known to most people as the "Moonie" cult, could show up in statistics as one of the main reasons for it. Founder Moon Sun-myung comes from Korea, and since he offers followers matchmaking in the form of instant marriage between strangers, a number of foreigners, particularly Japanese women, came here for that purpose. Reverend Moon believes he has the God-given ability to select a person's perfect partner, and his followers trust in him to do that. Through him, thousands of international marriages have taken place; many such couples participated in mass blessing ceremonies, which sometimes are so large that they are held in stadiums. Among the general population, however, the idea of marrying a non-Korean remained anathema. Even by 1990, only 1.2 percent of marriages in Korea had one foreign partner.

In the past two decades, business ties, overseas study, travel, and generally increased contact with the outside world has led South Koreans to change their attitude towards people from other countries and become more open, as a result. It is not unusual now for Koreans to have foreign friends or go on solo backpacking trips to foreign countries, staying in hostels and mixing with an international crowd. This has been accompanied by the increased acceptance of international marriage. Mixed-race children, once treated as pariahs, are now admired for their looks, and are in great demand as models in advertisements. The process is happening so quickly that foreigners who have lived here for four or five years remark on how perceptible the change has been in so short a time. There were 2.5 times more international marriages in 2008 than in 2002, according to Statistics Korea.

The Rural Revolution

South Korea's increasing globalism (openness to trade, travel, foreign culture, and so on) is only the second-greatest driving force towards Korean-foreigner marriage, though. Perhaps surprisingly, the real beating heart of multicultural Korea is to be found in the countryside, and it is not born of cosmopolitanism but rather the desperation of rural men for wives. The simple fact that most Korean women do not want to marry poor farmers is resulting in a huge influx of Vietnamese, rural Chinese, and Filipina women whose families can only dream of the kind of wealth even the poorest Korean men possess. It is very much like the "mail-order bride" phenomenon found in the West, but on a grand scale: in 2009, 43.5 percent of male farmers marrying in South Jeolla Province tied the knot with foreigners, the vast majority from one of the three aforementioned countries.

As a consequence, marriage brokerage has become a serious business. In rural areas, advertisements for agencies that will introduce Vietnamese wives, for example, are commonplace. Back in their own countries, these women are sold an image of Korea, and Seoul in particular, as a glamorous place. Korean TV shows and films that are popular throughout the region back this up. Financial expediency also means that many parents are eager for their daughters take the plunge.

Naturally, things do not always work out. A lonely farmer in his forties is not the same as a heart-throb TV actor, and South Jeolla, though beautiful, is not downtown Seoul. Reportedly, 53 percent of such couples live in poverty, by its South Korean definition. Tales of domestic violence, homesickness, the inability to communicate, and runaway brides are legion—so much so that one can sometimes see advertisements for wives who "don't run away."

However, according to research cited in an article by veteran Korea-watcher Andrei Lankov in 2009, the majority do not regret their decision to marry in Korea. Plainly, poverty in South Korea is very different to poverty in Thailand or Cambodia. 57 percent of the women are either "satisfied" or "very satisfied" with their new lives. The cynical will observe that this figure is probably not much worse than the general satisfaction rates among married people the world over. Furthermore, the government is actively engaged in programs to smooth the integration process, providing language classes and promoting publicity campaigns encouraging people to embrace multiculturalism.

Seoul Metro stations are full of advertisements showing happy multicultural families, and in particular, dutiful Southeast Asian wives who seemingly enjoy cooking Korean food and studying the Korean language for the benefit of their grateful husbands. The aim of these poster campaigns is to increase social acceptance of such women, by portraying them as warm, somewhat subservient (and thus non-threatening), and as near Korean as possible. In the long run, this will probably have to change: though the government's intentions are noble, they are portraying an outdated image of women, and only promote the idea of immigrants adapting to Korean culture, rather than of Korean society also learning something from them.

It Depends on What Kind of Immigrant You Are

According to Professor Chang Ha-joon, a more ethnically diverse Korea "is going to happen, like it or not." But do people like it? A Ministry of Veterans' Affairs survey on young people in South Korea, China, Japan, and the United States found that South Korean youths were in fact the most likely of the four to say that they welcomed immigration and multiculturalism in their country, despite the holdover effects of pure-blood theory. Broadly speaking, this acceptance is generational. As may be expected, the young are much more welcoming of change than the old. The implication, naturally, is that as the years go by, the acceptance of international marriage will continue to grow.

At the same time, attitudes often depend on the origin of the immigrant in question. In 2009, Professor Bang Hee-jung of Ehwa Women's University surveyed 121 Korean students and found that they tended to show positive bias towards white people, slightly negative bias towards black people, and more strongly negative bias towards Southeast Asians. Furthermore, in 2006, Amnesty International reported that Southeast Asians faced a much greater likelihood than other foreigners of being randomly stopped by police and searched than Koreans or other foreigners, such as Westerners.

The reason for strong prejudice against Southeast Asians is arguably economic rather than specifically racial. Westerners in Korea come from wealthy countries and work in fields like teaching or business, or for the U.S. military. Because of the poor financial circumstances of their own countries, Southeast Asians tend to come to Korea to work in low-wage, relatively unskilled jobs, regardless of their level of education or ability. Unfortunately, South Koreans thus tend to look down upon them. There have been many cases of abuse of Southeast Asian laborers by factory bosses, such as beatings and the withholding of salaries. Bonojit Hussein, an Indian academic who won a landmark case against a Korean man who racially abused him and a Korean female companion while they were traveling on a bus, was quoted in the Korea Herald newspaper as saying, "I interacted with many migrant factory workers and after my incident they said: 'This is nothing. The media are taking it up because you are a research professor. We face much more serious situations.'"

It is unfortunate that while South Koreans are opening up very quickly to people from abroad, the pace of change is much slower for those from places like Indonesia or the Philippines. Since discrimination against people from these countries is mainly a product of wealth disparity, it will probably remain in spite of the decline of pure-blood nationalism.

Inevitable and Necessary

In desiring an open, outward-facing economy, South Korea has already made an implicit choice in favor of multiculturalism. When countries develop advanced economies and feel confident in throwing open their doors to investment and trade, people will follow. They will come in the form of factory workers from poorer countries, students seeking to learn the language, wealthy foreigners seeking to invest, and others such as journalists, who go to satisfy the curiosity that settles on increasingly important countries like South Korea.

South Korea needs these new people, and it needs them to stay—assuming economic growth is desired. According to Professor Chang, "We need more foreigners to build a new nation." The reason is demographic: South Korea's boom generation of the late 1950s and 1960s is of course aging, while today's Korean women have on average just 1.2 babies each over the course of their lives. The consequence of these two trends is that South Korea is now the most rapidly aging country in the world. By 2026, it will be a "super-aged society," according to the UN, with 23 percent of its population above the age of sixty-five. The imbalance of relatively few workers paying the taxes that provide the pensions for a large population of elderly people will act as a drag on economic growth: according to the Korea Development Institute, South Korea's potential maximum annual GDP growth will reach just 1.7 percent by 2030, due mainly to what may be termed "Grey Korea."

There are several possible countermeasures to this problem, and, given its severity, all should be employed. They include raising the retirement age, using incentives such as a better childcare provision to encourage couples to have more children, and bringing more women into the workforce. The quickest way to counter the problem, however, would be to bring in more foreigners of working age. Immigrants will expand the workforce and, through their taxes, pay for the increasing numbers of elderly people, while having children of their own who will eventually support their parents' generation in retirement. Entrepreneurs who can create jobs should be especially welcomed. While members of the older generation may naturally wish to preserve Korea's traditional culture and so-called "pure blood," in opposing a policy of foreign integration they hurt their own pension pot, risking a situation like that faced by Japan—a super-aged society that lacks a sufficient number of younger adult workers yet persists in its hostility toward the idea of granting permanent residency to foreign workers.

Increased internationalization will provide other benefits. One problem for South Korea is a lack of recognition that borders on bad PR. A BBC survey of people from twenty-five different countries in 2011 found that only 36 percent had a positive view of South Korea, while 32 percent had a negative one. A further 32 percent had no opinion at all. Surprisingly, this is actually an improvement on previous scores. The only countries ranking below South Korea in this poll in terms of approval were controversial ones: Russia, Pakistan, Israel, North Korea, and Iran. South Korea is clearly not in the same league as any of those countries in terms of either real or perceived nefariousness. The only reason for its lack of popularity (other than a misunderstanding about its trouble with the North) is that people know nothing about it. The more people who have a Korean in-law, or indeed a Korean friend or business partner, the sooner the PR problem will disappear. And the more foreigners learn about South Korea and find things to approve of, the better it is for the nation's security. The potential value of Korea's soft power, like the value of its globalized business interests, is not to be underestimated.

Maturity

The trend towards internationalization within Korean society is a sign of South Korea's growing maturity as a nation. We can also see this maturity in the way that South Korea relates to other states—it has recently emerged as an aid-giving nation, a mere few decades after being an impoverished aid recipient itself. The amount donated is small in absolute terms, but it is projected to triple by 2015. This signals an acceptance by Koreans that their country is no longer a poor victim but a member of the wealthy elite and a responsible nation with an important place in the world. The sending of delegations to countries like Vietnam to advise on economic development demonstrates South Korea's increased desire to show leadership and share what the country learned from its GDP miracle; this will also no doubt be positive for diplomacy. Furthermore, the generous charitable response from South Koreans in the wake of the Japanese tsunami of 2011 was especially impressive, given the historic enmity towards Japan.

South Korea is growing up. And the fact that the number of foreigners married to Koreans rose by 85 percent between 2005 and 2010 does not signal a polluting of some metaphoric Han River—rather it is a sign of openness and maturity.

Chapter 26

"It's Our Turn"

Long perceived as insular and excessively Confucian, Korea and Koreans are now considered fashionable and cutting-edge by many people throughout Asia. This change is thanks to the phenomenon known as *Hallyu*, the "Korean Wave." From the late 1990s onwards, Korean films, TV series, and pop music have been finding great popularity in nearby countries like China and Japan, as well as Southeast Asian nations like Thailand, Cambodia, Vietnam, and the Philippines. In the late 2000s, *Hallyu* has even started making inroads in Western countries.

This trend has been encouraged by the government of South Korea, keen to increase the nation's soft power and develop cultural industries as a new source of export income. Pop stars like Rain are regularly used in government-produced tourism material, and subsidies have been given to support the promotion of *Hallyu* overseas. The Korean media have also contributed to the *Hallyu* hype.

Indeed, Korean pop culture has become so visible that backlashes have ensued in some countries. There have been anti-*Hallyu* protests in Japan, and restrictions have been introduced by the government of China limiting the amount of airtime given to Korean TV shows. Chinese premier Hu Jintao however once told a Korean politician that the only reason he did not watch every single episode of Korean drama *Daejanggeum* (Jewel in the Palace) was that he was too busy running the country.

Properly considered, though, *Hallyu* is something much broader than teen pop and melodramatic TV dramas, or those cultural products and cinema, as we saw in chapter 21. South Korea is gaining recognition and influence in a variety of other areas, from sports to science and technology. The country has been an acknowledged economic power for some years, having joined the OECD in 1996. What has been happening with *Hallyu* is that its cultural status is simply catching up.

"For a long time, we were the ones who were influenced. Now it's our turn" is how Park Jung-sook succinctly puts it. The former television presenter and actress, who played Queen Munjeong in *Daejanggeum*, is now professor of International Relations at Kyunghee University in Seoul and a sometime guest lecturer on the *Hallyu* phenomenon at Harvard University. Korea is a country with a unique, rich, and vibrant culture, and the increased confidence that comes with Korea's economic success and acceptance into world's elite club of wealthy, industrialized nations means it can now comfortably embrace genuine cultural exchange rather than merely accept an unequal, one-way flow of ideas. The power of *Hallyu* is in fact improving South Korea's international relations and prospects for a smoother eventual reunification with North Korea, should it ever happen.

One-way Traffic

Many Koreans are fond of pointing out that, many centuries ago, their country influenced Japanese culture and was a source of the Japanese royal bloodline. In the sixth century, the Japanese emperor Kimmei (r. 539–571) invited Korean experts in medicine, literature, and shamanism to introduce their knowledge to Japan. The Korean kingdom of Baekje is also known to have had links with the island nation, sending Buddhist texts for instance, in 552. Prince Shotoku commissioned Baekje architects to construct his personal palace and temple in 601. Emperor Kammu (r. 871–896) himself was a descendent of Muryeong, king of Baekje (r. 501–523), and in 2001, Emperor Akihito himself publicly acknowledged this fact. Akihito went on to state that Korea was the source of Japan's royal court music and had served as the conduit through which Buddhism and Confucianism entered Japan. During the Japanese Imjin Waeran invasions of Korea (1592–1598), Korean potters were abducted and brought to

Japan, where their work became known as Satsuma porcelain. Japanese Satsuma porcelain eventually gained popularity in Europe, after being displayed at the Paris Exposition of 1867.

The flow of cultural exchange between the two countries became one way, and in the opposite direction, with the beginning of Japan's colonial adventures in Korea in the late 19th century. Following the assumption of full control of Korea, Imperial Japan forced Koreans to speak Japanese, practice Shinto, and take Japanese names, particularly from the late 1930s onwards. By the early 1940s, as many as 84 percent of Koreans were legally known by Japanese names. Following liberation, the backlash was so great that Japanese cultural imports were prohibited for fifty-three years until 1998, when President Kim Dae-jung's government withdrew the ban. This action paved the way for the half-Japanese, half-Korean singer Tomoe Sawa to perform two Japanese songs in public, and since then Japanese anime, pop music, manga, films, and art have all found strong followings in South Korea.

Notwithstanding the enforced Japanization of Korea from 1910 to 1945, the influence of China has been even greater. China was the source of Confucianism, which impacts social relations in Korea to this day. It also provided the civil service examination system that governed selection to join the *yangban* class throughout the Joseon dynasty. The *yangban* aristocrats were generally in the thrall of all forms of Chinese philosophy, calligraphy, literature, and art. The *hanja* characters with which Koreans wrote until the creation of the *Hangeul* writing system in the fifteenth century came from China too. Even now, good knowledge of *hanja* marks a Korean as being cultured.

Since 1945, there has been a third major external influence on Korean culture. With the arrival of the U.S. military administration, followed by the pro-U.S. governments of Syngman Rhee, Park Chung-hee, and Chun Doo-hwan, the flow of American culture into Korea has been steady. It is because of contact with the United States that more than 20 percent of South Koreans are Protestant. The South Korean political system bears the hallmarks of American influence, as outlined in chapter 14. It is American English, not

British English, that is studied to excess. Some Koreans even used to refer to English as *Miguk-mal*, "American speech."

Koreans are able to brush up their English listening comprehension by following the endlessly repeated episodes of *CSI*, *Law and Order*, and *Prison Break* that fill up the TV schedules. The government even holds up American behavioral standards as worthy of emulation: from the late 2000s onwards, successive poster campaigns have encouraged people to walk on the right-hand side of corridors and walkways. Slogans for these campaigns always point out that walking on the right is customary practice in the United States. And for those eager to earn large salaries, an MBA from an American university is considered a prerequisite. When one meets a top lawyer, civil servant, or doctor, there is also a strong chance that they will have a post-graduate degree from a well-regarded American university; it is in fact considerably more difficult to reach such a position without an American masters or doctoral degree. Today's Korean elite is excessively influenced by American culture and ways of thinking.

That South Korea should bear the imprint of Japan, China, and the United States is no surprise, of course, as these countries have been historic shapers of Korea's destiny as well as masters of cultural export. What should draw our attention is the surprising strength of South Korea itself. This small nation is the inheritor of a continuous cultural tradition going back five thousand years. It is a modern miracle of nation building, democracy, and economic growth. And it is a world leader in the manufacture of a diverse list of products: from ships and automobiles to online games, semiconductors, cell phones, and cosmetics, for instance. Despite its achievements, South Korea flew under the radar for a long time. Yet since approximately the year 2000, something has changed.

From "Konnichi-wa" to "An-nyeong Haseyo"

Actress Park Jung-sook was first selected to represent South Korea as a Goodwill Ambassador for the Daejeon Expo of 1993. She recalls that, back then, whenever she promoted the event abroad while dressed in traditional *hanbok*, she would be met with choruses of "Konnichi-wa" or "Ni hao." When she replied that she was not

Japanese or Chinese but in fact Korean, her interlocutors would respond, "Ah, North or South?" Today she finds that people will spontaneously ask her, "You're Korean, aren't you?" and are able to rattle off a list of their favorite TV shows and pop stars.

This recognition is an effect of the international popularity of shows like the period drama *Daejanggeum* (in which Ms. Park played Queen Munjeong of the Joseon dynasty), singers like BoA (who has sold 20 million records across Asia and beyond), and actors like Bae Yong-joon, who is affectionately known as Yonsama to a generation of Japanese housewives. Yonsama is such a successful celebrity that he is worth a reported $100 million, making him one of the richest non-*chaebol* Koreans. Outside of Hollywood, he is one of the world's best-paid actors, and can command a fee of US$5 million per film.

Hallyu's first successes were TV dramas like *Winter Sonata* (2002), which starred Yonsama, along with female lead Choi Ji-woo. This particular series was so popular it aired twice in 2003 on the Japanese public television station, NHK. Producers followed up with cash-in books, DVDs, and other merchandise aimed at the Japanese audience. A Japanese version of a Korean novel based on the show sold over a million copies. When Yonsama landed at Narita Airport in 2004, 350 riot police were required to keep crazed female fans at bay.

Winter Sonata was the first major overseas hit, but others soon followed. Period drama *Daejanggeum* garnered number one viewership ratings in Taiwan and Hong Kong, performed well in Cambodia, Thailand, China, and Japan, and even became the most popular show in Iran for a time, with a 57 percent viewership rating. *Jumong* (2006), the story of the founder of the Goguryeo kingdom, was also a notable success in Iran, Uzbekistan, and Kazakhstan. Another series, *Coffee Prince* (2007), was dubbed into Spanish and sold to Latin American countries. Between 2006 and 2011, the three main Thai TV stations aired a total of 118 Korean soap operas; on average, Korean drama spent 100 minutes on those stations every single day during that period. This was apparently the major factor in convincing 97 percent of Thais that the image of Korea had improved during the same five-year time frame, according to a survey by the Korea-Thailand Communications Center.

Korean film exports were also becoming successful across the region. In 2004, Korea earned US$57 million from the export of drama series, but $58 million from movies. Much of the movie revenue came from war epic *Taegukgi* and *Windstruck*, a follow-up to the first Korean film to capture the imagination of non-Koreans, *My Sassy Girl* (2001). *Windstruck* and *My Sassy Girl* both starred Jun Ji-hyun, an actress who became a household name in China and went on to star in *Snow Flower and the Secret Fan* (2011), a U.S.-made film produced by Wendi Deng, wife of media mogul Rupert Murdoch. In 2005, a Yonsama film, *April Snow*, drew 2.2 million viewers in Japan within twenty-seven days of opening.

Korean TV dramas and films have a kind of aspirational value in poorer countries such as Thailand, Vietnam, Cambodia, and Indonesia. Storylines often feature a girl from a poor family, who ends up marrying a handsome, wealthy young man. This often-used cliché is sometimes criticized by Koreans, but it is not hard to see its appeal to people who struggle to make ends meet. Such Cinderella stories have the same sort of power as Korean consumer brands. For example, a flat-screen television from LG is a status symbol in some developing countries. As Park Jung-sook observes, "We cannot separate such brands from pure cultural content." They come as a package and constitute a kind of Korean Dream, of the sort that may convince young women from those nations to emigrate to South Korea for marriage.

Different countries have responded to the Korean Wave in different ways. The Japanese have no need to look up to Koreans in terms of wealth, but, in what the Japanese call *dorama* (TV dramas or shows in general), older Japanese women in particular tend to respond to Korea's sense of the emotional—that mixture of *jeong* and *han* culture that is so distinctive. According to Ms. Park, this kind of sentimentality perhaps used to exist in Japan but has now been lost, and so Korean dramas offer feelings of warm nostalgia as well. As one Japanese female fan of all things Korean explains, "Japanese guys are cold, and so unromantic. When I see Korean guys on TV, they always look like they have so much passion and emotion."

K-pop is a different matter. It is characterized not by emotionalism, but by slick dance routines, catchy American pop-influenced melodies, and the physical attractiveness of its performers. At heart, it is pure escapist fun aimed at teenagers. Korean pop is now eclipsing the power of TV drama and films, in a financial sense. The largest producer of K-pop music—SM Entertainment, founded by former singer Lee Su-man—is valued on the Korean stock market at around US$1 billion. SM's most popular solo singer, BoA, has sold millions of records across the region. Manufactured pop groups such as Super Junior and Girls Generation tour the world, and K-pop showcases in Madison Square Garden in New York have sold out. A group called SHINee even played in front of a crowd of 55,000 at the Tokyo Dome arena. In 2009, 5,000 Chinese fans, disappointed at being unable to enter the Expo Culture Center in Shanghai for a Super Junior show, stampeded. One fan died and hundreds were injured in the ensuing chaos.

The streets of Myeongdong, Seoul's busiest shopping district, are constantly crammed with female tourists from Japan, China, and other Asian countries seeking out trinkets emblazoned with the faces of Korean pop stars and actors. Those especially afflicted may even move to Seoul and enroll in Korean-language classes. At Sogang University's renowned Korean Language Center's higher-level classes, around half the students are Japanese women. There are also plastic surgery clinics that offer multilingual service to foreigners seeking to look like their favorite Korean celebrities.

On the surface, the popularity of a few actors and pop groups may seem to offer little that might benefit South Korea's status in the long run. However, unintended, positive consequences for this country's soft power have already accrued within the region. Ms. Park points to improved relations with Vietnam—a former enemy, owing to South Korea's assistance of the U.S. Army in the Vietnam War—which she cites as an example of how, if the people like something enough, the politicians have to follow suit. Korean TV has been "like a diplomat that delivers Korean culture without payment or coercion." President Lee Myung-bak was a clear believer in this concept, stating that the Korean Wave was one of the most important developments for Korea's status in the world. In February 2012, he brought Kim Jae-joong of boy band JYJ with him on an official visit to Turkey. Kim and President Lee dined with Turkish President Abdullah Gul at his residence in Ankara. JYJ made another appearance at President Lee's official residence in March 2012, to promote the opening of the Seoul Nuclear Security Summit. Cynics would surely have a point in questioning the connection between boy bands and nuclear security, though.

Importantly, South Korean films and TV shows are having a genuine impact on North Korean society as well. Jang Cheong-rae (not his real name), a North Korean defector living in Seoul, reports that "about half of North Koreans have seen South Korean TV." According to Mr. Jang, in around 2002 the North began importing cheap DVD players from China, and, to the extreme displeasure of the regime, illicit copies of Southern content began flooding across the border with them. Today, DVDs are being replaced with USB memory sticks, but still contain illicit South Korean content. Many North Koreans are now well aware that Seoul is not an enslaved wasteland, contrary to official propaganda. This piercing of the veil of North Korean mind control could possibly support or foment a desire for change from within, and, in the event of reunification, prepare people emotionally for the shock of seeing the true South Korea for the first time.

The Trouble With *Hallyu*

In December 2011, Culture Minister Choi Gwang-shik told reporters that he would be a "Hallyu minister," as he outlined plans to triple government spending on the promotion of Korean pop culture abroad. In recent years, the South Korean national government has enthusiastically sponsored international K-pop dance events, while the Seoul Metropolitan Government has made use of *Hallyu* stars like pop star Rain as cultural ambassadors. One civil servant at the ministry of finance says, "Per year, we increased our spending on promoting traditional Korean culture by around 2 percent but increased our spending on K-pop by 12 percent." This weighting reflects the philosophy of Korean governments since the days of Park Chung-hee that part of its role is to choose potential "national champions" and that it is a correct strategy to support them at the expense of others, as General Park did with Samsung and Hyundai. In this case, the winners are companies like SM Entertainment. Seoul Metro, the underground railway, even uses boy bands as "spokes-models" for its service, despite the Seoul Metro not being in need of any sort of promotion. This is essentially a transfer of wealth from ordinary metro users to entertainment companies, facilitated by a state-owned enterprise.

But can cultural products receive government support and still be "cool"? And is it good for Korea to be known as a country of manufactured pop music and melodramatic television above all else? In a poll of twenty Chinese people conducted by the author, more than half mentioned the pop stars or actresses who "all have plastic surgery" (in the words of one respondent) when asked to name things that come to mind about Korea. There is a risk that Korea—a country with a long history and rich culture—may become known as a shallow place. No British person would want their country to be known as the land of the Spice Girls, but it seems as though the Korean government would not mind if their country became known as the land of pop groups like Girls Generation or JYJ.

Excessive reliance on pop culture has an additional danger. If people ever tire of over-hyped Korean drama and pop music, the Korean Wave will be over. Already in Japan, China, and other countries, there have been anti-*Hallyu* backlashes, as mentioned earlier. In 2006, a comic book titled *Hyom-hallyu* (Hatred of the Korean Wave) sold 300,000 copies in Japan and became the top seller on amazon.co.jp. The story of *Hyom-hallyu* was of a boy who came to realize "the ugly nature of Korea" from coming into contact with its pop culture. And in July 2011, Japanese actor Sousuke Takaoka told followers on Twitter that he was tired of all the Korean dramas on Fuji Channel 8. In response, a boycott of the channel was organized. "It feels like Korean dramas brainwash you," wrote the actor.

Mr. Takaoka's agency terminated his contract as a result of his comments, but many Japanese agree with him, and six thousand people turned out for a protest against Fuji TV's *Hallyu* programming in the wake of his remarks. Some were reportedly shouting nationalist slogans like "Long live the emperor," and "Chase the cockroaches out of Japan." This incident was widely reported in both Korean and Japanese media, and certainly did no favors to Korea-Japan relations.

In February 2012, a planned promotional visit to Japan by actress Kim Tae-hee was canceled, due to anti-*Hallyu* sentiment as well as the hostility of right-wing Japanese groups to Ms. Kim's support for Korean sovereignty of the disputed Dokdo islets (known as Takeshima in Japan). In the same month, Korean boy band Block B caused anger in Thailand by appearing to make jokes about the 2011 Bangkok floods, in which 780 people died. A representative of the Korea Thailand Communications Center was quoted as saying that the incident may have "an adverse effect on the popularity of Korean culture and lead to anti-Korean sentiment" in Thailand.

According to film critic Darcy Paquet, *Hallyu* has had a negative impact on the Korean movie industry, as we saw in chapter 21. In the mid-2000s, he says, studios started to "put packaging before story": because studios came to believe that audiences in Japan or China would go to see any film starring Yonsama or Jun Ji-hyun, no effort was put into actually making good films. This eventually led to a steep decline in popularity. Film export revenues plummeted from US$76 million to $12 million between 2005 and 2007. "For the film industry, *Hallyu* is over. It has crashed," he states.

The Korean Wave has come under regulatory pressure too. In 2006, central and regional Chinese authorities restricted the amount of Korean TV broadcasters are allowed to schedule, in order to protect homegrown content. In 2012, the National Communication Commission of Taiwan as well (the official regulator) issued a call for local stations to play less Korean content, in order to give Taiwanese drama a better chance. Gala Television, one of the main Taiwanese drama stations, announced in response that it would comply and reduce the amount Korean-made content while devoting an hour of prime-time scheduling each day to domestic shows. Both cases show how Korean drama has become a victim of its own success.

It would be almost unthinkable for the South Korean media to question the value of Korea becoming known abroad as a source of television and pop music. Indeed, in the 2010s so far, there has been a relentless stream of articles in all main Korean papers trumpeting the overseas success of such products; the press even greatly exaggerates the success of K-pop in Europe and the United States on a regular basis. Media do not ask whether *Hallyu* may one day come to an end or provoke a more widespread backlash than has already occurred in some places, and also do not ask whether the government's promotion of the Korean Wave may end up becoming counterproductive. Such criticism or skepticism would seem unpatriotic, though South Korea would benefit from having such a debate.

The Real *Hallyu*

Perhaps it would serve Korea better if the authorities marketed the Korean Wave in a more comprehensive and balanced way, as indicated at the beginning of this chapter. Architect Hwang Doo-jin has observed that South Korea is "a small but complete world." It possesses a complete and unique culture, with a range of nation-specific dress, music, drama, cinema, art, and so on. An inevitable consequence of its economic success must be that a broad sweep of its cultural output will finally make its way overseas, just as Japanese culture did from the 1980s to the present day.

Already, we are seeing evidence of a broader Korean Wave traveling far beyond the bounds of East Asia. For the first time, a Korean novel has achieved success in the international mainstream. *Take Care of My Mother* by Shin Kyung-sook has sold well over a million copies worldwide and become a bestseller in nineteen different countries, including the United States. Korean brands such as Hyundai, Kia, and Samsung are gaining recognition both as leaders in their fields and as identifiably Korean. Previously, they were often assumed to be Japanese or elicited confusion about their origin. In 2010, Seoul hosted the G20 Summit of leading economic powers, for the first time. Half of the top ten WPGA golfers are Korean. UN secretary general Ban Ki-moon's Korean nationality has helped raised his country's profile and is also another indication of its increasing soft power.

In the furtherance of South Korea's reputation, the best thing officials have done has nothing to do with pop culture. In the 1950s and 60s, this country was a recipient of vast amounts of aid, principally from the United States. Today, it is a donor country. Where the Philippines once gave to South Korea, now it receives: in November 2010, for instance, the Korea International Co-operation Agency (KOICA) handed a grant of $22 million to Manila for agricultural projects. In 2011, the Korean government also announced that humanitarian aid to Africa, which stood at just US$5 million annually, would be increased to $50 million by 2013. As of the end of 2011, South Korea was the only non-Western country to be a member of all the major international humanitarian policy-setting forums, such as the Development Assistance Committee. And between 2009 and 2010 (the latest statistics available), according to the OECD, Korea increased its overall overseas development aid by 30.5 percent. The top recipient was Vietnam, which received US$82 million.

This aid diplomacy in some way echoes the efforts of the United States and other countries, such as Japan, to build soft power through monetary and other donations, but for South Korea there is one additional benefit. As a small country that dug its way out of poverty at a remarkably rapid pace, it can offer expertise—and a positive, feasible example—in the way that America cannot. Thus, when Korean officials armed with both checks and solid advice visit places like Vietnam, a country with a similar history of colonialism and division, people listen. Admittedly, it remains to be seen whether Vietnamese authorities will heed Korea's lesson on democracy as much as its economic lesson.

South Korea has completed an almost 180-degree turn. Having left behind poverty, inwardness, and a unidirectional flow of culture and aid, it is embracing its place as a wealthy, culturally rich country that has something to offer to the world. Neighboring Asian countries have certainly noticed, and the rest of the world will naturally start to do so as well. As Park Jung-sook says, a country's image is "something others recognize, not something you force upon them." It is now South Korea's turn to be recognized.

Chapter 27

"We Are Not Aliens, From Another Cosmos"

South Korea is considered an intolerant country where homosexuality is concerned. Yet throughout the Koryo dynasty, the union of "the dragon and the sun" (two male symbols) was fairly common among both kings and peasants. Even in the later Joseon period, where Confucian values prevailed, same-sex relationships were not unusual among village folk. It was only during the twentieth century that society began to consider homosexuality absolutely unacceptable.

That attitude of intolerance in the modern era did not generally take the form of active hostility, for homosexual acts were not banned by law, and there was no serious problem of anti-gay violence as in many Western countries. It was more the case that twentieth-century Korean society chose to pretend that homosexuality did not exist and only reacted against it—primarily through ostracism—when faced with people who wished to express their same-sex preference openly. Even today, the majority of gay Koreans lead double lives for fear of being disowned by parents, abandoned by friends, or facing discrimination in the workplace. Participants in "Gay Pride" marches sometimes cover their faces, to avoid being recognized.

It was in such an environment that Hong Seok-cheon, a rising actor, became the first Korean celebrity to "come out" in the year 2000. He forced Koreans to confront the reality that they all knew existed but preferred not to think about. The initial public response was rage: "At the time, ninety-five percent of the people hated me," says

Mr. Hong. Offers of TV work and sponsorship completely dried up, and friends deserted him.

Three years later, alone and poor and living in a small house near to the Itaewon district of Seoul, Mr. Hong opened a restaurant. The place was not a success initially. Today though, he presides over a mini-empire, with a portfolio of nine restaurants, each of which is extremely popular and profitable. He is back on television as well. This dramatic reversal of fortune is a direct result of changing attitudes to homosexuality. While society in general still does not approve of Mr. Hong's lifestyle, a great many young people now fully accept same-sex relationships.

Powder and Rouge

Homosexuality is hardly a modern concept. Anyone even remotely acquainted with Greek or Roman, not to mention samurai, history is well aware that homosexual love was accepted in many communities in the world. In Korea, Confucianism, a conservative moral code, put great emphasis on the need for individuals to marry and produce children to continue their family line. Yet, here too, despite Confucianism's long and profound influence, we can find evidence for the existence of homosexual relationships down through the centuries.

The most commonly cited example is King Kongmin, the Koryo dynasty monarch who reigned from 1351 to 1374. Scholars such as Professors Kim Young-gwan and Hahn Sook-ja at Pyeongtaek University state that, following the death of his wife, Kongmin kept a coterie of *jajewi*, handsome young men selected as lovers. One of Kongmin's predecessors, Chungseon, who reigned briefly in 1298 and then from 1308 to 1313, is also believed to have had a long-term male lover.

Though such relations were, according to some sources, quite common among the elite during the Koryo dynasty, tolerance of homosexuality declined in the Joseon era. King Sejong the Great himself was advised by ministers to disown his daughter-in-law for the crime of having sexual relations with maidservants. This case has the rare distinction of being recorded in royal documents. We can probably infer that the scarcity of such tales in official records is more a result of the aversion and taboo that had by then developed than an indication of the absence of homosexual practices. Indeed, homosexuality was still practiced widely, particularly among country folk.

Richard Rutt, an Anglican priest who spent many years in Korea and eventually became Bishop of Daejeon in 1968, wrote extensively about Korean culture and history. He stated that, in spite of official Joseon opposition to the practice, "homosexuality was well known in rural society during the Yi (Joseon) Dynasty (1392–1910)," adding that older men in Gyeonggi Province had told him that same-sex relations had remained commonplace among village folk until well into the early twentieth century. His informants reported that such relations had "very little stigma...and would not impair chances of marriage" later. If this is true, it would seem that society actually became more conservative with respect to some sexual practices as the twentieth century wore on—to the point where people not only disliked homosexuality, but also preferred to deny its very existence.

There are also those who claim that the Hwarang, the Shilla dynasty's proud fighting force (and a symbol of Korean militarism), was somewhat homoerotic in character. Verses celebrating particular Hwarang, such as "Song of Yearning for the Flower Boy Taemara," were "seen as illustrating a Hwarang penchant for sexual intercourse with same-sex partners," claim Professors Kim Young-gwan and Hahn Sook-ja. This may be a step too far, although it is worth noting the following comments by the Tang dynasty Chinese official Cheng Ling-hu, who wrote: "They selected handsome sons of the elite and adorned them with powder and rouge. They call them Hwarang. The people all revere and serve them. Good generals and brave soldiers are produced by reason of it."

Don't Ask, Don't Tell
During the Joseon era, *namsadang*—bands of itinerant male performers who would travel from town to town and sing, act, and do acrobatics—were popular among the general population, despite coming from the *cheonmin*, the lowest social class. It is believed that male-to-male prostitution and general homosexual activity were widespread among such troupes, especially among a class of

namsadang performer called *midong* (beautiful boy). The *nam-sadang* tradition continued up until the 1910s, when the colonizing Japanese put an end to it as part of their efforts to stamp out Korean culture.

One of the most popular Korean films of the recent golden era, *The King and the Clown* (2005), made great dramatic use of this theme. The story concerns one such *namsadang* performer, who would be described as a *kkotminam* ("pretty flower boy") in the current parlance. This young man, Gonggil, wins the affections of King Yeonsan, perhaps the most brutal monarch of the Joseon period. The film, which sold 12 million movie tickets in this country of 48 million, bears the original Korean title of *Wang-ui Namja*, which translates to the rather more direct "King's Man."

Lee Jun-ki, the actor who played said king's man, is one of several male stars who derive their popularity from their prettiness. In the early 1990s, the dominant style of male representation in the entertainment industry was macho, but for some time now the *kkotminam* has reigned supreme. There are also boy bands such as 2AM, whose style, which features heavy makeup and elaborate hairstyling, is undoubtedly androgynous and, to the eyes of the more worldly, homoerotic.

Yet, at the same time, any celebrity who chose to come out would be putting their career in jeopardy. Several very famous Korean stars whose homosexuality is an open secret within the industry would find themselves bereft of the lucrative advertising and sponsorship opportunities that provide the bulk of celebrity earnings if they ever actually announced the fact publicly.

Hong Seok-chon

The one person who knows this better than anyone is Hong Seok-chon, who to this day divides public opinion. On a variety show in September 2000, another guest jokingly asked him if he preferred men or women. Disbelief ensued when he gave them the honest answer. Producers edited this exchange out of the show, but a journalist later got wind of the story and asked him about it, and again, Mr. Hong, who had been thinking for some time that he "didn't want to live a double life" any more, decided to repeat his admission.

The result was public uproar. He had broken the taboo that "we didn't talk about the gay issue in Korea," and he paid the price. He received death threats and, despite being the most talked about person in the country at the time, "had no work for three years." To this day, with his career in recovery, he is still never chosen to represent Korean companies in advertising. For this reason, he defends other celebrities who refuse to come out, saying: "They know I lost everything."

Following the setback to his acting career, he opened a restaurant (Our Place) in the Seoul district of Itaewon. For the first twelve months, he consistently lost money because of a lack of customers, and, to make matters worse, many of the people who did show up merely came to shout abuse at him.

What Came Next
In time, Our Place enjoyed a turnaround in fortune. Over the next eight years, Mr. Hong opened eight more restaurants and became a wealthy man. Streets where he set up shop would be transformed as other restaurateurs and bar owners followed his lead. His personal brand, which had once been poison, started to work in his favor. TV producers, though never quite as ardent as in the days prior to September 2000, began to call him again.

The new interest from producers stemmed from what Mr. Hong calls the "big change, which happened so fast." While nobody would claim that homosexuality is truly tolerated by Korean society in general, there has been a shift in attitude, and Mr. Hong is the one person most responsible for it. His public announcement "forced [people] to think deeply...and start to talk." He believes that it is now becoming possible for a gay person to come out and not face the ruin of his career and the abandonment of friends, as would have likely happened in the very recent past.

These days he is regularly invited to universities to speak to groups of up to five hundred at a time. He says that young people do not care about his sexuality and respond well to his message that "we are not that different... We are not aliens from another cosmos." Among his public activities, he considers these speaking engagements to be the most important, because the young audience members "will be bosses ten or twenty years from now." He wants them to remember his message then and not refuse to hire people on the grounds of what they do in their private lives.

In 2010, a popular TV drama series entitled *Life Is Beautiful* featured a same-sex relationship between the two main characters. Less than a decade earlier, portraying even a minor character as homosexual would have been unthinkable. Indeed, writer Kim Soo-yeon tried repeatedly over the years to insert gay characters into her screenplays, only to be rebuffed by producers.

General Attitudes

No one should mistake such developments for change at all levels of society. Though many people—particularly twenty- and thirty-something urbanites and those of artistic or creative backgrounds—consider Mr. Hong a hero (or perhaps just enjoy going to his restaurants), have gay friends, or support the legalization of same-sex marriage, a poll by the Pew Research Center in 2007 found that 77 percent of Koreans believe that "homosexuality should be rejected." The change at present is among a particular subset of the population. Whether or not this group will remain tolerant as they grow older, and pass this attitude on to their own children, remains to be seen.

For lesbians in South Korea, life is by most accounts even more difficult than for gay males. In traditional Confucian thinking, a woman's duty is to marry and have children, even more so than it is a man's, and this belief still lingers in contemporary Korean society. According to some lesbians, even the male homosexual community is not particularly welcoming towards them. Mr. Hong and others term lesbians a "double minority," in that they suffer not merely from prejudice and misunderstandings about their sexuality but also from the remnants of general sexism that women are striving to defeat.

For both gays and lesbians, the legal environment is tough. Though homosexuality was never illegal in South Korea, the right to civil partnership for gays has never existed and probably never will. Mr. Hong feels that, despite the changes that are taking place, it unlikely that society will ever give him and his partner the same rights as heterosexual couples, because of residual Confucianism and the influence of a more recent arrival, fundamentalist Christianity.

In 2007, an anti-discrimination law was proposed in order to protect minorities, including sexual minorities. Christian activists, who, as in the United States, tend to be socially conservative and politically powerful, lobbied extensively against the bill. Due to this pressure, the parts of the bill pertaining to homosexuality were removed, and eventually the whole bill was withdrawn. The election of Presbyterian president Lee Myung-bak in December 2007 meant there was no chance legal protection for lesbians and gays would be introduced, for he himself has publicly described homosexuals as "abnormal."

Korea's first Christian martyrs were executed for refusing to perform Jesa, the Confucian rite to commemorate ancestors. Now the twin forces of Confucianism and Christianity seem to have combined to produce a brand of conservatism regarding sexuality that gay people will find very difficult to overcome. Yet Korea is a place where diverse philosophical and religious traditions have somehow learned to live with each other. The proportion of the population who are neither conservative Christians nor adherents of Confucian morality will grow increasingly tolerant of homosexuality. Society as a whole may never treat gay people equally, but it will be possible for them to live more honestly and openly as time goes by.

Chapter 28

A Woman's Place Is in the Office

Until very recently, a woman could not legally be the head of a household in South Korea. Under the terms of a family record system called *hoju*, each Korean was registered as belonging to a particular household, the head of which could only be a man. A woman leaving her family home to marry was removed from her father's record and placed on that of her new husband. Any children they had would automatically join the husband's record, and remain there even in the event of divorce.

Though introduced only in 1898 under the influence of the encroaching Japan, *hoju* fit well with the male-first culture that had existed in Korea since the rise of neo-Confucianism in the fourteenth century. Earlier dynasties like the Shilla and Koryo had some degree of sexual equality, but the Joseon dynasty (1392–1910) saw the status of women shrink dramatically. Women could not initiate divorce, though their husbands could divorce them on a whim; they had to strictly obey their husband's commands; they were not able to inherit property; and they were generally forbidden from participating in public life.

When the National Assembly voted in 2005 to abolish the *hoju* system, the change was hailed by women's groups as a landmark victory for equality. In the same year, though, the United Nations' Gender Empowerment Measure (GEM) ranked South Korea just 59th among 116 countries surveyed on the extent to which women are found in senior management, professional, and political roles—an unusually poor showing for an economically developed, democratic nation. Plainly, the influence of five centuries of Joseon government cannot be swept away with a few legal revisions.

However, times are beginning to change. The current generation of young Korean women is starting to explore opportunities that their mothers and grandmothers never had. This is not due to any women's rights mass movement—only 16 percent of Korean women call themselves feminists, according to a 2007 survey by the Chosun Ilbo newspaper—but rather "because people realized it is more efficient" to give women the chance to get out of the kitchen and into the workplace, according to 2008 Korean Woman of the Year, and first Korean in space, Soyeon Yi.

As with South Korea's growing internationalization, the transformation of women's roles in society is an example of this country's ability to set itself on the right track in a time of need. By 2026, 23 percent of South Koreans will be aged sixty-five or over. Their pension requirements will place a huge burden on taxpayers. Additionally, the low birth rate means that there will be a relative lack of young people of working age to make tax contributions. It is absolutely imperative then that the size of the workforce increases. Bringing women into the office is an obvious and inevitable part of the solution.

"If You Are Educated, You Won't Listen to Your Husband"

During the Shilla, Koryo, and very early Joseon eras, couples would typically follow a tradition of matrilocal marriage, by getting married in the bride's parents' home, and then living with them until they had children (following that, they would live with the husband's parents). Women had equal rights of inheritance and could remarry after divorce. The women of Shilla were able to travel more or less freely and "possessed more rights and privileges than women were to ever hold again in Korea until the twentieth century," according to Mary E. Connor, president of the Korea Academy for Educators, in her essay "Women and Marriage." The situation of women deteriorated precipitously with the rise of neo-Confucianist ethics, particularly from the fifteenth century onwards. The reign of King Sejong (r. 1418–1450) saw the introduction of rules that restricted women's ability to visit temples. Ironically, it was the elite *yangban* women who bore the brunt of the changes in the Joseon era: the administration of King Seongjong (r. 1469–1494) introduced a national code that stated, "Any woman from the *sajok* [*yangban* class] who attends a festival in the mountains or the riverside, or conducts a ritual ceremony, shall receive 100 lashes." Seongjong's reign also saw the introduction of regulations preventing the descendents of women who married more than once from taking the civil service examination, thus blocking their path to *yangban* status.

By the seventeenth century, women's inheritance rights were curtailed, as well as their ability to conduct ancestral commemoration ceremonies. The lower status of women had become fully entrenched and was supported by the growth of literature that promoted a kind of idealized, subservient neo-Confucian woman. In government-published textbooks like *Yeosaseo*, from the eighteenth century, women were encouraged to be virtuous and follow standards of Joseon etiquette, serving their husbands and in-laws at all times. They were expected to produce male heirs (failure to produce a male heir was considered a woman's fault and reasonable grounds for divorce). By this time, women were also legally obliged to cover their faces whenever they left their homes.

Not that they left their homes often. The status of women had eroded to the extent that the family home became the only domain regarded as suitable for a woman. It is said that the game of *nolttwigi*, in which participants jump up and down on seesaws, was created by women who wished to look over their walls to gain a view of the outside world—as there were few opportunities to do so otherwise. Even basic education was denied to women, and the realms of politics, business, intellectual affairs, and anything else deemed "outer" or "public" were reserved for men alone. It was also considered perfectly acceptable for a husband to beat his wife. Many old expressions exist that reveal the harsh nature of the times: "If you don't beat your wife every three days, she'll become a fox," held one. As in other countries, the fox was a symbol of cunning, wily femininity. In Korean folklore, the *gumiho*—nine-tailed fox—could take on the form of a beautiful woman, seducing men and eating their livers.

Some women were less restricted than others. Among the poorest classes, it was necessary for many women to work—in farming, for instance. Shamanist *musok-in*, most of whom were female, and *kisaeng*, (who, like Japanese geisha, entertained men with elegant dress, song, conversation, and sometimes sexual favors) performed their roles in the world outside the home. Such women could become powerful through their influence over men in authority. However, in rank *musok-in* and *kisaeng* were still considered to be of the lowest class of people and ostracized in public, regardless of their abilities and earning power. The ideal woman was the one who stayed indoors and faithfully served her husband and in-laws.

Joseon mores built up over five centuries and thus became deeply ingrained in the mindsets of Korean men and women. Even the upheavals of Japanese colonialism, division, and war did not correct the unequal balance of roles. From the 1950s onward, the government began moving towards the provision of schooling for all children, regardless of gender—yet many girls were prevented from benefiting from it by their own families. Soyeon Yi says that her own mother "was a victim of conservatism... My grandfather said, 'if you are educated, you won't listen to your [future] husband,'" and so she was not even allowed to attend middle school.

Changing Times

Dr. Yi's mother retained a life-long yearning for education and, like many people who are forced to go without something, pinned all her hopes on her children. She insisted that her daughter be treated as an equal to her brothers—something Dr. Yi's father himself did not oppose. "You are all just as precious to me," Dr. Yi quotes her mother as saying, with obvious emotion and pride. "She almost cried on my PhD graduation day," Dr. Yi adds. Thanks to such changed attitudes, women have had virtually the same access to education as men for some years now. By 2010, 49.1 percent of Masters' degrees awarded in South Korea went to women.

Nonetheless, the range of work opportunities presented to women following graduation did not grow at a comparable rate. South Korea's Gender Empowerment Measure rank in 1995, according to the UN, was 90th out of 116 countries surveyed, only marginally better than Arabic countries. A female civil service recruit in the early 1990s would have had to give details about her "wife" on official forms, since there was no slot for "husband" or "spouse." This is perhaps unsurprising considering less than 2 percent of civil servants at the time were women. Women who graduated in the 1980s or early 1990s were generally expected to marry as soon as possible and give up on any career aspirations to focus on raising children.

The unfortunate cohort of women who received all the advantages of education except the chance to actually use it are an anomaly. Men in positions of authority discriminated against them and ensured that they quit their jobs after marriage, regardless of whatever qualifications they may have had. Thus, the current crop of leaders in their forties and fifties is lacking in female representation. Indeed, only 4.7 percent of executives of large Korean firms are women. This is much higher than Japan, where the figure is just 1 percent, but by international standards, Korea does lag. For those who came later, graduating in the late 1990s and 2000s, the picture is strikingly different. Dr. Yi, an engineer by training, recounts that older supervisors would express surprise when her projects were successful, "even though you're a woman." They would always refer to her as a "woman engineer" rather than simply an engineer. However, male peers just considered her an engineer of equal status, reflecting the changed attitude that had occurred in the span of a generation. Hiring practices now are much more equal in many fields, especially the public sector. In 2010, 71 percent of newly appointed judges, and 56.8 percent of newly appointed prosecutors, were women. With figures like these, it may not be too long before young men start complaining of discrimination.

Private Korean firms do still lag relative to the state, but even the old-school *chaebol* have begun dramatically increasing their female headcounts. Between 2002 and 2006, for instance, the number of women at the largest ten business groups rose by 47.9 percent (though seven out of ten of their new hires still are men). Their increased interest in hiring women may be partly explained by the fact that the *chaebol* are looking over their shoulders at the Seoul offices of foreign firms, who have derived an advantage over them by taking their pick of the most talented female graduates, the kind of potential top performers the *chaebol* did not formerly pay attention to. In this way, greater opportunities for women have had little to do with campaigning for rights or positive discrimination, and everything to do with efficiency. People are realizing that talent should not go to waste.

Smarter from the Beginning?

Trailblazers like Soyeon Yi are helping change attitudes towards women in Korea. "All my friends were sure I couldn't make it, because I was a woman," she recalls about the selection process that saw 36,000 applicants whittled down to two—and then one, when Ko San, the male applicant originally chosen ahead of her, was disqualified for breaking the information secrecy rules of the Russian space program. Having shown that it was possible to come out on top, she regularly receives letters from girls, thanking her for showing them that "if you do your best, you can make it."

Recently, it has been something of a trend among Korean men to feel that women are "taking over." One look at the cabinet or the board of Samsung Electronics would tell them otherwise, but the men of this country have long harbored the suspicion that the women are in fact "much smarter than we are," and given the chance, will end up turning the tables on them, as Cho Jin-won (not his real name), a senior Samsung manager, noted to the author only in half jest.

The usual evidence of superior female common sense is that, even in the days before women were able to compete in the job market, they were generally left in charge of household finance in the belief that this would lead to better results. Typically, men hand their salaries over to their wives, who give them an "allowance" in return. Decisions on the purchase of homes also tend to be made by women. Furthermore, a survey by the Chosun Ilbo newspaper in 2007 revealed that 65 percent of married Korean women have "secret funds" that their husbands are unaware of. Women may keep a stash for a multitude of purposes, both good and bad, but stories are legion of such rainy day funds being used to save families from financial disaster. A friend of the author says that when his father's business went bankrupt, his mother produced a sum of money she had been hoarding for years, one large to enough to open up a restaurant. The hard work of both parents turned that one establishment into five, and the family is now well off again, thanks to his mother's wise deception.

The Jeju Woman

While it is hard to deny that Korea has been a historically sexist country, important regional variations make stereotyping difficult. The province of Jeolla, for instance, has always offered women more of a say than the more conservative Gyeongsang Province has. According to architect Hwang Doo-jin, many Joseon-era homes in Jeolla had reception rooms where both the men and women of the house could greet guests. In Gyeongsang, only men had such rooms. However, the best place for women in Korea was always considered to be Jeju Island, located off the south coast of the mainland.

An independent society prior to its conquest by the Koryo dynasty and eventual absorption into Joseon Korea, Jeju to this day is home to a dialect that other Koreans find hard to understand. One Seoul resident calls Jeju people "only about 90 percent Korean" in the way they think and act. Probably the most obvious way the island's culture differs from that of the mainland is in its traditional gender roles. Very often, a Jeju woman was the breadwinner of her family.

The iconic example of the Jeju woman, known to all Koreans, is the *haenyeo*, literally "sea woman." These women dove to depths of around sixty feet to retrieve abalone and other valuable sea creatures to sell at the market, while their husbands would traditionally stay home and look after the children. This culture was particularly vibrant on the small island of Mara (about five miles off the south coast of Jeju), where the economy was almost entirely dependent upon *haenyeo*. It cannot be said that women had power over men in Jeju—men still dominated political affairs, for instance—but as breadwinners they played an indispensable social role and were respected accordingly.

Paradoxically, encroaching modernity has reduced the economic status of Jeju women in recent years. The island is no longer remote. In fact, it is a tourist destination for Seoul dwellers, who can arrive via Gimpo airport in just one hour. The growth of tourism has resulted in the development of more classically male-dominated businesses like hotels, often run by large mainland Korean corporations, in which women are generally employed to clean rooms or sit at the front desk and smile. Furthermore, the typical *haenyeo* is now over fifty, and her daughter is not following in her footsteps.

Discrimination Is Going—But How Quickly?

Though sexism was undeniably prevalent in Korea, it was not uniform or simple—as the cases of female control of family finances and the economic power of Jeju women would attest. And as we have seen, times are changing, at least for young people. Women like Soyeon Yi are benefiting from this change already, but, when their own daughters are ready to enter the workforce, how equal will society be? If equality is increasing, the speed of that increase may be more important than anything else, and for the same reason we have seen in previous sections: this country is facing a demographic crisis.

South Korea is expected to become a "super-aged society" by 2026, with 23 percent of its population over the age of sixty-five. This is because of two separate factors. The first is a positive one—life expectancy is now beyond 80 years and rising. We can thus expect Korea's baby boom generation of the late 1950s and 1960s to live long lives. The second is the fact that Korean women now only have 1.2 children, on average, over the course of their lifetimes. In the late 1950s, they had more than six.

By the late 2020s and 2030s, a chart showing population numbers by age will look like an inverted pyramid, with large numbers of old people at the top, and fewer young people at the bottom. Economists talk of a "demographic dividend" when there is a preponderance of young people out working and paying taxes and relatively few old people for society to support. When the opposite becomes true, the result is an economic nightmare. With almost one in four people beyond working age and requiring pension payments and greater healthcare expenditure, the burden on wage-earning taxpayers—of whom there will be fewer than before—will be vast. Korea's maximum GDP growth rate will be just 1.7 percent per year by 2030, and by some estimates Korea's national pension fund, currently the fourth largest in the world with assets of over US$300 billion, will be completely depleted by 2040.

To increase tax receipts in order to pay for the growing legions of senior citizens, the 39 percent of university-educated women who do not work need to be coaxed back into the office. Some may have conservative husbands who discourage them from working, but the main problem stems from the lack of support for working mothers and the gender pay gap, which at 35 percent, is the highest in the OECD. These serve as disincentives and the result is a so-called M-curve pattern, in which young women begin working after school or college, give up after having children, then return to work after their children grow up, but in low-paid, low value-added jobs.

The right policies should lead to an increase in the female labor participation rate, and that would actually lead to a higher birth rate. The main cause of Korea's low birth rate is the shocking cost of raising children. Raising one child in Korea costs an average total of 260 million won (around US$230,000) according to the Korea Institute of Health and Social Affairs. This is a conservative figure: the Korea Labor Institute claims that the cost is actually over 400 million won. Outside of the wealthy, single-income couples are unable to afford this. If a couple wants two children, both of them have to work.

The examples of the U.K. and Sweden demonstrate that when generous maternity and paternity leave is offered and accepted, high rates of female labor participation and much higher birth rates (2 per woman in the UK, 1.9 in Sweden), result. In Korea, maternity leave is too short, and workplace pressure results in women not taking all of it. Paternity leave of five days is a legal right, but few men would actually go to their boss and demand it. A 2005 report by the OECD argues that better childcare policies (and genuine implementation of them) would result in an increase in the birth rate of 0.4 in South Korea, shifting it up to around 1.6 children per woman.

Since 2001, when the first maternity leave legislation was introduced, successive governments have been well aware of this logic, and some improvements have been made. There are now childcare vouchers for low-income families, for instance, and more than three hundred laws have been changed since 2005 with the specific purpose of increasing gender equality.

Killing the M-Curve

The current generation of young women holds the key to South Korea's economic future. They have access to education and work opportunities in an (almost) equal fashion to men in many areas. Women just ten years older than them sit at home or work in low-paid part-time jobs, prisoners of the M-curve. The question is, will increasingly positive social attitudes towards working women and policies aimed at supporting them be enough to help today's twenty-three-year-old college graduate a decade from now, when she contemplates having children? Will the M-curve level out enough to allow South Korea to support its elderly and increase its birth rate at the same time?

There are two reasons that lead to hope. The first is that a majority of policymakers as well as citizens in general are well aware of the urgency of solving Korea's aging society problem. 91 percent of Koreans consider the low birthrate issue very serious, according to a survey by the Korean health ministry in 2012. Sexism is not likely to be an obstacle to change either, as men themselves are no longer against the expansion of opportunities for women. The Pew Research Center has found that only 8 percent of Korean men are now against gender equality.

The second reason is simple market efficiency, as Dr. Yi points out. 50 percent of human talent is held by women, and people now finally realize this. Thus, the nation's four largest financial companies, the titans of an industry long considered a bastion of sexism, selected women for 52 percent of new management jobs in 2007. Such positions, which typically take seven to ten years of experience to attain, would not have been awarded to women in the past because of the belief that they would have to quit to start families. Precious few directors at these companies today are women, but within ten years, there will be many.

Cultural critics who are fond of painting Korea as a sexist country still make a valid point. Indeed, the media in this country is particularly regressive in the way it portrays women, as either helpless or overly sexualized objects. However, when the need is great enough, Koreans display a willingness and ability to be flexible, and that is a social trait that trumps this and many other problems. We are already seeing evidence of Koreans' ability to change under pressure with regard to the new opportunities being created for women. This is also partly why the traditional xenophobia is disappearing. More and more foreign workers as well as more women workers are needed to beat the demographic burden of a super-aged society.

Epilogue

Where Is the Champagne?

As a modern state, South Korea was born in a desperate condition. Impoverished, sapped by decades of colonialism, ravaged by war, poorly endowed with natural resources, and a mere half of a historic nation, it has nevertheless survived and gone on to become an unlikely success story. In fifty years—an incredibly short time—South Koreans have somehow contrived to transform their country into one of the most advanced in the world.

This success is not just economic, a matter of GDP figures, but also social and political. Democracy has taken root, artists have found their voice in cultural areas like cinema, and South Korean society is beginning to embrace a new era of openness. The most exciting aspect of these developments is that they are works in progress. This is a country whose days of greatest glory are still ahead of it.

South Korea's achievements have come in spite of the many conflicts and divisions that exist within its society. These include an extreme left-right political split; the thousand-year-old Jeolla-Gyeongsang regional rivalry; the conflicting religious traditions of Buddhism and Christianity; and, the contradiction between the everything-in-its-right-place mentality of Confucianism and the drive to overturn old traditions in the pursuit of economic growth. Today, new conflicts are emerging: with the rise of income inequality, there is an increasing divide between rich and poor; there is also now a rising lack of understanding between the older and younger generations.

A flexibility in the character of South Koreans and in their society has allowed conflicts and differences to coexist, and to be productive rather than get in the way of progress. This innate ability to yield to reality has enabled society to accept change when it becomes clear that change is needed. Other aspects of the Korean character, such as the ability to focus on goals and work relentlessly towards them, have helped Koreans bring about transformation in some areas at remarkable speed.

Yet the country's achievements have come with certain unfortunate costs. South Koreans work so hard in part because a spirit of competition infects virtually all aspects of life. The pressure to outdo other members of society is linked with a need to be seen as a top achiever. The result is that, while Koreans have much to be proud of, they remain an unhappy people. While the expression of pure joy (*heung*) is woven deeply into Korea's traditional culture, opportunities to manifest it have grown limited in modern South Korea. Workdays are long and tiring, holidays are short, and the perceived need for success makes time devoted to amusement or relaxation a luxury.

Though the country has achieved wealth to the point where its people might naturally be expected to start spending a little time doing nothing—in other words, being at leisure—Koreans continue to work the longest hours in the OECD. They overinvest in education and compete to have the best test scores and degrees. They compete for jobs at the most famous companies, and at those jobs—spurred by their own competitiveness and the company "spirit"—proceed to work around the clock and accumulate stress. This practice is counterproductive for firms themselves, since the pressure felt by staff ends up reducing workers' productivity.

A young Korean man in his twenties or thirties—particularly one of high social status—will likely have few hobbies relative to his counterparts in other advanced, industrialized countries. The vacations he takes will last a few days rather than weeks. Because of the perceived need to compete and demonstrate a high level of achievement, he will invest an unhealthy amount of time in bolstering his academic or work credentials. Should the eventual outcome of all this effort prove disappointing or even just average, he will most likely be assailed by feelings of extreme inadequacy.

It is scarce wonder then that statistics show depression to have reached crisis proportions. Suicide is the number one killer among young Koreans, and the fourth greatest cause of death in the population overall. Every year, 31 out of 100,000 people take their own lives. This rate is second only to Lithuania, which has 31.5 suicides per 100,000 people. According to the Ministry of Health and Welfare, 16 percent of South Korean adults suffered from some kind of mental illness in 2011. Regrettably, people do not seek help for such problems. Korean psychiatrists say that the need to preserve face and dignity stop people from admitting they are depressed or unable to cope.

South Korea ranks 102nd on the "Satisfaction with Life" index, alongside the far less developed Kazakhstan and Madagascar. The outstandingly disadvantaged Republic of the Congo ranks a mere three places lower. And in February 2012, polling firm Ipsos surveyed 18,000 adults in 24 different countries and found that South Korea ranked second to bottom in terms of the happiness of its citizens, outperforming only Hungary, another country that struggles with a high rate of suicide. In the poll, just 7 percent of Koreans described themselves as "very happy."

Most of the problems that beset this country—with the obvious exception of the issue of North Korea, which is outside of the South's control—are fixable. As we have seen, South Korean society and government now seem to be taking steps to forestall the potential disaster of becoming a "super-aged" nation. Tempering the spirit of competitiveness, particularly with regard to education and career, will be more difficult. Korean society is flexible, but can it rein in one of the attributes that made the country's take-off possible?

Unrelenting competition was beneficial for South Korea as a nation from the 1960s to the 1980s. The fact that the competitive spirit has become twisted and counterproductive on a personal level has not led to movements against it, though many people do question it. Spending on private, extracurricular tuition continues to rise every year, as does the number of graduates chasing the limited range of good jobs available. Amounts spent on cosmetics, elitist fashion brands, and plastic surgery—products perceived to elevate the social value of the buyer—are among the highest in the world. People go to extraordinary lengths to present the best possible version of themselves to the world, and yet unhappiness prevails.

Son Byeong-hui, 83
Song Kang-ho, 232
Songdo (city), 140
Southeast Asians (prejudice against), 275
street food, 226
suicide, 11, 110, 116, 175, 310, 311
  and celebrity, 116
  and reputation, 188
  and social expectations, 116
suneung (university entrance examination), 52,
  116, 203
sunshine policy, 148, 156
Tablo (musician), 118
Taegukgi (film), 233, 284
  and *han*, 122
Taiwan, 99, 283, 288
Taliban, the, 63
Tang Dynasty (China), 14, 293
Tapgol Park, 125, 255
Terauchi Masatake, 57
The King and the Clown (film), 233, 294
Third Line Butterfly, 247
Three Kingdoms period, 44, 128
Time Magazine, 97, 120, 248
"T-K Mafia", the, 95
Toyota, 40, 214
Toyotomi Hideyoshi, 18, 261
trade unions, 175, 176
  and post-crisis bargain, 266
Treaty of Ganghwa, the, 19
Tripitaka Koreana, 16, 36, 44
trot (bbongjjak), 243, 255
Twitter, 143, 158, 287
  and politics, 169
UCLA, 92, 97, 230
Uighurs, 129, 272
UN Gender Empowerment Measure, 298
UN Human Development Index, 111
UN Security Council, the, 154
under-circles (protest groups), 87
Underwood, Horace (missionary), 56
Underwood, Peter, 94, 182, 184, 186, 189, 191
Unification Church ('Moonies'), 273
United Democratic Party (UDP), 159
United Nations, the, 20, 84, 118, 263, 277, 302
United States of America, the, 9, 19, 20, 40, 52,
  56, 58, 59, 60, 63, 66, 86, 93, 97, 103, 116,
  133, 140, 150, 151, 160, 173, 177, 184, 203,
  204, 206, 207, 223, 228, 242, 262, 269, 270,
  275, 281, 282, 285, 289, 290, 297
  and Korean political framework, 160
  influence on South Korea, 281
University of Illinois, 113
upahana (Indian concept), 121
urbanization, 74
USSR, the, 20, 84, 152, 166, 262
Vietnam, 42, 228, 279, 284, 285, 290
Vietnam War, 68, 172, 243, 285

Wang Geon (King Taejo), 15, 36, 129, 130
  and regional divide, 163
Wealth of Nations, The, 94
weddings, 199
  financial considerations, 199
Western Han Dynasty, 13
White Day, 200
William of Wykeham, 43
Wilson, Woodrow, 58
women (status of), 17, 26, 50, 136, 214, 298
  and employment in modern Korea, 307
  and household finances, 303
  at work, 172, 179
  decline in Joseon era, 47, 299
  foreign brides, 274
  in modern Korea, 302
  Jeju Island, 305
Woori and *Nam*, 95, 182
  and Korea, 96
  and nationality, 271
  mistrust of strangers, 182
Woori Bank, 96
Woori Party, the, 96, 160
World Cup (2002), 126, 150, 254, 267, 268
  and *heung*, 120
  and national pride, 267
World Health Organization, the, 125, 251
World War Two, 9, 123, 160, 262
Yahoo! Korea, 115
Yalu River (China), 13, 21
Yan (Chinese state), 13
Yang Ik-jun, 235, 236
yangban (social class), 17, 19, 51, 79, 98, 105,
  113, 123, 130, 173, 182, 207, 213, 217, 281,
  300
  status of women, 299
Yeonhee-dong (district of Seoul), 90
Yeonpyeong attack, 2010, 154, 155
Yeonsangun (King), 80
Yeouido (location of parliament and financial
  district), 81, 112, 159, 162, 225
YG Entertainment, 248
Yi Seok, 132
Yi Seong-gye (King Taejo of Joseon), 17, 45,
  47
Yi Soyeon, 299, 303, 305, 312
  family and education, 301
Yi Sun-shin, General, 18
Yi Won, 133
Yoido Full Gospel Church (megachurch), 61
Yonsei University, 51, 57, 87, 109, 113
Yoon Po-seon, 66
Yu Su-won (scholar), 130
Yuan (dynasty), 16
Yuri, Shilla king, 129
Yushin Constitution, the, 87, 88, 229
Zhou Wenmo (priest), 55
Zhu Xi, 45, 46, 50

association with the USA, 56
fervency, 60, 62
megachurches, 61
missionaries, 63
relationship with Buddhism, 64
tithing, 63
Putin, Vladimir, 97
Pyeongan Province, 81
Pyongyang, 12, 148, 149, 150, 152, 153, 154, 155, 213
Qing dynasty (China), 18, 83
Queen Jeongsun, 56
Queen Min, 26, 29, 46
Rain (pop star), 97, 248, 279, 286
"real name" law, 118
red pepper, 222
religious syncretism, 84
Rhee, Syngman, 20, 51, 59, 84, 88, 104, 166, 262, 281
1960 downfall, 66
and anti-Communism, 149
and education, 102, 171
and ethnic nationalism, 264
martial law, 85
Roh Moo-hyun, 96, 99, 145, 148, 153, 164, 168, 269
and bribery scandal, 161
and Constitutional Court, 160
death of, 117
reduction of working hours, 180
Roh Tae-woo, 89, 90, 95, 151
death sentence and pardon, 90
room salon (hostess bar), 186
Ross, John (missionary), 56
Russia, 19, 57, 113, 263, 277
Rutt, Richard, 293
Saenuri Party (former Grand National Party), 155, 156, 159, 161, 163, 164, 165
Samga (founder of Deoksu Jang clan), 129, 272
Samguk Yusa, 12
Samho, 68, 75
Samsung, 40, 67, 69, 71, 72, 74, 75, 77, 109, 132, 140, 142, 172, 205, 231, 248, 287, 289, 303
and fast-follower strategy, 142
and Michael Breen lawsuit, 188
competitiveness, 75
presidential pardon of Lee Kun-hee, 162
samulnori, 126
Sangha (Buddhism), 39
and business culture, 40
and collectivism, 99
sangmin (social class), 17, 19, 37
Sanshin, 32, 34, 36
and syncretism, 32
sarangchae (room), 214
Satisfaction with Life Index, the, 111

Satsuma porcelain, 281
Sejong the Great (King), 17, 46, 56, 79, 130, 292, 299
Seo Tai-ji, 245
Seocho (area of Seoul), 105, 115
Seokguram Grotto, 35
Seollal (lunar new year), 135, 136, 187
seon (marriage interview), 193
Seonbawi (Zen Rock), 32
Seoul, 9, 11, 21, 31, 45, 50, 51, 55, 57, 60, 64, 74, 80, 82, 83, 89, 90, 93, 94, 96, 100, 104, 106, 110, 114, 115, 125, 128, 134, 136, 139, 141, 142, 148, 150, 151, 154, 155, 156, 164, 165, 170, 172, 175, 178, 180, 181, 184, 189, 192, 204, 207, 214, 217, 219, 221, 227, 230, 241, 242, 244, 250, 254, 255, 257, 258, 267, 268, 269, 274, 280, 285, 286, 287, 289, 292, 302, 304, 305
apartment prices, 164
population imbalance, 219
traffic out on national holidays, 135
Seoul Metro, 108, 142, 274
unnecessary hallyu sponsorship, 287
Seoul National University, 51, 72, 87, 104, 156
Seoul Olympics (1988), 267
sex slavery ("comfort women"), 20, 261
Shanghai, 84, 262, 285
Shilla (dynasty), 13, 14, 15, 34, 35, 36, 44, 128, 129, 163, 224, 293, 298
status of women, 299
Shin Chae-ho, 261
Shin Joong-hyun, 240, 241, 245, 249
and American music, 242
arrest and imprisonment, 241
Shin Kyung-sook, 289
Shin Saimdang, 48
Shinhan Bank, 76
shinparam, 124
Shinto, 20, 31
enforced practice of, 281
Siberia, 12, 24
sijo (founder of a clan), 129, 134
Singapore, 11, 78, 162, 219
Sinsi ("City of God"), 12
Sinyu persecution (1801), 55
SK Corporation, 152
and presidential pardons, 162
SK Telecom, 140
SKY (group of elite universities), 52, 207
SM Entertainment, 248, 249
smartphones, 72, 140, 144
Smith, Adam, 94
Socrates, 43
sogaeting (blind date), 194
Sogang University, 285
soju (drink), 98, 125, 183, 200, 225, 248, 251, 252, 253, 254, 255
Somang Church (megachurch), 93

and geomantic principles, 213
and recreation, 255
Muhan Dojeon (Infinite Challenge), 144
multiculturalism, 268, 271, 276
  and birth rate problem, 276
  and generational differences, 275
  and mixed marriage, 273
  and rural Korea, 273
  government campaigns, 274
  growth in, 271
Musok (shamanism), 10, 24, 32-39, 46, 61, 137, 280
  and flexibility, 32
  attacked by neo-Confucians, 46
musok-in (Korean shaman), 24, 25, 27, 28, 29, 31, 32, 208
  and Buddhism, 36
  and women's role in society, 301
myeongpum (luxury goods), 114, 311
myeongye hweson (defamation), 117
Myocheong (monk)
  and *pungsu-jiri*, 213
nakhasan ("parachute" appointment), 162, 168
  and the financial industry, 162
Nam Sang-ah, 247
name trading, 130
namsadang (itinerant entertainers), 293
Namsan, 31, 241
Naneun Ggomsuda (podcast), 117, 169
National Assembly, the, 60, 85, 112, 145, 149, 155, 159, 160, 220, 298
national curfew, 250
National Security Law, 85, 149, 150
naver.com, 72, 143
NCSoft, 72, 76, 143
neo-Confucianism, 16, 26, 37, 45, 47, 130, 298
  and homosexuality, 293
  and Park Chung-hee, 173
  and women, 299
  as state ideology of Joseon, 46
  hostility to Buddhism, 45
neo-*yangban*, 105, 207
New Orleans, 124
New York Times, the, 26, 75, 118, 172, 202, 227
Nexon, 181
NHN, 72, 76, 143
nol-ttwigi (game), 125, 300
noraebang (singing room), 125, 194, 254
North Korea/DPRK, 10, 17, 20, 21, 60, 66, 68, 71, 72, 81, 84, 85, 86, 95, 134, 148, 149, 151, 152, 153, 154, 155, 156, 166, 171, 219, 220, 252, 263, 277, 280, 311
  and *hallyu*, 286
  and Korean language, 210
  declining interest in reunification with, 156
  strong ethnic nationalism of, 272
nuclear family, 128, 135, 136
O'Rourke, P.J, 81

Obama, Barack, 97
OECD, the, 65, 109, 135, 164, 170, 179, 206, 280, 290, 306, 310
  labor market flexibility survey, 180
Ohmynews (news website), 143, 168
Old Korean (Godae Gukeo), 13
Olympus (Japanese company), 140
overseas aid, 278
  benefits of, 290
pa (kinship structure), 134
  loss of relevance, 134
Pakistan, 99, 277
Paquet, Darcy, 231, 234, 288
Park (family name), 128
Park Chan-wook, 230, 232, 234, 238
  and so-called "extreme Asia", 236
Park Chung-hee, 38, 66, 68, 73, 74, 85, 88, 95, 102, 103, 109, 145, 151, 159, 166, 172, 175, 207, 231, 250, 264, 265, 286
  and apartment living, 214
  and competition, 102
  and ethnic nationalism, 172, 264
  and mercantilism, 69
  and repression, 87
  and the film industry, 229
  and the music industry, 240
  and trade unions, 175
  and work culture, 170
  anti-Communism, 149
  assassination, 88
  coup, 87
  election victories, 87
  numerical economic targets, 103
Park Geun-hye, 155, 163, 165
Park Jong-chul, 89
Park Jung-sook, 280, 282, 284, 290
Park Won-soon, 60, 80, 87, 90, 110, 150, 165
  election of (2011), 165
Park Yeon-cha (businessman), 161, 165, 168
  corruption case, 161
Pearl Sisters, the, 242
People's Solidarity for Participatory Democracy (PSPD), 154
Philippines, the, 54, 228, 276, 279, 290
plastic surgery, 107, 287, 311
  and Gangnam district, 207
  and *hallyu*, 285
  as everyday phenomenon, 107
pojang macha (tent bar), 125, 225, 253, 254
poktanju (bomb alcohol), 183, 186
pollack (fish)
  and Shamanic practice, 29, 31
POSCO, 94, 96
Protestantism, 38, 281
  and education, 57
  and independence movement, 58
  and politics, 60, 61
  arrival in Korea, 58

jungin (social class), 17, 18, 131
jungmae (matchmaking), 192
Jurchens, 129
JYP Entertainment, 247
Kabul, 63
Kaesong (city), 45, 152, 213
kaizen (continuous improvement), 40
Kandahar, 63
Kia, 9, 75, 177, 289
Kim (family name), 128
Kim Beom-woo (Christian martyr), 55
Kim Chang-ryong, 86
Kim Chu-ja, 243
Kim Dae-jung, 75, 84, 87, 90, 95, 126, 148, 152, 153, 166, 269, 281
  and 'Asian Values', 78
  pardon of Chun and Roh, 90
Kim Gu, 11, 86, 262
Kim Hye-jeong, 192, 196
Kim Il-sung, 20, 21, 84, 152, 154, 262
Kim Jae-gyu, 88
Kim Jong-il, 148, 152, 154
Kim Jong-un, 148, 155
Kim Jung-mi, 243
Kim Kkobbi, 229, 235
Kim Kwang-seok, 244
Kim Min-gi, 244
Kim Ui-cheol, Professor, 40, 123
Kim Woo-choong, 68, 75, 188
Kim Young-sam, 84, 90, 151
  and *"woori-ga nam-iga?"*, 96
  pardon of Chun and Roh, 90
Kim Yu-shin, General, 14
Kim, Patti, 242
kimchi, 220, 221, 223, 254
  different varieties, 222
Kimhae Kim (clan), 18, 131, 134
King Yeongjo, 55, 225
kisaeng, 170, 301
Ko Un, 122, 124
  and Han, 121
Kong Fuzi (Confucius), 42
Konglish, 209
Kongmin (King), 292
Korea University, 51, 87
Korean Air, 153
'Korean barbecue' (*samgyeogpsal*, etc.), 224, 253
Korean cinema, 229-236
  'golden age', 1998-2005, 232
  and late 1990s venture boom, 231
Korean cuisine, 220-228
  and service culture, 227
Korean War, 10, 25, 41, 59, 66, 85, 86, 99, 101, 104, 122, 134, 148, 150, 155, 206, 233, 250, 263, 272
Koryo (dynasty), 16, 17, 36, 44, 45, 47, 98, 129, 163, 213, 224, 272, 291, 292, 298, 299, 304

K-pop, 240, 247, 284, 286
  media exaggeration of success of, 289
Kwon (family name), 129
Kwon Youngse, 155, 156
Kwon, Edward, 227
Kyunghyang Shinmun, the (newspaper), 161, 167
Lankov, Andrei, 274
Laozi, 129
Lee (family name), 128
Lee Byung-chul, 67, 72
  dealings with Park Chung-hee, 67
Lee Chang-dong, 233, 234
Lee Hyo-ri, 233, 248, 249
Lee Jin-ho, 225, 227
Lee Kuan Yew, 78
Lee Kun-hee, 132
Lee Myung-bak, 60, 61, 94, 103, 117, 119, 133, 155, 163, 169
  2007 election victory, 163
  and *hallyu*, 286
  and North Korea policy, 145
  and presidential power, 153
  and summer 2008 protests, 269
  imprisonment, 1965, 167
  views on homosexuality, 297
Lee Wan-yong, 57
Lelang Commandery, 13, 44
lesbianism, 296
LG, 69, 74, 75, 77, 142, 152, 172
  corporate song, 174
Liao River (China), 13
Liberal Party (Syngman Rhee), 85
Lim Jae-hae, Professor, 123
Lithuania, 11, 311
Lotte, 70, 74, 75
M*A*S*H, 9, 267
MacArthur, Douglas (General), 2, 20, 263
  and shamanism, 25
Mahatir Mohamad, 78
Mahayana (Buddhism), 39
makgeolli (rice wine), 253, 255, 265
Malaysia, 78
Manchuria, 12, 13, 34, 56, 214
March 1st Movement, 83
Marxism, 82
McKinsey Consulting, 114
M-curve pattern, 306, 307
Meiji Restoration (Japan, 1868), 19
"Membership Training", 98
Minerva (online forum user), 118
Ming dynasty (China), 17, 18
"miracle on the Han River", 11, 78
Mongols, 16, 36, 272
  and *soju*, 252
  influence on Korean cuisine, 224
mountains (importance in Korean culture), 30, 31, 32, 34, 62

Hong Gyeong-nae (peasant uprising leader), 18, 81

Hong Myung-bo, 267

Hong Seok-cheon, 257, 291, 296
  'coming out', 294
  turnaround in fortunes, 295

Hongdae (university district), 142, 240, 246, 247, 254
  development as a party destination, 254
  indie music scene, 246
  record shops, 249

Hu Jintao, 97

Hubaekje (later Baekje), 15, 163

Hugoguryeo (later Goguryeo), 15

Humax (company), 72

hwaishik (company drinking session), 250
  and health problems, 251

Hwang Doo-jin, 213, 215, 216, 218, 289, 304

Hwang Sang-min, Professor, 113, 116

Hwanghae (province), 55

Hwanin (Lord of Heaven), 12

Hwanung, 12, 221

Hwarang (warriors), 35, 44, 293

Hyundai, 9, 60, 71, 74, 75, 77, 132, 152, 168, 172, 174, 177, 179, 184, 189, 265, 266, 269, 287, 289
  and presidential pardons, 162
  Hyundai Motor Union, 180
  response to economic crisis, 266
  work culture, 174

Ichadon, 35

Imjin Waeran invasions (1592-1598), 18, 37, 54, 131, 222, 256, 261, 280

import substitution, 69

Incheon, 20, 25, 135, 263

Incheon Airport, 135

Individualism Index, 97, 99

industrial soldiers, 102, 109, 172, 174, 264

industrialization, 20, 102, 172, 218, 251
  and removal of hanok, 215
  and the sex industry, 172
  as 'sacred quest', 172

Inner Mongolia, 13

International Monetary Fund (the), 176, 177, 178, 265, 266
  and national pride, 265
  bailout, 177

Inwang-san (mountain), 31, 32, 62

iPhone (Apple product), 75, 144, 189

Iraq, 63

Itaewon, 256, 292
  development and reputation, 256
  gentrification, 256

jaeki-chagi (game), 123

jakmyeong (name-making), 137

Jang (condiments), 222

Jang Hoon, Professor, 159

Japan, 9, 18, 19, 20, 32, 35, 37, 40, 42, 51, 54, 55, 56, 57, 58, 67, 68, 70, 78, 83, 85, 93, 97, 99, 102, 116, 121, 123, 125, 130, 132, 142, 160,167, 176, 185, 209, 234, 240, 256, 260, 261, 262, 264, 267, 270, 275, 277, 278, 279, 280, 282, 283, 285, 287, 288, 290, 298, 302
  influence on Korea, 281

Japanese colonial rule, 19, 20, 38, 57, 62, 99, 132, 261
  and *han*, 121
  and ethnic nationalism, 260
  and Korean pop music, 242
  and *namsadang*, 294
  architecture, 214
  corrupt purchase of assets, in aftermath of, 67

Japan-Korea Treaty of 1910, 19

Jeju Island, 30, 82
  and eochongye, 99
  and women, 304

Jeolla Province, 82, 83, 89, 95, 163, 164, 165, 214, 221, 225, 274, 304, 309
  and regional rivalry with Gyeongsang, 163

jeom (Shamanic practice), 29

Jeon Tae-il, 175

jeong, 10, 40, 92-100, 120, 136, 182, 284
  and Buddhism, 39
  and elite social groups, 160
  and groups, 93
  and rationality, 95
  and *woori*, 93
  miun-jeong, 92

Jeong Bong-ju, 117

Jeong Do-jeon, 37, 45

Jeong Ju-young, 72, 132, 152, 174
  and Goryeong Bridge project, 184
  and self-belief, 73
  relationship with Park Chung-hee, 73

Jeonju (city), 83, 133

jeonse (housing deposit system), 137, 198

Jesa (ceremony), 49, 50, 55, 297

Jesus Christ, 64
  and Shamanism, 25, 28

jipan (family unit), 134

Jiri-san (mountain), 30, 62

Jogye Order, 38

jokbo (family record), 129, 133

Joongang Ilbo, the (newspaper), 154, 167

Joongang University, 159, 162

Joseon dynasty, 17, 18, 26, 28, 31, 37, 42, 44, 46, 47, 51, 52, 57, 79, 81, 83, 105, 113, 128, 130, 133, 137, 153, 173, 203, 233, 263, 281, 283, 291, 292, 293, 298, 299, 300, 304
  and female roles, 300
  Chinese influence on, 281
  relations with China, 260

Joseph Stalin, 20, 84

Jun Ji-hyun, 232, 233, 284, 288
  and *hallyu*, 233

Emperor Sunjong, 57
Emperor Wu (Western Han Dynasty), 13
Emperor Yao (China), 12
English obsession, 10, 106, 109, 202-209, 282
    and birth rate, 205
    and recruitment, 203
    native-speaking teachers, 208-209
ethnic nationalism, 260, 263
    and industrial development, 172
    and prejudice, 272
    development in early 20th century, 261
    growth post-Korean War, 263
eumju-ga-mu, 125, 250
    and overcoming, 125
Ewha Girls School, 57
Ewha Women's University, 257
Feast of Fools, 123
Federation of Korean Industries, 67
Federation of Korean Trade Unions, 175
fermentation, 221
fighting!, 101
Financial Times, the, 267
Finland, 206
First Sino-Japanese War (1894–1895), 83
five relationships, the (Confucianism), 43, 47
France, 19, 96, 99, 160
funeral, traditional, 123
Gabo Reforms, 83
Gaeseong, 45
Galaxy S (Samsung product), 75, 140, 142
Galleria Department Store, 114
Gangnam (district of Seoul), 52, 60, 100, 105,
    114, 207, 255
    and education, 207
    and 'Gangnam-guk' label, 100
Gangwon (province), 55, 72, 161
garlic, 12, 221
Genthe, Siegfried, 30
Germany, 30, 99
Gimje (town), 30
Gini coefficient, 104
GMarket (website), 137
godeung goshi (modern civil service exam), 53
Goguryeo, 13, 15, 34, 35, 44, 283
Gojong (king), 132
Gojoseon, 12
"gold miss", 196
Grand National Party (now Saenuri), 143, 154,
    155, 159
Guksadang (Shaman shrine), 31, 32
Gul, Abdullah, 286
Gung Ye, 15
gut (Shaman ceremony), 24, 26, 27, 28, 29, 31
    and Danoje, 125
    and overcoming, 124
gwangdae boseot (magic mushrooms), 30
Gwangju, 89, 163, 257
Gwangju massacre, 89

gye (mutual aid societies), 98
Gyeon Hwon, 15
Gyeongbokgung (palace), 31
Gyeonggi Province, 203, 293
Gyeongju (city, capital of Shilla), 35, 129, 133
Gyeongsang Province, 82, 95, 129, 161, 163,
    164, 165, 214, 304, 309
    and regional rivalry with Jeolla, 163
    reputation for conservatism and sexism, 304
Gyeryong-san (mountain), 32
Haeinsa (temple), 36
haenyeo, 304
    decline of, 304
hakwon (private educational institute), 106,
    108, 202, 203, 205, 208, 209
    and sleep deprivation, 205
Halla-san (mountain), 30
hallyu, 233, 234, 279, 286, 287, 289
    and diplomacy, 286
    aspirational value in Southeast Asia, 284
    government support for, 286
    hype and backlash, 287, 288
    successful TV dramas, 283
Hamgyeong Province, 82
han, 10, 120, 123, 127, 229, 235
    and appeal of *hallyu*, 284
    and Korean cinema, 235
    and Korean music, 245
    and melancholy in popular culture, 122
Han River, 27, 115, 272, 278
Han Seung-joo, 66
Han Young-yong, 221
Hanahoe, 88, 89
hanbok, 199, 216, 282
Hangul (Korean writing system), 17, 56, 79, 80
hanja (Chinese characters), 17, 56, 79, 261, 281
Hankyoreh, the (newspaper), 167
hanok (Korean house), 142, 212, 214, 215,
    216, 217, 218
    decline and rebirth, 215
    and sustainability, 217
    traditional vs. modern debate, 217
han-puli, 123, 235
Harvard University, 59, 84, 106, 116, 262
Hawaii, 66, 87
Hermit Kingdom (image of Korea), 19, 272
heung, 10, 120, 124, 126, 235, 310
Hiddink, Guus, 268
Hilton, Paris, 119
Hofstede, Geert (Professor), 97, 99
hoju system, 298
Homer B. Hulbert (missionary), 46
homosexuality, 291-297
    and rural Korea, 293
    celebrity, and double standard, 294
    current attitude to, 296
    in ancient Korea, 293

and relationship with North Korea, 153
influence on Korea, 281
Cho Bong-am, 86, 166
Cho Bong-gu, 75
Cho Seung-hui, 97
Cho Yong-gi, 61
Cho Yong-pil, 244
Choco-pie (snack), 145
Choi Je-woo, 82
Choi Kyu-ha, 88
Choi Min-sik, 232, 236
Choi Si-hyeong, 82
Chosun Ilbo, the (newspaper), 110, 123, 167, 197, 299, 303
Christian Council of Korea, 60
Christianity, 10, 18, 26, 32, 38, 54, 56, 61, 62, 80, 82, 84, 297, 309
and homosexuality in Korea, 297
and Korean-Americans, 64
and opposition to Japanese colonial rule, 57
and shamanism, 32, 62
Chun Doo-hwan, 59, 85, 88, 108, 166
'3S policy', 89
corruption, 75, 89
death sentence and pardon, 90
economic liberalization, 74
Gwangju massacre, 89, 163
Chungnyeol (king), 272
Chuseok (holiday), 49, 135, 136, 187
civil service examinations, 15, 17, 44, 46, 51, 105, 281
and divorced women, 300
coffee shop culture, 257, 258
collaborators (Koreans aiding Japanese rule), 19
and Syngman Rhee government, 167
Communism, 150
and National Security Law, 84
and Syngman Rhee, 85
competition, 101, 310
against other countries, 102
and income equality, 104
and labor productivity, 108
and mental health problems, 109
and overeducation, 109
education as primary outlet for, 104, 105
marriage, 110
physical attractiveness, 107
Confucianism, 10, 13, 14, 15, 16, 26, 35, 37, 41, 42-56, 62, 66, 70, 73, 74, 75, 78, 79, 82, 99, 101, 105, 112, 115, 130, 135, 137, 171, 172, 173, 193, 214, 260, 279, 280, 281, 291, 292, 296, 298, 299, 309
and age, 48
and business meetings, 186
and Park Chung-hee, 173
and paternalistic business culture, 70
and women, 48

and work culture, 47
complementarity with Buddhism (Shilla era), 44
corruption, 21, 66, 83
and development era, 69
and Korean politics, 160
and North Korea, 95
Joseon era civil servants, 82
Syngman Rhee government, 102
Corruption Perceptions Index, the, 95, 160
Daedong River, 13, 14
Daegu, 95, 164, 257
Daejanggeum, 279, 283
Daewoo, 68, 173, 188, 231
and 1988 Seoul Olympics, 152
collapse, 75
Dangun, 12, 126, 171, 221, 261
Danoje, 125
Darling, Alastair, 266
Dasan Jeong Yak-yong, 55, 133
defectors (North Korean), 14, 286
Democratic Labor Party, the, 159
and North Korea, 150
democratization, 78, 90, 176, 267
movement for, 80, 89
Deoksu Jang (clan), 272
division of Korea, 21, 38, 51, 134, 167, 262
and ethnic nationalism, 263
and *han*, 121
divorce, 200
dog meat, 14, 206, 213, 214
Donga Ilbo, the (newspaper), 165
Donghak (religion), 18, 82, 83, 84
Donghak Peasant Revolution, 82
Dongjak (area of Seoul), 115
Duo (matchmaking agency), 192, 194, 198
system of introduction, 196
East Timor, 54
economic crisis (1997-98), 75, 177, 231, 265
and bankruptcies, 177
beginnings of job insecurity, 178
impact on work culture, 178
Economist Intelligence Unit, the, 160
Ecuador, 99
education, 11, 41, 50
and choice of marriage partner, 197
and competition, 104
and Confucianism, 44, 50, 51, 101
and democracy, 79
and Syngman Rhee, 102
as status symbol, 114, 115
as ticket to social elite, 194
extreme cost of, 204
netizen 'witch-hunts', 118
women's access to (modern Korea), 301
women's lack of access to (Joseon era), 47
Eightfold Path, the (Buddhism), 38
Eighth U.S. Army, the, 242

Index

386 generation, 148, 151, 152, 155
38th Parallel, the, 20, 263
Afghanistan, 63
Ahn Chul-soo, 165
Ahn Doo-hee, 86
Allen, Horace (missionary), 56
An Hyang, Confucian scholar, 16, 45
Andong (town), 129
Andong Kim (clan), 19, 131
Andong Kwon (clan), 129, 130, 132, 133
Andong University, 123
'Angry 20–40', the, 165
animism, 30
anju, 253
apartments, 212, 215
  and alienation, 215
Appenzeller, Henry (missionary), 56
Apple (company), 75, 140
  and product recall, 189
April Revolution (against Syngman Rhee), 86
Armed Forces Korea Network
influence on Korean music, 242
Asadal, 12
'Asian values' debate, 78
Bae Yong-joon, 233, 236
  success in Japan, 283
Baejae Boys High School, 57
Baek Ji-young, 119
Baekdusan (mountain), 12, 30, 62
Baekje, 13, 14, 35, 44, 163, 280
baesanimsu (geomantic principle), 213
Bakhtin, Mikhail, 123
Ballantine's (whisky), 115
Ban Ki-moon (UN Secretary-General), 289
banmal and *jondaetmal*, 49
bballi bballi (quickly quickly), 139
Beijing, 16, 54, 55, 153, 261
bibimbap, 227
birth rate problem, 277, 299
  and cost of childcare, 306
  and working women, 305
BoA (singer), 283, 285
bodhisattva, 40
bone rank system, 14
Bong Joon-ho, 230, 235
bon-gwan (Korean clans), 14, 128-137
  and name trading, 18, 131
  declining importance of, 128, 133
booking (nightclub practice), 195
Borges, Jorge Luis, 126
Breen, Michael, 188
Britain, 19, 116, 189, 203
Buddhism, 10, 13, 14, 15, 16, 32, 34-46, 54, 62, 99, 224, 280, 309

  and overcoming, 41
  and *shinparam*, 124
  arrival in Korea, 34
  as state religion, 36
  commonality with Shamanism, 37
  decline in Joseon era, 37
  Korean influence on Japan, 280
  syncretism with shamanism, 39
Bukchon, 217
Bulguksa (temple), 36, 38
Busan, 20, 96, 161, 219, 225, 244, 257
Canada, 116, 203, 204, 207, 208
capitalism, 10, 11, 66, 69, 70, 71, 151, 166
Catholicism, 54, 58
  and insularity, 58
  arrival in Korea, 54
  martyrs, 55
Cha Ji-cheol, 88
chaebol, 29, 66, 70-77, 104, 110, 132, 143, 159, 166, 171, 173, 174, 175, 176, 177, 178, 180, 184
  and 1997-98 economic crisis, 75, 265
  and crime, 76, 161
  and debt, 176
  and economic growth, 73
  and female staff, 302
  and lack of competition, 72
  and layoffs, 178
  and post-crisis bargain, 266
  and press freedom, 168
  and the film industry, 231
  family rule, 71
  hiring practices, 179
  work culture, 173
Chang Ha-joon, Professor, 205, 206, 275
Chang Myon, 66, 87
charye (ceremony), 49
Chemyon (face), 112
  and education, 115
  and materialism, 113, 114
  and property prices, 115
  and social status, 114
  changing nature of, 113
Cheonan (navy corvette), 154
Cheondogyo, 84
Cheong Wa Dae (Blue House, presidential residence), 31, 86, 149
cheonmin (social class), 17, 18, 26, 37, 46, 131, 293
China, 9, 11, 13, 14, 15, 16, 17, 18, 21, 34, 42, 43, 45, 54, 55, 78, 83, 93, 99, 103, 113, 114, 129, 141, 152, 157, 206, 228, 233, 240, 254, 255, 260, 262, 263, 270, 275, 279, 282, 283, 285, 286, 287, 288